VICTORIAN SPLENDOR

VICTORIAN·SPLENDOR

Re-Creating America's 19th-Century Interiors

Allison Kyle Leopold

Photography by Elizabeth Heyert

Stewart, Tabori and Chang

New York

Additional photography © 1986 Carin and David Riley: pages 15, 16–17,
20, 31, 36, 37, 38, 42, 46, 47, 58, 59, 69, 70, 71, 76–77, 83, 86,
88, 89, 91, 93, 100–101, 102, 107, 116, 117, 122, 123, 127, 128,
129: both, 132, 135, 142, 143, 147, 148, 149, 152, 156, 157, 162: both,
163, 177, 190–191, 192, 214, 226, 227, 236, 237, 243, 244

Design by Laurence Vetu

Published by Stewart, Tabori & Chang, Inc.
740 Broadway, New York, New York 10003

Library of Congress Cataloging-in-Publication Data

Leopold, Allison Kyle.
Victorian splendor.

  Includes index.
    1. Interior decoration—United States—History—19th
century. 2. Decoration and ornament—United States—Victorian style.
3. Victoriana in interior decoration.
I. Heyert, Elizabeth.   II. Title.
NK2003.5.L46   1986   747.213   85-30267
ISBN 0-941434-69-9
ISBN 0-941434-83-4 (pbk.)

86   87   88   10   9   8   7   6   5   4   3   2   1

First Edition

Distributed by Workman Publishing
1 West 39th Street, New York, New York 10018

Printed in Japan

Introduction

In the course of researching and writing this book, I've come to realize that the meaning of the word "Victorian" is subject to dispute, not to mention a wide variety of prejudices. No one can agree, it seems, on what the term really means. Is "Victorian" a style of architecture, a type of home, a descriptive term for furniture? Is it a kind of decor—and, if so, what kind is it? Is it even proper to refer to American homes and interiors as "Victorian," since Victoria herself was an English queen? Or is the vaster, vaguer, and certainly less romantic label "nineteenth century" a better, if more prosaic, choice?

To those not professionally involved in the study of the nineteenth century's taste, "Victorian" conveys a much more fulfilling impression than do the blander, if more precise, substitutes. Although I use both "nineteenth century" and "Victorian," as well as the names of the various revival and reform periods, freely throughout this book, I find that the word "Victorian" most effectively evokes the vision of the rich and splendid world of the previous century. Because its use is subject to such debate, however, I feel called upon to define my terms.

"Victorian" refers not to a style, but to a period of time, held together, as are all eras, by certain accepted values and beliefs, a certain widespread code of behavior. It best describes a way of life that existed in America and Europe for the greater part of the nineteenth century. While the bulk of those years conveniently correspond with the 1837 to 1901 reign of England's beloved Queen Victoria, the roots of Victorian life in America can be found as early as the mid-1830s, and the era continued well past the turn of the century. Because daily life didn't undergo an abrupt change with the first dawning of the twentieth century (nor homes mass redecoration), the Victorian age's influences lasted into what we popularly regard as the Edwardian decade and lingered right up until the First World War.

Within that period, an unprecedented concern for the importance of interior design emerged. *House and Home Papers*, an influential little book written in 1864, for example, preached that "the man and woman who approach the august duty of creating a home are reminded of the sanctity and beauty of what they undertake." Nearly thirty years later, in 1891, *The Delineator* magazine expanded that view, equating bad housekeeping with bad morals. Such was the importance of home and decoration that even women crossing the frontier in covered wagons attempted to maintain the domestic standards that they had been raised with, adding a touch of color to the wagon's interior with a green lining cloth, laying rag carpets on the floors of sleeping tents to make them homey and cozy as well as snug.

As a result of this concern, many styles appeared, most of them revivals of one kind or another. For a while it must have seemed as if there wasn't a single moment of the past that wasn't re-formed, reinterpreted, or relived, resulting in a range of Victorian ornament nothing short of overwhelming. If there was any consistent reason for this opulence and excess, it was the expansion of American wealth as the young nation expanded; and if there were any consistent themes that connected the consequent mélange of styles, they were those of the romantic, the picturesque, the exotic, and the ornate. In a manner which would have been directly opposed to the later "less is more" school of design, the Victorians seem to have adopted the motto "For every space there is an object," and carried it out with absolute relish.

It is just these qualities—of orna-

ment, opulence, romanticism—that I see being reborn in this twentieth-century revival of the Victorian interior. Sometimes, especially for newcomers to this Revival, it is difficult to imagine the past splendor of the sadly neglected "white elephant" house that they see, or even the very fullness of ornamentation that was once taken for granted in middle-class homes—details like rich woodwork and moldings, carved fireplaces and brass hardware, beveled-glass panes. That's not to say that thoughtless Victorian excesses or bad taste didn't exist; of course they did, as they do in any style. But also, we are now in a position to evaluate Victorian interiors, like any other style of the past, by the best they had to offer, not the worst.

The Victorian Revival interior is here to stay, as a viable "style." Once its current trendiness has faded, it will be as firmly ensconced in legitimacy as any other style. The fact that the look rests heavily on the adornment of the room's shell—its windows, walls, ceiling, and floor—as well as on furniture and accessories, contributes to its applicability to a wide range of interiors, even those that are not Victorian to start with.

Only a few of the many beautiful Victorian Revival interiors that I saw were photographed for this book, but each one added to my perceptions about the Revival. I thank those people whose homes I was privileged to see and whose collections I admired, though they were unable to be pictured here. In particular, I would like to express my appreciation to Samuel Dornsife, who permitted me to see the extraordinary Victorian interiors of his own home, which because of scheduling difficulties could not be formally photographed. I would also like to acknowledge the many people around the country who, in hearing of my search for Victorian interiors, sent hundreds of slides, photographs, and wonderful letters detailing their own restoration efforts, or ones they knew of or had heard about.

Many people provided me invaluable assistance and guidance throughout this project.

First, I'd like to thank those members of the team at Stewart, Tabori & Chang who were helpful and encouraging during the many stages of this book. In particular, I'd like to thank my editor, Leslie Stoker, whose help was constant, advice invaluable, and assistance vital in shepherding an unwieldy project to its completion. I'm also grateful to Brian Hotchkiss, whose careful copy editing, thoughtful suggestions— and humor—helped me clarify what it was I wanted to say.

Special thanks go to my agent, Deborah Geltman, whose guidance on the project from the outset and whose support during its more turbulent moments, was appreciated.

Many thanks to Elizabeth Heyert, whose beautiful photographs make up most of the illustrative work in this book and who was able to translate through the camera my vision of Victorian life and then magically invest it with a special look of her own. Her understanding and perception of the nineteenth century added immeasurably to the quality of the project, and her courtesy and professionalism made a difficult job easier. I'd also like to acknowledge the quiet presence and steady assistance of Kristen Brochmann in the creation of these pictures, as well as the work of the other photographers whose pictures appear in this book, including David and Carin Riley.

In helping to compile the Appendices, I appreciated the assistance and enthusiasm of Megan Murray and, especially, CindyLynn Jones, who was able to step in at the eleventh hour to organize the overflow of information that had descended on my office as well as track down the stray fact, obscure quote, or lost date whenever I needed it.

Many other people assisted me in ways I would like to acknowledge: Susan Oberstein at *Vogue*, for her understanding through the duration and demands of this project; special friends, including Maria Hopkins, who made several trips to California more pleasant, and Lynda Graham-Barber and Liz Warren, both of whom helped me with advice, leads on sources, and most of all tea and sympathy; Roberta Scheer, who, if she sees this book, knows very well why I am thanking her. My special appreciation to Professor Dale McConathy of New York University, who, as my adviser, encouraged my research from its earliest stages. It was a stroke of good fortune that led me to him through the tangled mazes of NYU, and his insights into the taste and times of the nineteenth century helped me formulate many of the ideas I've incorporated in these pages. Plus, his confidence in me—in encouraging me with this book and in helping me enter the doctoral program—helped more than he can imagine.

For varied help and Victorian information, my thanks to Carolyn Flaherty of *Victorian Homes* magazine; Judy Snyder of The Victorian Society in America; Gail Winkler, who writes beautifully about the nineteenth century, for leads on houses and other valuable sources; Nada Gray, for her hospitality and graciousness in showing me the Victorian homes of Pennsylvania. My thanks to the many people who shared their knowledge and perceptions of Victorian splendor, including all the "Victorian" San Franciscans like Bruce Bradbury, Larry Boyce and his team, and Jill Pilaroscia; Margot Johnson, whose charm and personal enthusiasm for the offbeat side of the Victorian era is irresistible; Sheila Parkert at Saratoga's beautiful Victorian Adelphi Hotel; experts such as Barrymore L. Scherer; Dan Damon, for generously running notice of my search for Victorian homes in his catalog as well as rushing source books to me when I needed them; John Freeman, who lent me his copy of Clarence Cook's *House Beautiful* as well as the delightful *House and Home Papers*. The insights, wit, enthusiasm, and good cheer of Dan Diehl, a member of the "Victorian" community, also made a real difference to me.

I'd like to express special thanks to John Burrows, whose generosity in sharing his ideas and sources was a great help on many occasions. I especially appreciate his introducing me to Victorian San Francisco and opening up just the right homes to me there, his assistance on many of the California shootings, and his true Victorian spirit.

Also, I extend my appreciation to all the curators, antique dealers, and other experts listed in the Appendices, who took the time to respond both to my questionnaires and my follow-up interviews. Most of all, I'd like to thank the people who graciously allowed their homes to be photographed for this book and who, in the course of doing so, shared their considerable expertise and love of the Victorian century: Dennis Rolland, Nancy Stoddart Huang, Marilyn Buckland and Ralph Gillis, Kenneth Jay Lane, Jean-Marie and Neita Blondeau, Mark Rosen and Arlene Dahl, David Hocker, Alan and LaDel Clendenon, Tom and Tommie Veirs, Dr. Don Van Derby and Don M. Liles, Paul Pilgrim and Jerry Roy, Don Clay, Ralph DuCasse and Tom Roberts, Wandz Constanzo and Richard J. Tuff, and, in Cape May, Tom and Sue Carrol at the Mainstay Inn, Jay and Marianne Schatz at The Abbey, and Karen Andrus, who caters beautiful Victorian-style dinners and created the Victorian tea for this book. Special thanks to Julie and Jim Dale, for their graciousness on what were a very hectic two days in their lives; Richard Reutlinger, who literally gave us the run of his extraordinary Victorian mansion; and Joan and Dane Wells at Cape May's Queen Victoria Inn, both of whom made special efforts to make our stay there both productive and especially pleasant.

Finally, to my two very special "Victorian" friends, Jody Shields and Rita Baron-Faust, who are as taken with the beautiful, bewildering Victorian world as I am. Their knowledge and honest comments improved the book with the challenges they posed, and their understanding, support, and, especially, friendship mean a great deal to me. Also, to my sister Jody, who patiently listened to long chapters over the phone and whose good, natural ear and thoughtful responses helped me most of all. When time travel is perfected, these are the three people with whom I would like most to visit the nineteenth century.

And to my husband, Tom—for his stoic patience, for taking care of everything, big and small, in our lives for two years while I worked—this book is affectionately dedicated.

Chapter 1

The Victorian Revival: A Legacy of the Romantic Age

A true home should be called the noblest work of art possible to human creatures, inasmuch as it is the very image chosen to represent the last and highest rest of the soul, the consummation of man's blessedness.

House and Home Papers (1864)

The curve of this bay window in a restored nineteenth-century Anaheim home speaks of a primary Victorian Revival mood—nostalgia and domesticity. The room owes this old-time ambiance to the soft, layered draperies on table and windows, the Victorian wicker chairs, and the homey familiarity of much-loved objects scattered about.

icture this. Picture a rich parlor, bursting with romantic detail. Picture walls covered with a sensually dark wallpaper, its gilding lit by a flickering mellow light. Imagine fanciful Oriental rugs, piled one on top of the other; the twinkle of delicate etched glass; the patina of gleaming mahogany woodwork. Now, focus on the furniture—tall mirrors; low chairs with garnet-colored upholstery accented with tassels and silken fringe, drawn together here and there in intimate conversational clusters; draped side tables strewn with a magpie mixture of exotic carved boxes of jade, photographs in sinuous silver frames, bits of old ivory and amber, leatherbound books. Picture too the greenery, palms and leafy ferns filling the shadows, filtering the light.

It's a vignette right out of the heart of America's Golden Age, the Victorian years. Sumptuous, yet warm and comfortable, it is a very cozy sort of splendor. There's a sense of gracious invitation about it that recalls the life and pleasures of a bygone era.

Now, actually step into that parlor to hear the crackling fire, the glasses clinking, people talking. In-stead of soft murmurings about the opening of the Suez Canal, Mr. Edwin Booth's fine performance in last week's *Othello*, or whether the new Bell and Edison Telephone Companies will ever amount to anything, the conversation is about something called a VCR. Someone mentions income taxes. The Academy Awards. Shopping malls. We're in the *1980s*, not the 1880s, after all.

But for the content of the conversation, this newly redesigned living room in San Francisco's Pacific Heights could as easily have been found in the San Francisco of one hundred years ago; or it could just as easily be seen in a restored townhouse in Boston's South End, in one of Houston's ten thousand recently constructed "Victorian" homes, or in the suburbs of Stamford, Connecticut. It could be found in a Midwest Queen Anne, a New York City co-op, or a shingle-style mansion perched atop a New England hill.

While the Victorian era is long past, its heritage of style is in a period of rediscovery: designers, collectors, and homeowners are creating interiors that recall the ambience that flourished during America's nineteenth century. Called Victorian Revival, it's a style that's attracting a new and fervent following. Probably more people have reupholstered sofas in the past two years than in the past ten. More and more people are scavenging salvage barns for fanciful Victorian fretwork, stained-glass windows, stately marble mantels, and embossed brass doorknobs. It is particularly interesting to observers of taste to see how wall treatments, once rejected as fussy or oppressive, now seem alive with fantastic pattern and color; how carvings, once scorned as overblown, have come to resemble complex sculpture. Even the floorplans of old Victorian homes are finding favor again. Their nooks and corridors are no longer branded as wastes of space or as evidence of poor design, but rather are sought after for their individuality, prized for their lingering rustle-of-taffeta charm. For the first time in the history of twentieth-century design, people have begun to prefer the splendid to the simple, the intensely personal to the safely neutral, the freely flamboyant to the austere discipline of minimalism.

Finally, the time has arrived for the return of the Victorian interior. Given the passage of many years, the Victorian era in all its facets—its fine and decorative arts, its politics and scientific accomplishments—is being reevaluated and reassessed. Today, spirited bidding on Belter and Bougereau fills the auction houses; Victorian furnishings and art have an honored place in museums from New York's Metropolitan to the High Museum in Atlanta.

Time is not the only reason for the return of the Victorian-inspired interior, either. The romance that clings to our perception of the nineteenth century, which masks its defects and softens its reality, is another reason for the appeal of Victorian interiors. The years spanning the 1830s to the turn of the century bring to mind certain clear pictures: the gallant clip of horse-drawn phaetons, landaus, barouches, victorias on cobblestoned streets; wasp-waisted ladies, their white shoulders gleaming as they move under the lights of great crystal ballroom chandeliers; the faint mixture of lavender mingling with bay rum; children playing with hoops and china-faced dolls.

But the Victorian era was also one of contrasts and contradictions, asking that the passionate and the proper, the sensual and the sentimental exist side-by-side. Victorian America was far from being all satins and laces. It embraced the bravado of the entrepreneur, the rugged independence of the Wild West, the perfumed allure of the opium den, as much as it did the genteel manners of polite society.

All of this was reflected in the development of the Victorian interior; there has never been anything to compare. There was—and is—a rhyme and a reason to all its elements, for it was very much an out-

This family of dolls, decked out in lace and finery, evokes the charm and innocence of the Victorian era. The "lives" of dolls like these were a favorite theme for writers of children's books in the second half of the nineteenth century. Today, dolls of this vintage are of tremendous value and appeal to collectors.

Overleaf: *Carmine-colored walls and deeply tufted upholstery point to the nineteenth century in this grand, urban expression of the Victorian Revival. Actually the studio apartment of a New York City designer, this Victorian mix is as intimate as it is elegant—with unmatched Victorian chairs, rare nineteenth-century brass tables and needlepoint rug, and the elegantly carved center table attributed to Alexandre Roux. Yet one also senses the undercurrent of tongue-in-cheek humor from the unexpected combinations.*

Above and opposite: *The sophisticated spirit of nineteenth-century exotica is evoked by the shimmer of crimson-colored pillows and the all-out splendor of a city co-op drawing room in a six-story townhouse built around 1898. All the items in the room demonstrate Victorian design precedents: the busts on the oversized marble mantel; the light-filtering greenery; the profusion of picturesque personal bibelots; even the classic nineteenth-century arrangement of furniture in various conversational groupings.*

ward expression of the Victorian inner self. Each and every detail of Victorian rooms was intended to convey a message and to reveal the values of the inhabitants. One might even say that the Victorian parlor served as a "résumé" of sorts, proclaiming with each bibelot its owner's status, cultural aspirations, family ties, and level of taste. Family portraits attested to ancestry; shells and bits of driftwood propped up in the étagère betrayed both an appreciation for nature and finances permitting summers at the shore; a fan and a peacock feather resting casually on the mantel informed visitors of at least a nodding acquaintance with the new fad of Aestheticism; while heavy crimson draperies looped up with thick gold tassels left no doubt that behind it all was a bank account to be reckoned with.

Because the Victorian interior represents not merely a decorating style, but a historical decorating style that evokes the atmosphere of a very specific time, its true appreciation is best reached by understanding the life and tempo of Victorian times. Without that understanding, the rooms, in many cases, can remain a confusing, even meaningless jumble. Therefore, in the pages that follow are discussions of the social underpinnings that inspired the Victorians to create the kinds of rooms they did, as well as

what life in those rooms might have been like. Because Victorian interiors were reflections of Victorians themselves, knowing something about timely social issues, such as the effects of industrialization or the domestic position of women, as they relate to the development of the interior, can help in unraveling what may appear to be paradoxes in the style. Once one has a picture of what each room was originally like, and why it was that way, one can more readily understand the Victorian Revival counterpart.

There is no question that today's Victorian Revival interior has its differences from the original, but this fact just tends to reinforce the idea of a "revival" in the authentic Victorian sense of the word. Just as the original nineteenth-century styles were derived from a series of interpretive revivals based loosely on historical example, then embellished and modified to suit contemporary tastes, so the current Victorian Revival is a creative revival rather than a literal one, capturing the spirit, not the letter, of the age.

Victorian Revival interiors pay homage to their century of inspiration, but from a twentieth-century point of view, carefully blending the furniture, the arts, and the ornamentation of the era to produce the warm, romantic atmosphere of the

The graceful wood frame of an early Victorian sofa in a seaside cottage is set off, not with a traditional horsehair, velvet, or brocade, but with a colorful contemporary fabric shirred for extra detail.

last century. While it wholeheartedly employs the nineteenth-century love of comfort and luxury and its delight in color rather than in monochromatic or neutral tones, the result is a less heavy look than that of a hundred years ago. While Victorian Revival design occasionally indulges in the "line-by-line" documentation suitable to historic-house restoration, it more frequently does what the Victorians themselves might have done had the minimal look and the Neo-Colonial Revival never intervened. Today's Victorian Revival designers are creating new designs (in the proper Victorian spirit), while reinterpreting old ones with imagination and verve. In addition, today's design elements are more balanced than those of a hundred years ago, and the density of the rooms has been pared a bit to satisfy twentieth-century tastes and space.

Because the Victorian period spanned so many years and encompassed so many styles and attitudes, and because the interiors usually present such a richly "inhabited" look, it's often difficult to understand these rooms at first glance— to appreciate what they are all about. The nineteenth century (unlike the eighteenth century, which seems to have expressed values of reason and order through the understated symmetry of its interiors) appeals much more to the emotions

than to the intellect. This response is more visceral, based on mood and impression rather than on analysis. It is with this awareness that Victorian Revival interiors can best be divided into four nineteenth-century–inspired "moods" that reflect their overall spirit.

• The first such mood derives from the opulent, urbane aspects of the Victorian interior. It is these luxury-oriented interiors that present the finer nineteenth-century antiques, wonderful overstuffed upholstery in satins and brocades, gilt mirrors, sumptuous drapery, and imaginative trompe l'oeil work.

• The second aspect of the Victorian Revival projects the mood of the exotic and picturesque. Interiors such as these are highly personal rooms, often the homes of avid collectors or world travelers who have filled them with the vibrant colors and rich patterns of faraway places. These unconventional Victorian Revival interiors have very literal antecedents in the globe-trotting tendencies of many nineteenth-century Americans, with their fascination for other cultures, particularly those of China and Japan, Thailand (then Siam), Turkey, Egypt, and the Arabian lands. Very often, too, this look combines with the opulent, luxury-oriented style to produce a very dramatic and exotic effect.

• The nostalgically domestic Victorian Revival interior—cozy, homelike, filled with eclectic clusters of wicker, soft fringed shawls, and profusions of pillows—presents still another side of the style. Like all the best Victorian rooms, it exudes comfort. One can easily imagine fresh lemonade being prepared in summer in the next room, or the family dog curled up by the winter fire. Often this type of room, with its strong sense of turn-of-the-century charm, has a more accessible feeling than does either of the two former types. Frequently it tends toward the use of the lighter tones prevalent in the first decade of the twentieth century, with golden oak, touches of creamy lace, and sentimental framed chromolithographs of favorite Victorian scenes.

A closely related substyle of this look is the Victorian Country interior. A more casual side of the Victorian Revival, yet less so than the traditional country look—with its hand-made baskets, rustic decoys, and potpourri of folk-art accents— Victorian Country rooms tend to reflect the country-estate living of the nineteenth-century well-to-do, not that of the strictly rural or rustic folk. In a Victorian Country kitchen, a carved mahogany sideboard might be used instead of an unpretentious pine cupboard. Or, in a parlor, a country French armchair and plaid camel-back sofa share space with a colorful silk and velvet crazy quilt and embroidered mid-Victorian firescreen. The mingling of simplicity and civilization adds the Victorian urban edge without eliminating the country impulse.

• The final, and perhaps most interpretive, view of the Victorian Revival is the selective use of nineteenth-century antiques, accessories, and collections in a non-Victorian setting where their opulent appeal joins surprisingly well with slicker contemporary edges. Often, a single piece of Victorian pedigree can stand alone as the focal point of a modern room, softening and personalizing its surroundings. A glittering turn-of-the-century Baccarat chandelier can add a touch of drama to an otherwise cool, contemporary dining room. The curving silhouette of a Victorian frame sofa may pleasingly startle against a pale wall, or the same piece could add a touch of human dimension to a sprawling loft space. Victorian collections alone can also bring the warmth of the nineteenth century into the twentieth. Exquisite Victorian silver, brilliantly colored Majolica, tawny pottery, all present an appealing contrast when set against a background of stark modern art.

The following pages demonstrate many of the personal expressions of Victorian style which can be seen in Victorian Revival interiors across the country. Here are interiors seen as total living environments, the best examples of how the look of the Victorian decades has been revived and interpreted as a viable style for twentieth-century living.

In an effort to document and display the burgeoning enthusiasm for the Victorian Revival, homes from all over the country were sought. Those that were chosen reflect a wide range, from a gingerbread home restored by its owners to documented nineteenth-century authenticity—walking into it was like stepping back into a glorious time tunnel to the past—to a Manhattan studio apartment that was a witty glimpse of the Belle Epoque. All these points of view are valid in the context of Victorian Revival; all have in common the re-creation of the flavor and feeling of the nineteenth century.

In selecting these homes, museum authenticity was not an important criterion. Creativity and comfort, concepts that the Victorians themselves championed, were. Once one is looking for them, suggestions of Victorian style can be discovered in many contexts: a pale lavender-gray border stripe circling the upper reaches of the walls of a

bedroom recalls the nineteenth-century frieze. The loving display of collections of all kinds—souvenirs of foreign travel or family portraits and pictures—always suggests its Victorian antecedents. Of course, these glimpses of Victorian interiors express no one's "certified" vision of what Victorian Revival really is, except their owners' and my own.

A second, equally important criterion for inclusion was that all these interiors be rooms that are currently lived in. None are museum setups or historic re-creations, and therefore all must stand up to the rigors of daily use, entertainment, and family life. In a few instances, inns, rather than strictly private homes, were photographed. The Victorian splendor of their interiors was, quite simply, too good to miss. But most are *family* inns in which the owners live as well as work. And in two cases, details from a historical home have been inserted—but only ones that a homeowner could re-create today.

The interiors, then, were photographed to express, in some way, the ongoing life of the present: you'll see a set of keys on a nighttable, scripts on the floor, invitations and mail propped up on a hall table. Occasionally one of the family members may even have slipped into camera range, further demonstrating that these rooms are as much a

Above: *The rich, tawny shades of nineteenth-century pottery combine with a variety of eighteenth- and nineteenth-century tortoise-shell boxes—intended for matches, snuff, cards, needles, or tea—creating an exciting contrast to the artist-owner's stark, modern paintings.*

Opposite: *Creative thinking produces an innovative Victorian Revival room in the back parlor of an 1882 catalog house (originally built from blueprints obtained through a mail-order catalog), with elements that symbolize three centuries of design: eighteenth-century Napoleonic seating; picturesque zebra-skin pillows and an exotic table inlaid with ivory and mother-of-pearl from the nineteenth century; and a twentieth-century symmetry and balance along with a white-on-white palette.*

Many mirrors, rather than just one or two, and a whole collection of early-nineteenth-century fruit compotes of gold-and-white porcelain, all massed to resemble a Victorian art unit, add to the Victorian feeling of this interior.

part of the living present as of the historic past. For convenience and comparison, the book is divided by rooms—living rooms (drawing rooms), dining rooms, bedrooms, hallways, "special" rooms (sitting rooms, libraries, smoking rooms, and the like), kitchens, and baths—rather than in a home-by-home manner. And they vary in style from the almost pagan atmosphere of an exotic den to the hushed serenity of an Arts & Crafts dining room.

Perhaps the most interpretive of the interiors are necessarily the kitchens and baths. The appeal of few, if any, derives from their period authenticity. Rather, it is their successful solutions for creating a functional room not at odds with the rest of the home and invoking the spirit of the nineteenth century that make them so apt and inviting.

A substantial portion of this book has also been devoted to a Victorian directory, which consists of a selective listing of more than 100 historic Victorian homes and house-museums open to the public, all of which provide excellent opportunities to see the Victorian interior as it was. Most offer guided or personal tours, and many have special holiday events that re-create traditional Victorian customs. Also included is a listing of museums with outstanding collections of Victorian furnishings,

as well as a list of organizations and publications geared toward providing further guidance in the area. Finally, there is a listing of the most prominent antique dealers specializing in nineteenth-century antiques, as well as a listing of craftspeople working in the Victorian tradition today—textile restorers, stained-glass and stenciling experts, and restoration specialists—as well as Victorian Revival design consultants.

Due to the length of the Victorian era, its style is often designated as Early Victorian, Mid-Victorian, and Late or High Victorian, which generally indicates a progression toward the more elaborate and more ornamented—and more idiosyncratic—as the century advanced. Except where specifically noted, I have concerned myself primarily with the post-Civil War period, from the late 1860s through the 1890s, the so-called Gilded Age, when Victorian eclecticism was at its height. This was a purely personal choice: The latter part of the century was the period of the richest overlay of interior style and the most flamboyant, most complex mix of tastes.

In addition, I feel we still maintain a certain bond with the late nineteenth century; those decades are not so far removed in time that they have become remote or unreal. It's hard to say whether anyone can really fathom the lives or hopes of seventeenth-, or even eighteenth-, century Americans. But the Gilded Age, despite its differences, is still within reach. Familiar street names and buildings jump out at us from maps and documents; we can recognize products the Victorians used, companies they traded with. These were people who ate Mr. Graham's crackers, enjoyed Quaker Oats, washed with Ivory soap, bought furniture from W. H. Sloane's store, and shopped at R. H. Macy; whose lives spanned the eras of both the covered wagon and the Chrysler. There are Americans still living who remember the inauguration of Roosevelt—Teddy—and whose parents were married soon after the Civil War; and as distant as Victorian days sometimes seem, many of the threads that make up the fabric of our own lives and behavior were spun during the Victorian decades.

The attitudes that shaped the life and style of the American home, as discussed here, belonged to the country's emerging middle and upper-middle classes for the most part. While Victorian society was greatly stratified, with its vast underworld of the poor—homeless children, illegal immigrants, freed slaves—it was the values of the rapidly growing prosperous classes and the highly acquisitive nouveau riche that created and ruled the taste of nineteenth-century America, and it was

therefore those attitudes I chose to concentrate on.

This book has no pretensions to being a scholarly treatise on antique furniture, restoration of authentic Victorian interiors, or nineteenth-century American life. Books have been written by very competent scholars on all those subjects. Those inspired to delve more deeply into the nuances of nineteenth-century life and style are encouraged to consult the bibliography and the listing of organizations that have been especially helpful to me as references on American Victorian life and decorative arts, which are included at the back of the book. As the period is undergoing reexamination and redefinition at present, new works will no doubt be forthcoming.

The world and taste of Victorian America is still a rich and fertile field for all kinds of exploration. There are even those who will argue a case for it as the first truly American style. But less than one hundred years past its heyday, so much of American Victorian culture and so many of the aspects of its everyday life have disappeared from collective memory. Once well-known customs and traditions have become obscure. In its own way, the rediscovery of Victorian America in the Victorian Revival style may stem from hopes of recalling and honoring and enjoying this heritage from our past.

Chapter 2

Victorian Splendor: The Elements of the Style

Home! the place where all man's best and happiest hours are passed. Where in our language shall we find a word of four letters that stirs the sweet pulses of life, like this of home—our home.

Sarah Josepha Hale (1868)

The element of brilliant color unifies this provocative setting in a San Francisco home, ca. 1882, where rich, nineteenth-century-inspired stenciling, fabric-covered walls, and tasseled draperies make the room almost luminous. Keeping everything in just one tone prevents visual jolts, despite the amount of furniture and the number of accessories, including the impressive Victorian overmantel mirror, chandelier, and rare Renaissance Revival settee with eight kinds of needlework.

The Victorians approached the decoration and adornment of their homes with a seriousness that bordered on evangelistic fervor. From society matron to plantation mistress, people devoted an unprecedented amount of time and energy to their homes. In 1874, when Mark Twain opened the doors to his newly built Connecticut home, a picturesque "palace" with turrets and gables—and again, in 1881, following its sumptuous redecoration by Louis Comfort Tiffany—guests, curious bystanders, and eager members of the society press were all there to gawk at—and carefully record—its splendors. For months, craftsmen and cabinetmakers, art dealers and upholsterers had formed a steady stream in and out of the solid doors of the entry, bringing with them bolts of fabric shot through with gilding, furnishings, light fixtures, art glass, and paintings. But Twain was not the only Victorian who slaved over his home. Scores of lesser known folk were busy having curtains looped high with fringe, polishing mahogany tables to a high shine, plumping the cushions on their settees. Home decoration was frankly "in"; it mattered; it was dis-

Harmonious eclecticism is the key to the furnishing of this restored nineteenth-century drawing room, where an antique chintz wall-border, Rococo Revival settees, exotic screen, raccoon-tail rug, and tables draped in gold-threaded damask all complement one another in a gentle coexistence. A suggestion of the outdoors, glimpsed through the open door and stained-glass transom, anchors the grand setting with allusions to the Victorian love of nature.

cussed and analyzed everywhere.

Behind this decorative activity and interest was a good deal more than initially met the eye. Elevated to a level far beyond that of mere shelter, the home revealed nobility of character, solidity of morals, as well as nuances of taste and position of its owners. Painstakingly assembled, American Victorian interiors were fraught with expressiveness, not only reflections of their owners, but also images of the events and nature of their times. Thus, American Victorian interiors can tell us as much about codes of social behavior and human relationships as they can about paint colors and veneers.

Separated by a gulf of a century or more, however, how can one begin to unravel the mysteries of the Victorian interior in order to enjoy, appreciate, and finally re-create its style? Fortunately, the Victorians themselves left many clues behind that help us interpret the ideas that animated their rooms. Examining nineteenth-century photographs, for example, is a good way to begin, but one that should be approached with caution. Just as these vintage pictures often present a stiff, unyielding vision of the Victorians themselves, they also provide a false or misleading picture of their homes. Primitive camera techniques tended to convert shadowy romantic Victorian corners into gloom,

homey clutter into chaos. More important, the Victorians' love of rich color is totally lost; the flamboyance of patterns and prints, details of fabrics, and lavishness of ornamentation are barely discernible.

The various magazines, newspapers, and household-decorating guides of the time help flesh out the picture. For the first time in America's history, such publications fervently discussed home decoration. Industrialization had provided greater material wealth and more leisure time to more Americans, both of which led to higher social aspirations. The middle classes and the newly rich clamored for guidance on taste and improving their living styles.

Etiquette books from the period also prove an enlightening source as to why the Victorians decorated their homes as they did as well as how they viewed their own interiors at the time. For example, the stricture that a lady's steps should be short on entering the drawing room, not to exceed the length of her foot, makes sense considering the plentiful amount of furniture in the typical room. One could hardly have walked gracefully—or safely—otherwise. The unusually large number of small chairs scattered around the parlor can in part be traced to manners, specifically the fact that it was considered indelicate for a seated gentleman to rise and offer a lady his chair: the seat cushion might retain his body warmth. Instead, a fresh chair would have to be provided, making the existence of many spare chairs in the room a safeguard against the occurrence of such an impropriety. In fact, etiquette and style were so closely linked in the nineteenth century that it is sometimes difficult to tell where taste began and manners left off.

The American Woman's Home, written in 1867 by Catherine Beecher and her younger sister Harriet Beecher Stowe (better known for her best-selling *Uncle Tom's Cabin*), is an example of the home-management books that help fill in the outline for the ideal arrangement and appearance of the nineteenth-century home. It is important to keep in mind the intended audience for these books—*The American Woman's Home*, for instance, was directed at the middle-class homemaker—and that the how-to books, like the magazines, offer us the Victorian ideal and not the reality. An editorial written in the 1890s, for example, which advises readers to try to imitate Japanese simplicity with a minimum of knick-knacks and bric-a-brac, also implies by that advice that most women of that time were, in fact, doing much the opposite. Reading between the lines of the advice-givers, in other words, one can catch glimpses of the truth.

Finally, fiction written during the century adds immeasurably to the picture of what the Victorian home was like. The writings of Edith Warton, Henry James, William Dean Howells, Louisa May Alcott, and others allow us to see Victorian interiors function within the framework of their society. It's in such works that the actual layout and use of the drawing room, for instance, becomes far more real than it does through the recitation of rules one might find in an etiquette book.

These sources, as well as diaries, memoirs, and reminiscences of everyday Americans, help us to understand the ideas that created Victorian style. Foremost among these concepts is the idea of the American home as a retreat. In order to achieve the illusion of the home as sanctuary, the specific elements it contained were chosen to accentuate the differences between the security inside and the commercial howling without. The increasing solidity of Victorian furniture, for example, emphasized the unshakeable nature of Victorian family virtues; the effect of pattern everywhere was a soothing, subliminal lull. Dark, stained woodwork and paneling; heavy curtains and carpeting; leafy plants, breaking and diffusing the light—all enhanced the emotional sensation of the home

Nineteenth-century home guides frequently suggested using natural objects—pine cones, mosses, shells, leaves, or an arrangement of feathers—as adornment for the home.

as a comforting, almost womblike enclosure. In addition, the familiarity of the dozens of objects that filled the room provided further anchors, reinforcing the inhabitants' sense of their own place in society.

The sense of emotional well-being fostered by the Victorian interior was combined with an equally strong interest in material comfort, and this, too, is a key element in today's Victorian Revival. The comfort "ethic" that developed in the later part of the century was forthrightly expressed through overstuffed easy chairs with well-padded backs and seats, thickly stuffed sofas, rocking chairs and recliners, scattered footrests, and soft, draped shawls. Victorian chairs were often low out of concern for just such comfort (not because the Victorians lacked physical height, as is often supposed; dining room chairs and tables, after all, were of standard size). The lower seats permitted the easy lounging posture that many fashionable young men affected. Even though women, strictly corseted in an upright position, were prevented from this indulgence, slightly lower parlor chairs served their purposes too. By keeping the feminine center of gravity closer to the ground, the chairs made it easier to rise from a seated position when under the encumbrances of heavy skirts and numerous petticoats.

The Victorians did not emphasize only the separation between the inside and the outside worlds. Further distinctions were made through divisions within the home itself. Space was divided into spheres for the private lives of the inhabitants, for public entertaining, and for service areas. In addition, just as the Victorians accorded distinct roles to men and women, they similarly labeled the rooms of their homes. Rooms like the parlor, sitting room, conservatory, and music room—all centers of social and family life—were considered feminine spheres and were decorated in appropriately curved, delicate, highly ornamented, frivolous, or showy styles. Masculine areas, on the other hand, including the hallway, dining room, study, and library, as well as the billiard and smoking rooms in wealthier, larger homes, were furnished with solid, substantial items. The kitchen, contrary to more modern notions, was not considered a feminine domain, but rather a functional one, a place for servants, who were not regarded in terms of gender, but as a class. As a space devoted to work, the kitchen had only to be neat, clean, and efficient.

The visible effects of Victorian home-pride were also a key to the look of the nineteenth-century interior. One of the dominant cultural features of the last century, home-

The Victorians drew on all the previous centuries for design inspiration. True to that tradition, the sixteen-foot triple-vaulted ceilings in the parlor of this 1904 Belle Epoque mansion were hand painted in a design taken from a Louis XV carpet. The monumental Victorian walnut mantel is original to the home. (© Chad Slattery)

This subdued Victorian corner embodies several traditional Victorian themes: nineteenth-century home pride is evidenced by the family photographs and album, an awareness of artistic motifs is demonstrated with the arrangement of lacy peacock feathers, while the bust stands for the virtues of culture and learning. The nineteenth-century desk, originally a bedroom piece, now makes its home in the back parlor.

pride was evident in photographs, magazines, newspapers, how-to books, and novels. The Victorians strongly identified with their surroundings, believing their homes disclosed not only their taste and status but also their very virtue and worth. This attitude is most apparent in the Victorians' taste for sheer abundance of things in their interiors. Unlike their Puritan forebears, the Victorians reveled in display, and abundance was considered evidence of one's moral superiority and good works. Furniture, china, silver, glassware, paintings, sculpture, objets d'art were regarded as tokens of God's special favor, tangible signs of one's achievements and position.

Awareness of their own material achievements also contributed to Victorians' home-pride. With unwavering optimism about the future, the Victorians flaunted their faith in progress in the rooms of their homes. "Store-bought" furniture and "machine-made" lace were badges of material pride, as were the goods that poured in from all over the world: teak and brass tables from India, Sèvres porcelain, Chinese jades, all proclaiming an ever-increasing global reach. Victorian interiors blossomed further with nineteenth-century inventiveness, as demonstrated in the first glow of gaslight over cozy parlors, and later the miracle of electricity.

Closely related to the sanctioning of abundance and materialism is the nineteenth century's appreciation for ornament. Perhaps this is the element that most distinguishes nineteenth-century decoration from the design styles of the twentieth century preceding the current Victorian Revival. The nineteenth-century love of ornament resulted in the creation of elaborate exterior decoration, ranging from grand façades rippling with gingerbread, scrolls, and hectic fretwork, right down to the embellished stampings on the faces of brass doorknobs and the tiniest of keyhole roses. In light of the fact that plain or white surfaces were generally looked on with disparagement, it is not surprising that collective Victorian taste demanded such extensive detail. Henry James describes an interior as a "bare, bright, common little room [with] ugly, undraped" windows, clearly regarding its bareness with almost moral censure. This dislike for blank surfaces caused Victorian women to adorn their walls with opulently patterned wallpapers, which then were covered with so many paintings and prints that the wallpaper was often reduced to little more than a frame. Even the ceiling became a canvas to be stenciled, "frescoed" (the Victorian term for painting), or patterned in an intricate combination of wallpapers.

The love of ornament, integral to Victorian taste, is here evinced by the deeply tufted green velvet chair, with its inlaid frame; the Victorian portieres; and the unusual griffin-headed walking stick, which provides visual enrichment.

What is often surprising to observers today is the relative sophistication of the nineteenth-century eye to encompass such copious ornamentation. In fact, the Victorian design sense was surprisingly mature, possessing the ability to take in and appreciate an unusually complex mix of ornamentation, pattern, and motif. As a result, the passion for Victorian ornament extended to the most mundane areas. Even bathtubs, toilet tanks, and plumbing elements were treated to the decorative touch, and such functional hardware as door hinges were thought to gain a more ethereal quality when their brass was embossed with a design inspired by hummingbird wings.

What was developing, at least in some cases, was an environment perilously close to visual and sensory overload—intoxicating, almost alive with ornamentation, a provocative climate made all the more stimulating by its contrast to the surface propriety demanded by Victorian etiquette. In drawing rooms of the 1870s, 80s, or 90s, the psyche was teased on all sides, the equilibrium unsuspectingly capsized. Underfoot, carpeting blossomed forth from its grid of comparatively sober stripings, popular in the earlier years of the century, into gardens of stylized flowers or bold geometrics. Overhead, enthusiastically sculpted crown moldings, cornices, and spreading ceiling medallions (which increased in size with each decade) provided a visual feast. Emotionally charged furniture completed the picture: massive dining room sideboards sported realistic renditions of wolves' heads snarling from cupboard doors, or ladies' faces with small, seductive mouths appeared from the undersides of chair arms. Even the dinner table provided no respite. Plain white china, rejected by the Victorians for what was perceived as its tendency to produce a cold and stark-looking setting, was replaced with elaborate patterns and gilding. The sensuality of these rooms—their warm, dark corners, their tempting, touchable textures, their exotic imagery—provided an undercurrent of ripeness that was unmistakable.

DECORATIVE TREATMENTS FOR THE VICTORIAN REVIVAL INTERIOR

It is through individual elements of Victorian style that Victorian design philosophy achieved a practical application. The rich colors, textures, and patterns; the treatment of the walls, windows, and floors; such exquisitely crafted details as stained glass, tilework, and trompe l'oeil treatments—all instantly distinguish nineteenth-century taste. The following outline offers an overview of these elements, derived not only from historical precedent, but also from the creative context of today's Revival—one that is more relaxed in its scope and that possesses the design vitality that necessarily accompanies a fresh perspective on tradition.

Color

When examining the various specific treatments for the Victorian Revival home, the one that seems to stand out most is the Victorian color sense—a palette that consists of such warm, enriched colors as vivid bottle greens, blues, and golds; wine tones like deep burgundies, clarets, reds, roses, violets, and mahogany-browns; an ivory closer to the color of fresh, yellow top-cream than to pure white. There are also the Victorian earth tones and other colors of nature—terra cotta, ochre, and that particularly "Victorian" shade of muted stone green. What is important to realize about these colors is that most should be *deepened* rather than darkened. It was felt that deep colors enhanced the importance of the space, while light colors diminished it. For example, a Victorian dining room that was left bare and pale-walled was perceived as cold or cavernous, as impressive as a barn to Victorian eyes. Warmed and enriched by any of the deeper colors

and shades mentioned above, the room became more inviting, a stage set on which to entertain lavishly.

That's not to say, however, that Victorian homes abandoned the use of white or light tones. The nineteenth century tended toward lighter colors in bedrooms, for example, especially restful pinks, soft sea greens, light blues, and grays. Although white was generally in limited favor to Victorian tastes, it does have its precedent as a background color in the formal, French-influenced Victorian drawing room, where the use of ivory with gold or blue constituted two favorite color schemes. In addition, those Victorian Revival rooms that reflect the lighter, less formal feeling of early-twentieth-century life can certainly accommodate white accents like filmy white curtains, touches of embroidered white linens and laces—with their look of treasured heirloom pieces—or a cool, white-tiled kitchen dado.

Traditional Victorian colors also translate into Victorian Revival when lessened somewhat in intensity. Because electric light tends to cast an infinitely harsher light than did gaslight, with its orange-yellow tones, some toning down is often needed to compensate. It is, in fact, this failure to recognize that the Victorian interior was illuminated with a duskier, more muted light than

Victorian portrait heads adorn the carved arms of this nineteenth-century chair.

our incandescence and fluorescence that has so greatly contributed to Victorian colors being labeled garish and its style misunderstood as over-cluttered.

It is also important to remember that a degree of flexibility in color was inherent in nineteenth-century attitudes and that personal taste was always taken into account. Various tones and shades each had their periods of popularity, much as they do today. The April 29, 1893, issue of *Vogue* illustrated the changeability of Victorian color schemes when it mentioned that the newly fashionable colors of the season—lilac and pale green—were prominent not only in bonnets and gowns, but also in such interior accents as curtains, lampshades, and even table decorations.

Pattern and Texture

The Victorian appreciation for the simultaneous use of a wide variety of patterns and textures, particularly in those areas devoted to public entertainment, has also been adopted by the Victorian Revival. When one summons forth images of a generalized "traditional" nineteenth-century interior, it is the rich velvets, patterned brocades and damasks, and silky tassels and trim that almost inevitably come to mind. It's this rich visual texture that not only adds a patina of tradition to the Vic-

torian-inspired interior, but also serves as a foil to the uncommon blend of furnishings. Another application of such layering of pattern on pattern can be found in the piling of deep-textured rugs and carpeting one over the other, perhaps even adding animal skins for still another texture before throwing nests of hand-worked pillows dangling with fringe on top of it all.

The key to the use of multiple patterns and textures in the creation of the Victorian interior is the belief that at no time should any single pattern or texture gain dominance over the others, but should instead combine harmoniously in a single cohesive decorative statement. To achieve this, the patterns and prints used should generally be of equal strength. This rule of thumb applies to the size of the motifs as well as the brightness of the tones. Naturally, they should all relate somewhat in the basic colorings.

In a historic design sense, it's not surprising that the Victorian interior developed this characteristic overlay. The opulent lines of its furniture, discussed in the next chapter, tend to be displayed most effectively against an equally rich backdrop of pattern. The Victorian interior's traditional clustering of objects and accessories can be seen as an outgrowth of the facility with pattern-mixing and layering as well. A

Treasured objects arranged on a draped table fill one corner of this Victorian Revival apartment in New York City. Of special note is the backdrop of a nineteenth-century screen. Screens of all kinds were admired throughout the Victorian era for being both functional and ornamental; they could create rooms within rooms, conceal exits and entries, and protect against drafts.

This perfect example of the meshing of textures in a highly traditional Victorian parlor includes such details as parlor chairs upholstered with the original black horsehair, an embroidered velvet lap robe, and a Renaissance Revival wallpocket. The Neo-Grec border on the embossed velvet curtains was hand-stenciled to match the frieze by the owner of the house, and then fringed and valanced with braid. Wire was inset into the hems of the draperies to help them hold their shape. Hydraulically pressed woodwork adds an unusual touch.

plain sliver of a vase, when set against a vibrant, enriched Victorian background, could easily be lost. A grouping of two, three, or more such vases, on the other hand, could hold its own, creating an appropriately dramatic effect.

Woodwork

Much of the appeal of the Victorian tradition is derived from the appearance of its interior woodwork—the fine old staircases with their handsomely turned and ornamented spindles, balusters, and newel posts, the paneled wainscoting lining the halls, the hand-carved mantels, baseboard moldings, window and door frames, and other wooden trim. Stripped of what often amounts to a century's worth of paint layers, these elements are most effectively Victorian when they take on a highly finished look, rather than a raw or "natural" one. Tones of deep ebony, red mahogany, warm walnut, cherry, or golden oak, for example, tend to strike just the right period note.

Beginning in the 1850s, varnished, hand-grained woodwork gained a popularity, especially for an inexpensive wood like pine, which the Victorians would have painted to simulate the look of a costlier material, such as mahogany. Woodwork was also painted in imitation

of marble or other types of stone, and it frequently was even gilded or stenciled. Painting the woodwork in a variety of colors picked up from the room's wallpaper, upholstery, and furnishings (a treatment known as polychrome) was also popular for wood and plaster ornamentation, such as ceiling medallions, corbels, and cornice moldings.

Wall and Floor Coverings

Wall and floor treatments are also important to the look of the Revival home. Wall-to-wall carpeting, in large, geometric patterns, was popular in early-Victorian homes, the most typical being ingrain carpeting—a flat-pile weave—which was woven in strips, then sewn together to cover the entire floor space. Looped-pile Brussels carpeting, which was more expensive, was seen also, particularly in the parlor. By the 1870s, the fashion for wall-to-wall gave way to area rugs, which exposed the parquet-wood border around the floor's perimeter. These rugs, like the rest of the fabrics and furnishings in the home, were ornate in design and distinguished by intricate, often romantic patterns. Needlepoint rugs, imported Aubussons, Axminster rugs in Turkish designs, Oriental rugs, and Wiltons (a cut-pile carpet) were all used. Although rag rugs and hooked rugs to-

Carved, richly stained woodwork is a much-desired feature of the nineteenth-century home. The ornamentation of this woodwork is effectively set off against the textures of an antique screen and ribbed crimson portieres.

day are commonly associated with colonial-era homes, they were also found in Victorian interiors, in the upstairs hallways, in some of the bedrooms, and in country Victorian residences. Today, of course, nearly all these varieties are produced, many of them in authentic nineteenth-century designs, and the look of richly colored rugs, often layered one over the other, is an important part of the Revival.

Victorian style also had a strong association with unique and unusual wallpapers, especially with strong, highly decorative designs toward the later part of the century. Widely distributed and affordable from the 1840s on, wallpapers with scenic designs, lush overall patterns, or accompanying dado and border prints, and even those of embossed leather and faux-leather varieties, brought a bounty of color and excitement into the American home for the first time. Early-Victorian wallpapers featured small- to medium-scale patterns, frequently with vertical stripes, delicate florals, or scenes. Later, larger, more daring patterns, as well as combinations of different papers used in a single room, came into vogue. Wallpapers were so popular during the Victorian decades that a Victorian Revival room lacking this decorative treatment often seems to be missing an essential part of its make-up.

In the late nineteenth century, the wall itself consisted of several distinct parts: the dado; the patterned "fill," which covered the largest area of the wall; borders; and frieze. Re-created today, these divisions act much as they did in the nineteenth century, binding together the room's decorative elements and allowing its often eclectic furnishings to settle firmly into place. In addition, Victorian-inspired combinations of two, three, or even more wallpaper patterns used within one room can add a strong sense of architectural and decorative character to even the most stripped-down of modern spaces.

While decorative stenciling is more closely associated today with pre-Victorian decoration, it played an important part in the Victorian home as well. Although mass-produced wallpapers replaced overall wall-stenciling in most homes, stenciling continued to be used as an accent on the walls and ceilings. One might have found a stenciled border topping off a chair rail or wainscot in the dining room or hallway. It would traditionally have been varnished over to protect it from stains. Stenciled borders could also be found below the ceiling molding and frieze and on floors, while gilded stenciling might be added on top of door or window frames in more elaborate homes.

Other types of painted finishes were also part of the Victorian interior, such as glazed painted effects, popular in hallways, and sponge painting, which was more apt to be found in country homes. Trompe l'oeil graining for simulated wood and stone finishes, as well as faux-tortoise shell, marble, and even malachite also added distinction from a decorative point of view. Finally, fabric can also be used on walls to create an authentic nineteenth-century environment, especially when the silks, damasks, or brocades are quilted, shirred, draped, or lightly upholstered on the walls.

Windows

An elaborately draped and sumptuously layered window treatment is an important part of the style of the Victorian interior. Certainly a pronouncement of status and wealth, the overlayering of the Victorian window was also a practical barrier to light and heat, wind, cold, and street sounds. Because the severity of these practical problems has been greatly lessened, perhaps even eliminated, the typically heavy window treatment of the nineteenth century has been somewhat lightened in its Victorian Revival interpretations, but the windows usually still retain a highly finished look.

The typical window treatment

included four layers of curtains. Closest to the window pane hung what was known as a glass curtain, a thin, sheer curtain, usually of delicate net, marquisette, or point d'esprit. Covering that was a filmy lace undercurtain, which was then topped by a lush outer drapery, often made of velvet, damask, silk, brocade, or another similarly lavish fabric. This outer stratum was often imaginatively and asymmetrically draped with swags and festoons and generously embellished with embroidered borders or tassels, braid, and fringe. An ornamental valence, usually made of a slightly stiffened material, came next. This was called a lambrequin and was suspended horizontally from the great, often gilded wooden cornice, which stretched across the top of the window. Window covering didn't stop here either; beyond all these layers, the window would also have been heavily shuttered, often with "pocket" shutters, which folded into the window frames.

Alternatives to this admittedly opulent treatment existed, of course. Wooden Venetian blinds were a part of the era (dating back to colonial days), and instead of a glass curtain, a muslin roller shade might have been used. Roller shades, in fact, were one of the most attractive treatments the century devised, and they frequently were

Surprisingly brilliant colorings and lively mosaic-inspired patterning distinguish this reproduction Victorian parlor carpet—a wall-to-wall Wilton—in a historic nineteenth-century rowhouse. Both color and design are faithful to the 1867 original, however. (© Mel Adelglass, courtesy Old Merchant's House)

painted or hand-stenciled with scenes, sayings, and designs.

During the summer, the heavy draping of the Victorian window was considerably lightened. This was called "disrobing" or changing to "summer dress," and accompanied other seasonal changes in the interior. Summer dress for windows consisted of changing the heavier drapery layers to lighter silks or cottons or to airy lace panels that permitted the flow of light and air. Another choice was thin white muslin, which softened the harsh effect of the summer's direct sunlight at the same time that it excluded insects and dust.

Tilework, Stained Glass, and Other Crafts

Decorative tilework, which was popular from the 1870s onward, has also become a key part of the Victorian Revival interior. Tiles were used all over the Victorian home, not only at fireplace and hearth surrounds but also on hallway floors and wainscots, in bathrooms, and in kitchens. In some instances, the fascination with exotically painted tiles was such that entire rooms were sheathed in elegant tile mosaics. Tile was also used on some kinds of Victorian furniture: it was seen on sideboards, hallstands, washstands, and firescreens, as well as in accessories.

Framed tiles were hung as "pictures" or mounted on stands set up on a mantel. They were even used practically, as trivets for tea.

Victorian tile patterns reflected the full range of the century's eclectic taste. Anything at all was fair game as subject matter: classical Greek or Roman portrait heads; Renaissance or Gothic themes; William Morris-style motifs; Egyptian, Aesthetic, Arts & Crafts, or Art Nouveau designs. Stylized fruit, flowers, animals, birds, landscapes, and even scenes from literature were all depicted. It wasn't unusual either to find a hearth surround spelling out a motto or saying in tile, while fireplace tiles in a child's room might show characters from fairy tales or nursery rhymes. Tile painting, in fact, eventually became something of a Victorian fad, and blank tiles were manufactured with directions and designs for ornamental painting featured in women's magazines.

Stained glass, which was known as art glass or decorative glass, also lent its sparkle to the Victorian interior, especially during the 1890s and the first decades of the twentieth century. It, too, has been wholeheartedly revived. Whatever the design, in fact, whether romantic, intricate florals or sterner geometrics, it tends to impart nineteenth-century ambience and ornament to today's homes. The Victorians

Above: *An impressive handmade tassel, a modern reproduction of a Victorian original, ties back the draperies in this historic early-Victorian home.*

Opposite: *The same attention to detail can be seen in the private home, where fabric bows and tassels adorn wall hangings and draped tables. The stenciling on these doors represents just one of many decorative paint finishes that the Victorians indulged in. (© Mel Adelglass, courtesy Old Merchant's House)*

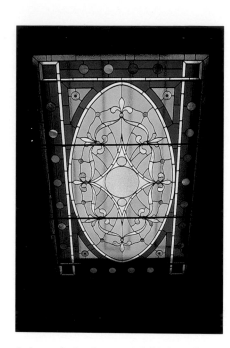

A thorough cleaning revealed this heretofore undiscovered stained-glass skylight overlooking the top floor of an 1890s townhouse.

themselves used art glass liberally, in interior windows as well as exterior, and panes were even sold through the Sears Roebuck catalog. Typical Victorian uses were in dining rooms and bathrooms, surrounding the front doors in sidelights and transoms, and as interior transoms and door panels. A stylish home of the 1890s might have also installed a colored-glass skylight, rich with Art Nouveau tendrils and vines, while iridescent glass in Eastlake-inspired or neo-Gothic geometrics would have framed a front bay window in light and color.

Horticulture

The Victorians also loved to display their gardening efforts in their homes, and no nineteenth-century abode would have been considered complete without a conservatory of sorts or at least some artistic touches of greenery scattered about. This became particularly prevalent in the later decades of the century when the potted palm became an almost universal symbol of Victorianism. All flowers and plants were welcome in the home, however, and botany, horticultural arts and crafts, and flower arranging were highly approved hobbies. Ferns, vines, and leaves were collected and pressed between panes of glass, forming what were called "transparencies,"

and hung in the windows or the sidelights of hallway doors. Flowers were dried to make lush winter bouquets or arrangements that were protected under domed glass containers.

"Natural" frames were another popular convention. These were made from twigs, vines, and pine cones (or even beans, corn, or straw) and decorated with fruit clusters, berries, and leaves. In this vein, an 1875 book devoted to "tasteful home decoration" suggests creating "a very pretty frame for an engraving . . . from the long, tough stem of the common cat tail found growing in profusion by streams and marshy places." This taste for natural frames stems from the Victorian desire to match the picture frame with the subject and the medium being framed. A skating scene, for instance, might take a "frosted" frame; a seascape, one made from coral or shells; while, we're told, oil paintings or chromolithographs called for gilding.

The enjoyment of nature within the home grew out of the Victorian love of ornament and was evident at all levels of nineteenth-century society, from the prominent lady to the newly arrived immigrant kitchen maid. But especially when the costly use of velvets, gilding, and brocade was beyond one's means, the fruits of nature provided an inexpensive and appropriate substitute for beauty within the home. Catherine Beecher and Harriet Beecher Stowe were among those who held this view, considering few things lovelier for the home than nature's own ornamentation:

If you live in the country and have your eyes open and your wits about you, your house needn't be condemned to absolute bareness. Not so long as the woods are full of beautiful ferns and mosses [or] while every swamp shakes and nods with tremulous grasses.

The Victorians' susceptibility to nature also flourished despite, or perhaps because of, the century's industrial enthusiasms. Both fascinated and intimidated by progress, their extensive horticultural efforts can be regarded as attempts to withdraw from an increasingly mechanized, complex world and return to the values and charms of a simpler society. Many Victorians, in fact, adopted utopian philosophies and pastoral back-to-nature community experiments, and these were an important part of the century too. In light of the eclecticism of their interiors, however, it's likely that the more mainstream Victorians saw no contradiction in seeking satisfaction for bucolic longings while maintaining their devotion to mass production. The Victorian vision was so vast and multifaceted, it could easily encompass both.

The unusual silhouette of this nineteenth-century wicker chair on the side porch of a Gothic summer cottage, ca. 1875, was chosen for its subtle reflection of the cottage's architecture.

Chapter 3

Victorian Eclecticism: The Furnishings

As home is the place where our best and happiest hours are passed, nothing which will beautify it or adorn it, can be of trifling importance.

Manners; or Happy Homes and Good Society (1868)

Victorian Revival eclecticism—the assembling of many key nineteenth-century themes into a satisfying and comfortable whole—is beautifully demonstrated here, in what the owners describe as an elegant Victorian "farmhouse." Included are a ca. 1890 wicker chair draped with a paisley shawl, an unusual 1850s needlework footstool on Bennington-pottery legs, brocade-covered tables, a tufted green velvet Renaissance Revival chair, and a nineteenth-century French-inspired walnut clock. The Tiffany-style lamp dates from the early 1900s, as does the Edison cylinder phonograph.

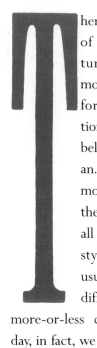here was no single style of Victorian furniture—no one design, motif, type of wood, or form of ornamentation—that can be labeled simply "Victorian." Instead, the quality most representative of the era was its free-for-all cultivation of many styles and design trends, usually stemming from different sources, into a more-or-less cohesive whole. Today, in fact, we tend to use the word "Victorian" to accommodate the astounding variety of nineteenth-century substyles, fads, revival and reform movements that caught the Victorian fancy from one year to the next during the era's long duration. As a term, it includes lacy wicker, coiled and frilled, culled from the porches and verandas of such nineteenth-century resorts as Newport and Saratoga. It includes curiosities like animal-horn furniture, crafted from antelope and deer horns and often upholstered in natural hide. Victorian furniture even goes as far afield as the rural "cottage" style, which embraced painted pine cupboards and spool-turned beds, just as it took in the opposite—elegant, urban masterpieces in the historic revival styles, produced with loving care by the great furniture makers of the century. The results: Victorian eclecticism, and an interior both splendid and irreverent, but, above all, highly livable.

The receptivity of Victorians to the series of changes in furniture styles that filled their homes was indicative of the emerging, and likewise changing, Victorian character. The sparer rooms of the 1830s and 1840s, for example, featured American Empire furniture, a look that retained strong vestiges of the classicism that had marked the pre-Victorian years. The style had yet to develop into the more flamboyant taste of the mid-century and later—a taste that nurtured the richly ornamented Rococo Revival and Renaissance Revival styles.

Even in the earliest Victorian interiors, however, the incipient rejection of the strictly classical is evident. Intimations of gilding, discreet touches of Gothic romanticism, and, certainly, nods to encroaching ornamentation are all there. It wouldn't be long before the domination of European classical motifs would be tumbled, succumbing to the lure of an American brand of romanticism.

The eclectic "High" Victorian interior was in part the nineteenth-century equivalent of "keeping up with the Joneses," fueled by an attraction for the latest, the biggest, and the best. This attitude was, in fact, a direct product of the machine age. Especially after the 1850s, the strides made by industry helped produce not only the vast fortunes of the superwealthy but also the lesser fortunes of the striving nouveau riche and an increasingly prosperous middle class, all clamoring for new, fashionable home products to support their hard-won status and position. Popular taste became subject to unusually rapid changes; new styles came and went. There was now no need for furniture that would last for generations. Not only had industrialism produced an extraordinary demand, it had also enabled furniture makers to supply it. New technology allowed for the easy and quick reproduction and interpretation of many different styles of furniture, drawing on the whole history of taste, in order to meet the rapidly changing taste of the nineteenth-century marketplace.

The simultaneous existence of Victorian substyles further fed the tendency toward eclecticism. Notable exceptions, such as Lyndhurst, in Tarrytown, New York (conceived, built, and furnished as a total Gothic Revival vision), the overall aestheticism of Château-sur-Mer, or Frederick E. Church's "Persian" Olana notwithstanding,* Victorian homes rarely were decorated to re-

flect a single vision of interior design. More often, homes were filled with furniture from all the different Victorian styles. Chicago society leader Mrs. Potter Palmer had a Louis XVI drawing room, an Old English dining room, a Spanish music room, and Turkish, Greek, and Japanese parlors. Alice Gwynne Vanderbilt's 137-room Victorian palace was an even more lavish example of the eclectic trend. Its tile-walled Moorish smoking room was crowned by a Tiffany stained-glass dome, a Chinese room was filled with porcelains and scrolls, and it even included a Louis XV salon and a patriotic colonial cache of early-American memorabilia. On the floors above these "ideal" rooms were the proper Victorian interiors occupied by the family: cozy bedrooms with soft green velvet walls and dark green-and-gold upholstered furniture; sitting rooms made gentle and intimate with lace, flowered fabrics, bright Turkish rugs, and plenty of family portraits and soothing pastoral paintings.

An even more common form of Victorian eclecticism, however, was the practice of adding token examples of each newly fashionable substyle to the existing decor. During the 1870s, with the advent of interest in the cultures of the Far East, for example, hand-painted fans, Japanese screens, and draped Chinese

*See Historic Houses listing on pages 253–265 for further details.

A harmonious Victorian blend typical of the late century's eclecticism is found in the hallway of this suburban home, where an informal Victorian wicker settee and a carved Renaissance Revival hall mirror complement each other perfectly. The dado is the original embossed leather, beautifully preserved and darkened with age. To the left of the hall mirror is a nineteenth-century boot scraper.

silks appeared in otherwise French-style Victorian drawing rooms.

Victorian eclecticism also ushered in a hybrid kind of Victorian furniture. Not only could one combine different styles within a home, or within a room, but one could also combine several styles in a single piece of furniture. For example, Eastlake ideas and the Renaissance Revival style were frequently merged, producing a chair that could be described as Renaissance Revival with Eastlake influences or as an Eastlake chair with Renaissance Revival touches, depending on which influence was dominant. Sometimes three, four, even five different styles were rolled and scrolled into a single piece. This type of furniture, though fun to look at and live with, is understandably hard to label and falls most readily into a special category—"proper Victorian"—and nowhere else.

In order to make sense of the Victorian substyles, it is convenient to divide them into three main groups. The period of the 1830s through the 1860s encompassed a series of historic-revival styles, all creative evocations of the past. The overall revival spirit, the turning to the past as a design source, was best summed up by Owen Jones in 1856, in his influential *Grammar of Ornament*, which stated: "We can find inspiration only in the past. The

present has nothing to teach us and the future is not our concern." The period of the 1870s through the 1890s, on the other hand, found its styles in a series of reform movements, rebelling against what that generation felt was the derivative and often florid nature of the revival furnitures. While preaching spareness and "honesty" in furniture and home design, however, these reform movements often unwittingly produced a visual clutter all their own. The third major trend, which coexisted with both the revivals and the reforms, falls under the heading of Victorian "invention" and involved the use of materials other than wood—papier-mâché, horn, wicker, and various metals—in the cause of innovative furniture design.

On the following pages is a summary of most of the major substyles that make up Victorian furniture design. The dates indicated refer to the general periods of time when each specific type of furniture was most popular in the United States. Because the Victorian substyles flow from one into the other, however, these time periods should be regarded rather loosely. American Empire furniture, for instance, continued to be manufactured throughout most of the nineteenth century, although its heyday was in the 1830s. Rococo Revival parlor suites could be found in homes from the 1850s through the 1890s, but the look was certainly not in the vanguard of style by the later decades.

Before proceeding to a discussion of the various Victorian furniture substyles, we must note an important element in the Victorian Revival interior by way of warning. Despite the freedom that Victorian eclecticism offers, not every nineteenth-century furniture substyle was meant to work happily with the others. The revivals tend to hang together; the reforms work nicely in tandem; and exotica can mix rather freely with them all. However, the most successful Victorian Revival interiors are those that explore aspects of the eclectic spirit in terms of their furniture, and often in their art, while maintaining a consistency of period in the shell of the room— the wall and floor coverings, moldings and mantelpieces, window treatments, and lighting. Juxtaposing an ornate Rococo Revival chair with a brick hearth of the Mission style does not revive Victorian eclecticism, but results in a misdirected hodgepodge. Furniture of the reform styles—Eastlake-inspired pieces or Anglo-Japanese—would be both visually and philosophically out of sync if paired with an ornate Rococo Revival chandelier and a cabbage-rose printed rug, although all these elements are certifiably "Victorian."

THE VICTORIAN REVIVALS

American Empire (1830–1840)

Sturdy American Empire furniture led the way into the styles of the Victorian "century." Although the look was losing favor even at the era's outset, American Empire is important in that it serves as a bridge style. While it barely qualifies chronologically as Victorian, it nevertheless links the formal and symmetrical taste of the eighteenth century to the more sumptuous and developing idiosyncratic one of the nineteenth. Although later pieces were made with the assistance of machinery (particularly the bandsaw, creating Empire's much-admired veneers), American Empire is further set apart from most of the succeeding revival styles by virtue of the fact that much of it was handmade. Such hand construction and its simplicity in comparison with subsequent styles have resulted in its being considered by many today as the most "respectable" of the Victorian Revival styles.

In the first quarter of the nineteenth century, Americans favored Greek Revival furniture—a style also known as Empire—for their homes. By the 1830s, this style had taken on a look that was heavier, more solid and substantial, and less

refined, in the process losing much of its surface ornamentation. It is this later-period style, characterized by simple rectangular shapes and massive, largely unornamented mahogany forms, that is known as American Empire. Its use of S-and-C-scrolls and turned pillars and columns has caused it to be nicknamed the "pillar-and-scroll" style.

Although American Empire furniture was still used in the Victorian home in a fairly traditional way (lined up along the walls in a standard classical arrangement), the style also introduced new pieces of furniture into the American interior. Notable among these were the marble-topped console table and sideboard, the classically shaped klismos-style chair with its curved saber legs and concave back, the pier table, the Grecian sofa with round bolsters, the sleigh bed, and the S-and-C-scrolled footstool. The weightiness of these pieces, coupled with the taste for brilliantly colored upholstery fabrics—especially red, but also bright gold and sapphire blue—marks the beginning of the Victorian-styled interior.

American Empire attained its high point in popularity in the 1830s and 1840s, but it continued to be produced throughout the century, even when other styles came and went. In fact, it even enjoyed a full-scale revival of its own—called Sec-

An American Empire walnut bureau. (Greenfield Village and the Henry Ford Museum, Dearborn, Michigan)

A Gothic Revival secretary, ca. 1836–1850, in rosewood and satinwood, attributed to J. and J.W. Meeks. (The Metropolitan Museum of Art, Purchase, Rogers Fund, 1969)

ond Empire or Empire Revival— near the turn of the century.

Gothic Revival (1840–1850)

Considering the Victorian romanticization of the Middle Ages and its glorification of the picturesque, it is no surprise to find that the Gothic Revival style was the next of the early-Victorian revival styles to develop. Victorians of the 1840s were wholeheartedly caught up in the Romantic Movement: Thoreau's meditating at Walden Pond captured their fancy; images of medieval pageantry and chivalry conjured up by the popular novels of Sir Walter Scott stirred their imaginations; and the mystical aura of the Gothic Revival forms themselves appealed to their growing romantic perceptions. Gothic Revival received a further boost through the efforts of architect Alexander Jackson Downing, whose book *Cottage Residences*, first published in 1842, envisioned a beatific rural American countryside dotted with picturesque Gothicized homes.

Victorian Gothic Revival furniture is perhaps the easiest of all the nineteenth-century revival styles to identify. It immediately calls to mind the pointed arches and delicate spires, pierced tracery and fairy-tale crockets and finials that make up the Gothic cathedral.

These details, as well as the quatrefoil and trefoil—also traditional Gothic hallmarks—repeatedly turn up in Gothic Revival furniture. Such religious overtones also presented the early Victorians with what must have seemed a proper decorative symbol of Christianity, as opposed to the pagan Greco-Roman background of the earlier classical styles. Gothic Revival furniture contrasted with American Empire in form as well as philosophy: its elegant, attenuated shapes appeared to be even more so when compared with the solidity of American Empire.

Although Americans always found the look a bit foreign and intimidating, Gothic Revival furniture did open the door to succeeding decades of Victorian ornament, and when it was used in small touches, it lent a special charm to the still spare American interior. A Gothic Revival chair, a pinnacled hallstand, or classical American Empire furniture adorned with touches of Gothic ornament made elegant additions to a fashionable home. Gothic Revival accents also turned up on accessories and home furnishings throughout the century: Gothic-inspired designs appeared on wallpaper and fabrics; Gothic arches were found on lamps, clocks, and other objects. Ultimately, of course, admiration for the Gothic was the basis of the "modern" Gothic underpinnings of the reform movements of the 1870s and 1880s.

The academic and religious overtones of the Gothic style bestowed a masculine quality, causing Gothic Revival furniture to be considered most proper for the hallway or dining room, and especially the library. A Gothic Revival library, in fact, eventually became something of a cliché in American Victorian taste. Unlike the more public rooms of the house, which were redecorated constantly to conform with the many styles that appeared, the library remained a Gothic sanctuary for most of the nineteenth century, with leather-upholstered seating, sturdy oak bookcases, and walls painted in quiet, neutral, "scholarly" colors.

Rococo Revival (1850–1865)

Nothing better expresses the undiluted decorative intentions of Victorian taste than the swirls and curls of the Rococo Revival furniture from the era beginning with the 1850s and extending through the end of the Civil War. Florid, curved, carved into sumptuous wreaths, rocks, shells, fruits, and flowers, it is probably the style most often brought to mind by the word "Victorian." Medallion-back sofas, balloon-back parlor chairs, bowlegged center tables with white marble tops, and multishelved étagères

were all typical of this style.

Rococo Revival furniture and the other lavish accouterments of the style also mark one of the clear turning points in American Victorian taste, for they were among the highlights of New York's Crystal Palace trade fair in 1853. Following that exhibition—itself a landmark in decorative taste—interior design began its advance toward the heavy, multilayered mix now associated with High Victorian style.

Rococo Revival furniture was the embodiment of Victorian exuberance. Constructed primarily of rosewood, it seemed to fairly burst from its well-made seams with all manner of undulating curves and naturalistic carvings. At the outset, Rococo Revival furniture was in great demand by the fashionable, urban well-to-do classes. Later, machine-made versions of Rococo Revival styles were easily obtained by the middle classes, and it was these simplified forms that dominated the parlors of small-town America for much of the remainder of the century.

Rococo Revival furniture also marked the beginning of certain significant changes in the Victorian interior itself. Its popularity suddenly released parlor furniture from its formal along-the-wall line-up, for example. People began to move their furnishings all over the room,

Rosewood Rococo Revival slipper chair, attributed to John Henry Belter. (The Metropolitan Museum of Art, Gift of Mr. and Mrs. Lowell Ross Burch and Miss Jean McLean Morron, 1951)

Above: *A parlor corner, with Rococo Revival settee and Renaissance Revival desk and gambling table.* **Opposite**: *A closeup of the desk illustrates the Victorian love of nooks, crannies, and cubbyholes. The stereoscopic viewer resting on the top shelf was used for looking at the three-dimensional storytelling cards scattered below, a popular Victorian pastime.*

often drawing them to the center in a casual, almost haphazard, way. This was partly because the strong, but delicate-looking furniture was actually amazingly light; almost dainty, it could be carried from here to there in a way the ponderously heavy American Empire furniture could not. This new mobility was enhanced by the introduction of castors to furniture. They were found to be such a practical convention that the height and shape of castors thereafter became important considerations in overall design.

Rococo Revival brought the padded-back chair into the Victorian parlor as well as the marble-topped center table. The style also heralded a furniture innovation that appealed greatly to the middle classes: furniture sets for bedrooms, dining rooms, and, especially, the parlor. A typical parlor suite consisted of one or more sofas, often with medallion or serpentine backs, a center table and an étagère, several arm and side chairs, as well as assorted footstools, thereby enabling one to furnish the entire living room in one fell swoop. Regal parlor suites in hand-carved and gilded rosewood were *de rigueur* in city mansions and country plantations alike, while lesser versions in walnut or mahogany and cheap ones in oak, pine, or maple were even sold by mail order. And, although the Rococo Revival style was always

thought of as more appropriate to the parlor than the bedroom, magnificent Rococo Revival beds can be found in many Southern historic homes, especially in the vicinity of New Orleans.

At its best, the Rococo Revival style provided a showcase for the skills of the century's finest craftsmen. It has become most closely associated with the work of German-born John Henry Belter, a New York cabinetmaker whose name has become almost synonymous with the most lavishly carved Rococo Revival furniture. Belter made exquisite works from the gleaming rosewood, his style being almost unmistakable in its lacy intricacy. In fact, it is a prime example of the blending of man and machine in the production of art, for his work depended on a patented lamination process by which thin sheets of wood were first pressed and glued together, then steam-molded into curving, cushiony shapes, and finally embellished with his intricate carvings and pierced openwork.

Renaissance Revival (1865–1885)

Predictably, it was only a matter of time until the Rococo Revival had a rival for star status in the fashionable American home, the style called Renaissance Revival. Although it was seen at New York's Crystal Palace in

1853, Renaissance Revival didn't attain its peak of popularity until the late 1860s and 1870s. Like Rococo Revival, it was often sold in suites, but there the similarity ended. Where Rococo Revival was delicate and elegant, Renaissance Revival was brash and bold.

Height and size were emphasized by Renaissance Revival furniture. Towering china cabinets or bedstands in walnut and walnut burl* were often as much as seven or eight feet high, while a carved sideboard might stretch the entire length of its wall in an average dining room. Its ornament was equally impressive: this was furniture in a grand manner, with heavily applied ornamentation such as cartouches, volutes and stylized anthemions, inlaid medallions and sculpted portrait heads, and, almost always, incised gilded lines.

The Renaissance Revival style, the choice of the American aristocracy of dollars, was more than just this mass of pediments, crests, and gaudy gilding. There was a strength and self-confidence inherent in its showiness that marks this period of unprecedented growth and nation-building. In the hands of fine cabinetmakers like John Jeliff of Newark,

Daniel Pabst of Philadelphia, and Leon Marcotte of New York, its artistry and craftsmanship rival those of any other maker and style. The label was, of course, something of a misnomer. Although based vaguely on the architectural styles of the Renaissance, it was actually a typical Victorian composite that bears little resemblance to the furniture of the Renaissance or to that of any other time.

The banner of the Renaissance Revival style was also taken up by manufacturers in Grand Rapids, Michigan, who outdid themselves producing machine-made versions of black walnut beds with built-up headboards and marble-topped dressing bureaus with gas brackets. The role of that city as a furniture center escalated as Americans moved westward, and its efforts can be credited with popularizing Renaissance Revival among the middle classes. While these provincial versions weren't comparable with the elegant work of Marcotte or Jeliff, they fully satisfied the taste of the general public. Although the families in these new Western towns had a different way of life from that of the settled Eastern Establishment, demands and tastes for their parlors were much the same.

*Black walnut, in fact, became the favored wood of the Victorian era. Not only did it provide a fine, dark contrast for the brightened upholstery fabrics, as well as lending itself to any amount of carving, but it also showed less wear than other woods. Curly maple and birch were seen as lacking the richness required for the parlor, and pine and cherry were scorned as frankly rustic.

Above: *Renaissance Revival walnut and walnut burl dresser with marble top. (Greenfield Village and the Henry Ford Musuem, Dearborn, Michigan)*

Opposite: *This carved and inlaid Victorian cabinet is found in a Boston rowhouse. Its outlining with incised and gilded lines is typical of the Renaissance Revival from the 1870s. At the right is a nineteenth-century sewing table and a Victorian reception chair. Sliding pocket doors divide the parlors.*

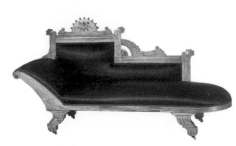

Above: Victorian cottage furniture—a day bed upholstered in horsehair is a simplified version of grander Victorian forms. (Greenfield Village and the Henry Ford Museum, Dearborn, Michigan)

Opposite: A modern interpretation of the nineteenth-century taste for the exotic reflects both the Victorian passion for travel to Eastern lands and the rising importance of richly upholstered furniture. Typical elements of exotica—the Turkish-inspired divans with their heavy burdens of fringe, pillows from India, and a rich assortment of unusual objects—combine to create this highly sophisticated "bazaar." The room's architectural elements bear witness to the apartment's former status as main salon in a Stanford White building, ca. 1896, now converted into co-operative apartments.

Cottage Furniture (1830–1900)

Thanks to the twin miracles of mass production and mail order, all manner of enticing goods was available to Victorian Americans. It was no wonder that more and more furniture was created with shelves, tiers, and niches in order to support and display these myriad goods. As early as the 1830s, little catalogs illustrated with woodcuts also engaged in the gentle art of selling goods to rural America. The furniture was usually of a type known as "cottage" furniture, pieces crafted from pine or perhaps from hickory, maple, or other inexpensive woods. It could be purchased in local villages or was available at modest prices through the mail.

Outside the major metropolitan centers, country versions of the most popular furniture styles were produced, and therefore cottage furniture doesn't represent a separate style, but a scaled-down, simplified version of its city cousins. The elegant city étagère, for example, was turned into the humbler whatnot, which displayed the family treasures equally well. A cottage version of a Renaissance Revival bed might not have been as imposing as its original, but the look was immediately recognizable. Instead of being oiled and varnished, however, cottage furniture usually was painted in enamel pastel shades of gray, white, lavender, light blue, or lemon. It was often enhanced with stencil work or other designs, and painted finishes, such as sponge painting or graining in imitation of a more expensive variety of wood, were favored.

Even in its own time, Victorian cottage furniture appealed to sophisticated folk who enjoyed it in their country homes. Highly ornamented and enameled cottage furniture was even presented at New York's Crystal Palace by several manufacturers, some pieces painted in white and gold, and one "chamber," or bedroom, set was enameled in an unusually dark color.

Victorian Exotica (1870–1900)

During the 1880s, *The Decorator and Furnisher*, a leading home magazine, wrote about a certain "change in taste [that] dates from the Centennial Exhibition." This change, it said, had come about through travel, which had created a "desire for decoration [that] amounts to a perfect craze. No one can tell where it is going to end."

What was being discussed was the developing taste for Victorian exotica—furniture designs inspired by visits to foreign lands like Morocco, Egypt, Turkey, and especially Japan—that assailed the Victorian

Above: Exotic Victorian table in the "Japanese" style. (National Trust for Historic Preservation, Lyndhurst)

Opposite: Mixing styles, piling pattern on pattern, was the key to the nineteenth-century exotic room and is carried off here with consummate assurance. The multicolored rugs, unusual fabrics, beadwork sofa pillow, and even casually stacked paintings, which contribute to the carefully controlled density of possessions, all hearken back to their Victorian antecedents.

interior and once again changed its appearance. Parlors came to resemble colored and gilded illustrations from *The Arabian Nights*. Proper ladies took tea in seragliolike surroundings, amid samovars, swords, and swaying palms.

Travel had become an important part of fashionable Victorian life, and once culture-hungry Americans of means saw something of Egypt or Japan, decorative possibilities beckoned. Souvenirs from exotic countries testified to one's ability to indulge in this fashionable wanderlust, and they crowded their way into the home. For those who couldn't afford to wander far, the great Centennial Exhibition of 1876 in Philadelphia was an eye-opener, bringing glimpses of faraway storybook lands to thousands of middle-class Americans. The improved transportation of the 1870s enabled many more Americans—200,000 more, it was said—to attend this fair than the Crystal Palace exhibition, which had taken place twenty-three years earlier.

Victorian exotica for the home took many forms: small inlaid tables from Persia, fringed and tasseled upholstered Turkish chairs, slender, ebonized Japanese-style tables with stylized latticework, and hallstands made of golden bamboo. Egyptian Revival furniture sported gilded sphinxes, palmettos, and other Nile-

inspired designs, and embroidered Chinese silks and tapestries provided elegant coverings. While the wealthy often were able to create total exotic environments known as "ideal" rooms, people of all economic means added touches of exotica to their parlors of revival furniture.

Fifty foreign countries were represented at America's Centennial Exhibition, and one of the most popular booths was that of Japan, with bronzes, ivories, bits of pottery, and porcelains among its treasures. It inspired the Anglo-Japanese look—Victorian interpretations of the stylistic simplicities of the Orient in furniture, accessories, even wallpapers. Despite such claims to simplicity, however, these furnishings were as ornamented as any other Victorian offering; they were just done with a distinctly Asian flavor. Even more popular than "Japanese" furniture were the "Japanese" accents one could add to one's home: screens, endless examples of blue-and-white china, hand-painted fans to pin to picture frames or perch on the mantelpiece, and parasols to shade a crystal chandelier.

The Turkish Bazaar at the Centennial was also a roaring success, and its brass trays, incense burners, piles of cushions, and inlaid tables were adapted by Victorian homemakers as fashionable "Turkish

An Eastlake-inspired organ with Aesthetic inlay work. (Grand Rapids Museum, Grand Rapids, Michigan)

touches" for the home. Everyone, it seemed, had to have a Turkish corner—a den or other area of the home devoted to these eccentricities. Every Turkish corner also had a Turkish chair or at least a puffy, upholstered, Turkish-style ottoman or divan. Turkish-upholstered furniture was a major trend in the late-nineteenth-century home. This furniture was upholstered in billowy shapes, tufted into oblivion, and then fancifully hung with loops, braided tassels, and plenty of fringe. Not surprisingly, it was remarkably comfortable.

THE REFORM MOVEMENTS

The Eastlake Revolution (1872–1885)

As Victorian interiors began to overflow with the revival styles and with exotica, people were beginning to become sated. Charles Locke Eastlake, an Englishman, was not alone in his pleas for a reversal of the frenzied quest for splendor, but perhaps his voice was the loudest, especially in American homes. In his best-selling book, *Hints on Household Taste*, published in England in 1868 and in America in 1872, he strove to turn the tide of decoration and ornamentation in the interior, preaching "honesty," "plain ornament," and a simplicity of design. "For many

years past, there has been, as I have said, a great deficiency in public taste . . . but by degrees, people are beginning to awake to the fact that there is a right and a wrong notion of taste."

Eastlake's book was an instant hit on American shores and quickly became the household bible for every young couple who had pretensions to good taste and wanted everyone else to know it. Eastlake's ideas were directed, in fact, at the young, "artistic," well-to-do, the refined and sensitive people who supposedly had both good sense and the intelligence to appreciate these ideas. They wanted nothing of the fussy old Victorian stuff in their parlors. In Edith Wharton's *Age of Innocence*, Archie Newland dreams of the house he and his fiancée will someday have, finding comfort in the fact that, though she probably will want to keep their parlor conventional, he probably could do as he pleased in his own library, which would of course have "sincere Eastlake furniture and the plain new bookcases without glass doors."

A mania for Eastlake furniture pervaded the home in the 1870s. Because Eastlake didn't design furniture himself, and his book had only a few illustrations, manufacturers had to take it on themselves to interpret his ideas. What emerged was not exactly what Eastlake had in mind.

In essence, what Eastlake advocated was a cleanup, a return to the economy of rectangular shapes over wasteful curves, to carved as opposed to applied moldings, to simple incised lines (known as railroad tracks) over excess ornamentation. He also favored hand-construction over what he felt was slipshod machine work, although few of the Eastlake-inspired pieces we have today were actually made by hand. His ideas were considered by many to be a kind of "modern Gothic."

Despite his intentions, Eastlake's ideas were largely misinterpreted by American manufacturers. Anything that was even vaguely straight-lined, or that was simply less ornate than its predecessors, was slapped with the magic Eastlake moniker. Most manufacturers found it difficult to follow his ideas to the letter. Fearful that pure, unadulterated Eastlake would be too radical to sell, they replaced the usual curved shapes with more boxlike lines, only to go ahead and apply the familiar machine-made curlicues and ornament that they knew and loved. When one looks at "Eastlake" furniture today, it's hard to believe it was a reaction against excess ornament, so ornamented is it in its own way.

What is called Eastlake, or more properly Eastlake-inspired, furniture today is usually made of sturdy oak or walnut and consists of clean, simple lines—or what were then thought of as such. Shapes are undoubtedly squared, and ornamentation includes jigsaw scrolling, spindles, and incised lines. Eastlake versions of horsehair-upholstered parlor sets, bedroom furniture, desks, pier mirrors, platform rocking chairs, pump organs, hall trees, and sideboards were all made.

Although Victorian America never really lost its taste for opulence, a slew of sham Eastlake furniture flooded American homes. So much of it was contrary to what Eastlake himself envisioned that he was forced to issue a formal denial of the furnishings being traded under his name.

The Aesthetic Movement (1880–1890)

Also originating in England, the Aesthetic credo of the 1880s succeeded the Eastlake movement. The symbol of its style was the sunflower. Emblazoned on countless home furnishings, from sideboards and bedstands to brass fireplace andirons, it was the symbol of artistic sensibility. Along with the lily, it proclaimed the presence of Aestheticism loudly and clearly to any who were listening.

Aestheticism actually stemmed from a combination of several Victo-

An ebonized and stenciled cherrywood night table, ca. 1880, by Herter Brothers, bears witness to the Aesthetic influence in America. (The Metropolitan Museum of Art, Gift of Paul Martini, 1969)

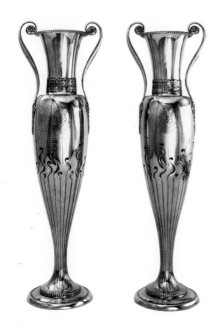

Silver Art Nouveau vases by Tiffany & Co., ca. 1894. (Museum of the City of New York)

rian reform movements whose aim was the regeneration of the Victorian interior and the arts. It encompassed Eastlake's Gothic Revival tendencies (specifically his interest in the handcrafts movement), at the same time as it took in the ideas of poet, painter, and designer William Morris and his set, ultimately acquiring a patina of elegance and simplicity derived from the arts of the Orient. In a sense, the Eastlake movement and the art reforms of the 1870s fused in the 1880s to embody a social phenomenon that embraced dress, poetry, literature, as well as all the fine and decorative arts.

The banner of Aestheticism was "art for art's sake," and the man who unfurled it was Oscar Wilde. While he wasn't the "originator" of the aesthetic philosophy per se, he can be credited with latching onto it early and with being its most ardent public proponent. Wilde brought Aesthetic ideas into the American home during his much-publicized lecture tour in 1882, speaking about interior design and the decorative arts. Of course, by that time Americans had already been exposed to some variations of the reforms: Eastlake had made his mark a decade earlier, as had the Japanese bazaar at the Centennial. By 1879, forward-looking converts were already adding Aesthetic peacock feathers, fans,

and blue-and-white china to their parlors. Through his tour, however, Wilde divested Aesthetic motifs of their implication of belonging only to elite, sophisticated circles, and made them accessible to the general public, making every level of society feel the Aesthetic pull.

Aesthetic-inspired furniture was strikingly beautiful, making use of simple, Japanesque lines, ebonized woods richly ornamented with inlaid designs of flowers—often sunflowers—and leaves. Some stylish pieces were inset with hand-painted tiles. Furniture made of bamboo also had Aesthetic overtones, even when it was of the often-used faux-bamboo (actually turned bird's-eye maple). This faux version was so realistic and sought after that it's often hard to realize that it isn't the real thing. Because the Aesthetic movement was short-lived, furniture with identifying Aesthetic motifs is rare and highly prized today.

Art Nouveau (1890–1915)

Swirling, swanlike lines, graceful curves and tendrils, entwined vines and flowers, and other romantic forms all add up to Art Nouveau, the design successor to the Aestheticism of the late nineteenth century. Like its visual opposite, the earlier American Empire style, Art Nouveau is sometimes considered "borderline" Victorian, since it leads nineteenth-century taste into the brave new world of the twentieth century. Not only does it qualify chronologically as Victorian, however, it is firmly Victorian in a decorative sense, for it represents a return to the flowers, leaves, and other organic, natural forms of the 1850s Rococo Revival, but though in a more abstract, sinuous, flowing manner. The sensual, curvilinear forms and richly naturalistic ornaments are fully in the High Victorian spirit, and thus expand our definition of what Victorian style encompasses.

As an international design movement, Art Nouveau began in Europe around the 1870s. Its force in America wasn't felt until twenty years later, however, when Art Nouveau motifs turned up as ornaments on cabinets, bookcases, and desks of the 1890s. A modified version of Art Nouveau furniture was even mass-produced in Grand Rapids in the early twentieth century. The romantic return-to-nature forms of Art Nouveau also entered the Victorian home through the decorative arts—in glassware and graphics, in metalwork and jewelry, in late-Victorian wallpaper and textile designs, and, of course, in the singular lighting and glassworks of Louis Comfort Tiffany—more usually than through furniture.

Arts & Crafts (1900–1920)

What could come next? Inevitably, the Victorians turned to a total change. At the end of the century, the Arts & Crafts Movement challenged popular taste as a major "reform" movement, meeting with quick success. Suddenly it was popular to try to produce furniture that was as plain and simple as possible. The very plainness of the furniture contributed in a way to its quick rise and fall in popularity. It seemed so simple to make that an army of do-it-yourselfers and quickie manufacturers were encouraged. Quality degenerated, and like other Victorian fads, this type of furniture quickly went out of style.

Before this happened, however, Arts & Crafts furniture attracted many supporters. Like the earlier Eastlake style, on whose philosophies it was built, this was furniture with a message, something the Victorians knew about from past experience. Arts & Crafts pieces were meant to be products with integrity of craftsmanship—durable, attractively proportioned pieces that honored the dignity and labor of their makers. In other words, it was a protest against the industrialized mass-production that had characterized furniture making in previous decades. Although several craft communities were established in the

Above: *At the height of its popularity in the first decade of the twentieth century, everything from standing clocks to living room furniture was fashioned in the functional, unadorned Mission style.*

Above and opposite: *The comfortable slatted Morris chair and stately Roycroft cabinet are part of a superb collection of American Arts & Crafts furniture in Cape May's Queen Victoria Inn. They are accented by antique Southwestern textiles, glazed Arts & Crafts pottery, and a subdued William Morris wallpaper. The room's brick hearth also finds its spirit in the Arts & Crafts style.*

United States to further these lofty ideals, the best-known proponents of the style were Gustav Stickley; his brothers Leopold and George, who started a rival firm under the label L. and J. G. Stickley; and Elbert Hubbard and his Roycroft community. Of course, each thought the others to be humbugs. American Arts & Crafts furniture is often also called "Mission" furniture because of its severely plain, rectilinear appearance. Legend has it that the name was derived from the idea that this was furniture with a mission—to be used. The name also refers to the fact that Arts & Crafts furniture resembled the simply constructed oak pieces found in the Franciscan missions of California.

Arts & Crafts furniture usually was made of hand-finished quartersawn oak, with a straight-lined and geometric construction. The impression it gives is one of solid, sturdy usefulness, while the working out of its proportions lends it an unexpected, almost sculptural grace. Details include wooden knobs, hammered copper or iron hardware, leather or canvas seat covers, and exposed nailheads. Roycroft pieces are often prominently marked with its Gothic letterhead. The same Arts & Crafts principles that applied to furniture design were put to work producing metalwork and leatherwork and were also used in printing.

Undeniably, Arts & Crafts furniture was radical for its time, but the Victorians were in a period characterized by a searching intellectual curiosity, and for those with a reformist bent, Arts & Crafts presented an answer. They responded to it wholeheartedly, coming to appreciate furniture whose only adornment was, in the lingo of the age, the beauty of "good proportions, mellow finish and harmonious decoration," and it became extremely popular in the first two decades of the twentieth century. Gustav Stickley characterized his work this way: "There is no seeking for flashy or cheap ornament. Nothing is stuck on. It is simple and dignified and frank."

The Mission look was lauded in the leading home journals of the day, and, for a time, tastemakers believed that here was a style with staying power. However, like the other Victorian substyles, its fame quickly faded as imitators produced the look, but without the quality, thereby cheapening its image and hastening its demise.

Golden Oak (1880–1920)

Turn-of-the-century Golden Oak, with its deep yellow finish that exposes the rich grain of the wood, is in sharp contrast to the dark-stained look of handcrafted Mission oak,

Roll-top Golden Oak desk from the late nineteenth century. (Greenfield Village and the Henry Ford Museum, Dearborn, Michigan)

which was produced at approximately the same time. Always a factory-produced style, there were no philosophies or messages implicit in it. When a little extra design was wanted, for instance, no thought of hand-carving was entertained. If a dining room chair wanted ornament, it was pressed into the back of the chair; if a sideboard needed an extra touch, applied ornamentation was the answer. Here, in other words, was good, sturdy, fairly simple furniture with some pretty curves, such as serpentine fronts on dressers, that made no pretense to being "fine furniture." Frequently sold through mail-order catalogs, its sturdiness, appealing lines, durability, and, most of all, affordability—in 1902, a set of four pressed-back chairs with caned seats and spindles was priced at $1.60 the set; a dresser with a beveled mirror and cast-brass handles, $9.85—gained for it a wide following, which has resulted in wide availability today.

Golden Oak's less formal, but still solid appearance made it ideal for the less ornate interiors, sans gilding and frills, that were becoming popular in the early 1900s. At the same time, it evoked the homey warmth and strong family values that still persisted. Typical pieces included massive, old-fashioned roll-top desks, claw-footed pedestal tables, dressers with cubbyhole glove boxes

and swinging mirrors, cane-seated chairs and servers, washstands and shaving stands, and even such Victorian hybrids as a combination bookcase/writing desk.

VICTORIAN INVENTION

Throughout the late nineteenth century, as the revival, reform, and exotic styles vied with one another for prominence, innovative new furniture was also being designed and produced, primarily intended as accent pieces for the larger body of established Victorian styles. Often these were made of non-wood, and otherwise nontraditional, materials, including wicker, metal, horn, and papier-mâché. Sometimes they fell within the realm of the new, technological novelties of patent furniture. Although always outside the mainstream of so-called serious furniture, this category gave a vital, distinctive look to the Victorian interior that corresponded with the rich experimental tempo of those later years. At this time, individual pieces of nonmatching furniture, rather than matching suites, had come to be preferred, a fact that lent a new and fashionable air of informality to the home, making a wicker settee, a papier-mâché tilt-top table, or a horn chair fit right in. The following types of furniture, then, can best be regarded as exclamation points for the more entrenched styles, punctuating the era and adding accents to its rooms.

Papier-mâché (1850–1900)

Furniture made of paper—papier-mâché, that is—was one of the earliest of the furniture innovations that the Victorians indulged in. After mid-century, it became quite the status symbol, scattered throughout the fashionable Victorian drawing room. The elegant nineteenth-century hostess, for example, would have been sure to serve tea to her guests on a gleaming, black lacquer papier-mâché tea tray. A papier-mâché firescreen inlaid with sequins and mother-of-pearl would have been poised by the fire, while a papier-mâché chair would have occupied a favored corner of the boudoir.

It is no surprise that papier-mâché appealed to fashionable Victorian taste from the start. It had all the feminine curves and decorative adornment of the Rococo styles as well as hints of the exotic. Most of the items made of this material were small: snuff boxes, tea trays, screens, dresser-top mirrors, and small chairs were among its most popular applications.

Papier-mâché was composed of paper pulp. Strips of paper were mixed with glue, steam-pressed in a mold, hardened into shape, then layered with coat upon coat of lacquer before being painted with decorative scenes or inlaid with small jewels and mother-of-pearl. Despite its delicate appearance, it was quite durable if protected from water or dampness. It was occasionally used to construct a larger piece of furniture, like a love seat or a settee, which would require bracing the pulp materials on a wooden frame for strength.

Horn (1865–1890)

There existed a more rugged side to the petticoated age, and this is in part exemplified by the horn furniture of the day. Like papier-mâché furnishings, it became something of a status symbol in the American home, particularly during the 1890s. The opening of the American West and the exploits of its settlers were sources of unending fascination to Victorians, and such adventures provided this inspiration in turn. Along with the dime novels that breathlessly recounted the daring adventures of Jesse James, people demanded for their homes rough and rugged-looking chairs made of buffalo and steer horns, tables inlaid with horn veneer and resting on antlers, or horn hat racks. Upholstery for horn furniture was usually derived from natural skins, such as

Leather-seated steerhorn chair. (Greenfield Village and the Henry Ford Museum, Dearborn, Michigan)

This Victorian garden bench made in cast iron reflects Rococo Revival motifs. (Greenfield Village and the Henry Ford Museum, Dearborn, Michigan)

cowhide, sheepskin, goatskin, or even jaguar, although, in a strange mixing of opposites, horn chairs were sometimes upholstered in silk plush and adorned with fringes.

Metal (1840–1900)

When we consider that cast iron was *the* building material of the day, it was just a matter of time before it turned up in the homes of the industrial nineteenth century. From the 1850s onward, cast-iron pieces, usually suggesting the lacy Rococo look of Belter or the slender spires of the Gothic Revival in metal, made proud new additions to the proper Victorian home.

Cast-iron furnishings included umbrella stands and doorstops, hat racks and towel racks, washstands, garden furniture, and beds. In addition to cast iron, however, other metals assumed their place indoors. Twisted wire, for example, less expensive than cast iron, was used for flower stands, serving carts, and chairs. The glow of brass also brightened the Victorian interior, especially during the second half of the century as brass beds, cribs, towel racks, and hat racks entered the home.

Wicker (1875–1910)

Few items stand out in today's imagination as more quintessentially Victorian than wicker. This light, airy-looking furniture, which graced late-nineteenth-century porches and piazzas during languid turn-of-the-century summers, hasn't gone out of style since. Considering the fact that it was originally intended for resort or outdoor use, it is somewhat surprising that Victorian wicker found a place in the parlor as well as in the garden. Few items were thought to be more chic, however, than a cane-seated wicker settee or rocker added to an overstuffed parlor, although a keen eye was called for to keep such a mix in good taste. Wicker was also used in children's bedrooms and was often combined with Mission furniture in the casual living areas.

"Wicker" is a generic term that refers to any of the twisted-fiber furniture the Victorians produced of rafia, reed, rattan, or willow. At first it was relatively plain, but it eventually evolved into the intricate masses of balls, twists, and curlicues, painted or stained, that we associate with the style today. All manner of items were produced in wicker—sofas and settees, chairs, benches, tables, hanging porch swings, even cribs—which was admired for its lightness and delicacy. A big thronelike wicker chair, today known as a peacock chair, also became a standard fixture in the late-century photographic studios, and vintage photographs frequently show infants propped up in these fanciful wicker chairs.

The popularity of Michael Thonet's bentwood furniture was related to the wicker passion. This furniture, specifically the famous bentwood Thonet chair, was imported to the United States from Austria and became immensely popular after the Civil War. Thonet, like Belter, used the steam press to bend and curve wood into delicate and graceful fluid shapes, resulting in a look that appears at once contemporary while reminiscent of Rococo Revival forms.

Rustic furniture is also related to wicker. This category includes Victorian twig furniture (highly collectible today), as well as the more organic rustic furniture made of roots, stumps, branches, and even bits of driftwood. Before the advent of mail order, this furniture was common in rural homes, but it was later seen on more sophisticated country estates, where it was intended to evoke the aura of what the Victorians felt were simpler, more natural times.

Patent Furniture (1860–1900)

The nineteenth century has been acknowledged as a time of invention, and nowhere is this more apparent than in what was called patent furniture. In an age in which the patent offices were overwhelmed with applications for everything from revolving castors to electroplated napkin rings, a good percentage of such patents were for some very odd furniture—vibrating chairs or sofas that doubled as bathtubs, for example. But there also were some practical ideas, as well as some that have a strange and wonderful appeal of their own. To imagine the wide variety of innovations, both good and bad, consider the following Victorian patent innovations: tilt-back invalid chairs; high chairs that folded into strollers or cradles; recliners; adjustable platform rockers designed so that the runners wouldn't slice into new, costly parlor carpets; beds that folded into desks, wardrobes, or bookcases; and, of course, the Murphy bed, which popped out of the wall.

One of the best-known makers of patent furniture was George Hunziger, who held over twenty patents for various types of folding and mechanical furniture. His work stands as a unique Victorian homage to the machine age. His Hunziger chairs, which looked mechanical and collapsible, but weren't, are perhaps the best known of his designs today. Somewhat related in appearance to Renaissance Revival furniture, they seemed also to be composed from the spare parts, gears, and gadgetry

Above: Patent furniture—a walnut side chair by George Hunzinger, ca. 1869, a substyle of the Renaissance Revival. (The Hudson River Museum)

Overleaf: As well as furniture, the Roycroft community produced metalware, glassworks, and books. The leather-topped Arts & Crafts table studded with nailheads, hammered copper bowl, angular lamp, and even suede bookcovers are typical of the community's output.

Some Victorian furnishings don't fall into any specific category. Such is the case for this exquisite screen made of scraps of wallpaper, cards, and other illustrations, all pasted and varnished onto a frame.

of an engine.

The Wooten desk, designed in 1874, is another example of the more distinguished patent furniture that the era produced. This was a massive, elaborate "home office" designed by William S. Wooten that had something of a "Horatio Alger" spirit to it. It was a response to the nineteenth-century worship of the entrepreneur, and the prototypal owner was just that: a successful industrialist who needed a secure and private place for his records and papers, but who also longed for something elegant and extravagant as a symbol of his position and wealth. Nothing filled the bill like a grand Wooten desk.

The magnificent Wooten desk, a symbol of power and plenty, aptly sums up the fast and furious march of Victorian furniture styles, which, along with the special, embellishing treatments, were the decorative building blocks of the Victorian home. The appearance and use of the various styles of furniture were complicated by the Victorians' susceptibility to fads, especially during the 1880s. At one point during that decade, for example, *The Decorator and Furnisher* announced that dogs with fur the same shade as one's furniture were all the rage in fashionable homes (whether the dogs were dyed to match the upholstery—or vice versa—is not known). Another time, the news was leaked that the latest shade of yellow was called "chicken down" and that "geranium red" had replaced "cardinal red" in chic—a distinction, perhaps, that only the Victorians could appreciate. Even with this fickleness, however, the basic social symbolism of the furniture and objects remained consistent throughout the Victorian period. Carefully arranged throughout the individual rooms—the hallway, the parlor, the bedroom—they garnered an even broader range and deeper meaning, which we'll explore in the chapters ahead.

Chapter 4

The Victorian Hallway

The hall is the keynote to the whole house, therefore everything about it should be dark and solid. Light colors are frivolous and gilding is out of place. Dark, rich colors with a dash of deep red are mostly used for wall and ceiling decorations.

The Household (1881)

The owners of this 1874 home reproportioned the overlong hallway by highlighting the division suggested by the archway. The effect is created by using two different wall treatments (here, the original embossed Lincrusta-Walton forms the dado), a series of small rugs instead of a single continuing runner, and by switching from tile to carpeting. The hallway becomes more personal and intimate as one delves farther. The fringed, tasseled, and braid-trimmed banner which highlights the arch is similar to the ornamentation in Queen Victoria's Pullman car.

Above: *A scaled-down hall tree, the slightest suggestion of layering (a patterned rug over a plain carpet), and a splendid collection of Victorian walking sticks conspire to become the perfect treatment for the small vestibule of the Mainstay Inn in Cape May, ca. 1875.*

Opposite: *As was typical in the later Victorian decades, every inch of the hallway in this beautifully restored 1882 Anaheim home is layered with carpeting, wallcoverings, pictures, throws, and bric-a-brac. The patterned carpet is of authentic design, recreated from a swatch discovered in a hallway closet during restoration.*

The hallway, the first "room" in the American Victorian home, was more than the strictly utilitarian space in which one wipes one's feet and drops one's mail that it is today. In every way, the hall was its own room, a space to be reckoned with. Solemn, solid, designed for sober dignity and definite effect, it was a room that proclaimed in no uncertain terms just how important its owners were.

Because the Victorians firmly considered their home to be an expression of their status as well as their taste, the decoration of any of its public areas was approached with particular deliberation. The hallway was given as much attention as were the main living rooms or dining rooms. Every object, every color, every pattern, was selected with a full consideration of its ability to create the desired impression. In an age when taste was inalterably linked with morality and ethics as much as with status and style, the first impression received on entering the hallway of the home was crucial for communicating the owner's place in society. The idea of "mere decoration" was a meaningless concept in Victorian America; more, it

A sample of Lincrusta-Walton wallpaper in the hallway of this restored South Dakota historic home, ca. 1889, is painted and richly glazed to show off its high relief. This thickly encrusted wallpaper, today reproduced in a variety of patterns, was typically found in the hallways of Victorian homes and was admired for its durability as much as for its more ornamental qualities. (© John Burrows)

was patently absurd. Decoration was a serious business, an emblem of a way of life.

Just as all the rooms in the home were decorated with an eye to expressing the full range of Victorian values—social, moral, and cultural—the hallway was designed to be the first suggestion of the worldly, "solid citizen" security that Victorian society held so dear. A bare or sparse entryway would have labeled its owners as common; one too overdone or too "gilt-ridden" was the sign of the arriviste.

In order to truly understand the full impact of the Victorian entryway, however, it is necessary to briefly retrace our steps and approach the Victorian home as it would have been approached then, observing the marble and the carved-stone detail or other ornamentation on the facade. These were the first signals of luxury and substance within. After we have climbed the tall gray stone steps and squarely faced the high, dark, wood-paneled doors looming in front of us, we reach out and pull the bell, then wait. The doors open and we are ushered inside, past the leaded glass side panels, through a small vestibule. The maid takes our coats, our cards, and we wait again. Now, inside the hallway of the Victorian home, we are in a position to see the life of the

home unfold.

The moment the tall, polished front doors close behind us, the first impression would be that of a dark and sheltering enclosure, not a sensation of forbidding or unpleasant darkness, but a deliberately comforting, secure one. Churchlike and quiet, the hallway was designed to make one feel shielded and protected from the clamor of the horses' hooves clattering on cobblestoned streets, the clanking of metal cart wheels, the shouts of street vendors, in short, the commotion of the teeming nineteenth-century world on the other side of those doors.

This sense of there being a firm barrier separating the outside world from the home was, in fact, an effect fostered intentionally by the Victorians. Even the huge front door, swinging on great hinges and noticeably solid bolts, was designed to emphasize this perception.

Once inside, our eyes would take a second or two to adjust to the dimness of the light filtering through small stained glass windows and insets which frame the front door. This shadowy half-light, barely supplemented by hanging lanterns, would cast a rich gloom on the satiny finish of the deep wall treatments, reflecting off the dark wood wainscoting or the shiny, varnished low relief of an embossed dado of Lincrusta-Walton (one of the new simulated-leather wall-papers). It would pick up, too, the heavily patterned wallpapers above the dado, their fertile greens, ox-blood reds, or burgundies.

Taking a step or two forward, one of the first things we would see would be the massive hall tree, with its twisted, horned, or spiraled "branches." Another wall would sport a grandfather's clock, looming there to inspire thoughts of culture and learning in the home's visitors, as well as filling a need in the days before everyone owned and wore a watch. The art work would have been chosen with care. Sculptures staring out from niches, a family portrait, perhaps an etching or two—all recognized immediately as proper and appropriate. The ab-sence of major or elaborate oil paintings on these walls was in keeping with the custom and tastes of the times. The influential book written by Edith Wharton and Og-den Codman, Jr., *The Decoration of Houses*, was very clear on this point: "Where the walls of a hall are hung with pictures, these should be few in number and decorative in composi-tion and coloring. No subject re-quiring thought and study is suitable in such a position."

Despite the impression of musti-ness we receive today from nine-teenth-century archive photo-graphs, a sniff of the air in a well-maintained Victorian home might well surprise one with its freshness. The Victorians, as evidenced through their writings on the house-hold, seemed to exhibit an almost obsessive fussiness about proper ventilation, devoting pages, even chapters, to this topic. Their obses-sion is not surprising when one re-calls that stale air was then widely believed to breed disease. The rugs in the hallway (deemed healthier than laid carpeting because they were easier to clean frequently) would have been turned and beaten regularly and often. The sharp odor of homemade furniture polish—probably one part turpentine to equal parts linseed oil and vinegar—would emanate from the center stairway, with its gleaming dark wood spindles and shiny balusters, its steps paved with runners held in place by brass carpet rods. In the most meticulous of households, stamped brass stair corners might have also been used. These eliminat-ed dust- and dirt-collecting corner spaces and made the stairway easier to sweep clean. At the same time they provided the refined, Victorian nicety of a decorative touch in an unexpected place—as did orna-mented and embossed door pins and hinges, door knobs, and escutcheon plates—a theme we'll see again and again throughout the Victorian home.

Above: A collection of walking sticks and canes was a fashionable accouterment for the nineteenth-century man-about-town. Elegant ones were made of ivory, marble, or even onyx, their handles of chased silver or gilded metal. Rarest are those with concealed compartments to hold a compass, or perhaps a pinch of snuff.

Opposite: The elegant entry in this New York co-op owes much of its character to the decorative traditions of the last century. A palette of rich crimsons, toned slightly darker in the dado, sets the mood, while the stairs to the gallery/library, the doors, and pilasters are handgrained to create an impression of nineteenth-century luxury. The small cove created by the gallery would typically have been furnished as a Turkish corner, a sitting room, or as a showcase for art. Partially enclosed by the low glass-topped screen, here it is set up as an intimate dining spot.

Essentially there were two schools of thought regarding the proper decoration of the Victorian hallway. Early in the period, the hall served as a transition area, dividing the house spatially while symbolically distancing it from the outside, and outsiders. For the family, it was basically a thoroughfare en route to more important areas of the home, in which to deposit parcels and packages, a dripping umbrella, a cloak and hat. For visitors, whether invited or unknown, the hallway was a place to wait to see whether or not they would be "received."

In larger, more imposing homes, however, the hall soon came to be seen almost as an adjunct to the drawing room. Originally unheated, some larger halls even began to be constructed with fireplaces. Furniture also entered the hallway, usually in the form of straight-backed chairs, a bench, or a cushioned settee or two. It was in a hallway such as this that a gentleman might conceivably feel comfortable enough to smoke in the presence of a lady without risking banishment to the library, smoking room, or billiard room.

This later, more roomlike concept of the Victorian hallway came to predominate, and by the height of the Victorian era, status-conscious Victorians had come to regard the hall as the means of setting the tone and demeanor of the entire home. This applied only to private halls and entryways, however. In the middle-class nineteenth-century apartment houses just beginning to be built in the 1870s, it was felt that public lobbies, hallways, and stairwells were best left simple. To furnish the public hall as one would an ornate private parlor (this grave social error having been committed in several buildings erected at the time) was to risk the potentially awkward social situation in which residents might feel obligated, by the very nature of such a homelike space, to exchange greetings with other residents to whom they hadn't been properly introduced. The borders of Victorian hospitality were clearly drawn: the welcoming embrace was enjoyed only upon moving from the public hall into the private one.

Once inside the home or apartment, an impressive entryway was pivotal, so much so that even the most modest nineteenth-century dwellings seemed to allot disproportionately large spaces for that purpose. As early as 1842, the eminent architect Andrew Jackson Downing designed a four-room cottage, described as being for a family of only moderate means, and reserved an eight-by-twelve-foot area for the hallway. In blueprints for a larger, Tudor-style home, the hallway expanded to a full twelve-by-sixteen-

A towering Renaissance Revival hall mirror on a marble-topped base dominates the entryway of Cape May's Mainstay Inn. Reflected in the mirror is a restored Victorian gaslight chandelier and a massive Renaissance Revival sideboard crested with antlers.

foot space—more than is often allotted for a typical apartment dining room or bedroom today.

The Victorians also used visual tricks to increase their hallways' grandeur and effect. One, particularly applicable today as well, is that of adding false doorways in the hall, which created the illusion of additional wings to be reached through these new passages.

In tackling hallway decor, Victorian tastemakers preferred dark, strong colors. For example, if painted walls were desired, a glazed sage green field, topped with a stencilwork frieze, would have been ideal. Dark-colored, boldly patterned wallpapers were also favored, not just for their look of substance and wealth, but because only such forceful colors and well-defined patterns were considered strong enough to be taken in at a single glance when passing quickly through the hall to the parlor or dining room.

At the same time, there was a very practical attitude at work in the choice of the hallway wallcoverings. The typical treatments recommended for the lower portion of hallway walls was a covering either of wainscoting (mahogany or oak or a softwood grained to resemble one of these) or leather or one of the popular simulated-leather wallcoverings, which were then painted and varnished. Occasionally, depending on the taste of the owner, a flashier treatment was accorded. For example, in Molly Brown's Denver home, built in the 1890s, the hallway anaglypta as well as the cornices and ceilings were totally sheathed in flamboyant gilding. Not only did such treatments provide the entryway with an immediate impression of richness, but they also bowed to the hallway as a high-traffic area, one that was subject to scuff marks and handprints and therefore was difficult to keep clean. A painted and varnished dado, or one that was wood paneled, could simply be wiped free of soil. The practice of graining the hall woodwork in black-walnut imitation (another suggestion of Downing's) shows this same mix of priorities at work: it provided the desired "greater effect," at the same time serving to disguise soil and scuffing. Floor treatments too were evaluated with similar reasoning. Although inlaid wooden floors, rugs, runners, and India matting were all popular, authorities like Charles Locke Eastlake recommended tile flooring for the hall, pointing out that it was durable, attractive, and cheap—all the better to withstand the trampings of muddy boots.

In many Victorian hallways, the stairway became a major feature of the decor. According to *Godey's*, the Victorians liked to ornament the sides of the stairway with tiles or painted panels, stenciling, or even squares of white India matting painted in tilelike designs, which could be changed when one got tired of them. Another *Godey's* idea, suggested during the 1880s, was to adorn the stairway with a motto of a "homely and instructive nature" spelled out along its side, running down the staircase. This was in keeping with the use of mottoes elsewhere in the home, such as a "Welcome" over the entry door or a framed message or sampler in a cozy hallway nook. Religiously oriented mottoes on the staircase were considered to be in bad taste, but any variation on "Home, Sweet Home" and other such sentiments met with approval.

The most notable feature of Victorian hallway furniture was that it was massive, impressive, even slightly oversize or overbearing, rendering the space more "masculine" than "feminine." The grandiosity of the hallway furniture was counterbalanced, however, by the Victorians' simultaneous efforts to diminish and humanize the very majesty that they were enthusiastically creating. It is in this kind of decorative paradox that the complexity of the Victorian temperament, as expressed in the domestic interior, becomes apparent. By artificially subdividing

their long, winding hallways—whether by segmenting them with bridges of ornamental fretwork, by breaking up the visual effect of their length with a succession of small rugs rather than using a single long runner, or by distilling the whole effect to a more human scale with conceits like decorative arches or flags of tasseled draperies, or portieres—they strove to reduce the hallway without trivializing it, thereby giving it a more comfortable, manageable proportion.

Perhaps the most frequently encountered piece of hallway furniture in the typical American Victorian home was the hall tree, sometimes called a hat tree. With its brass or iron hooks, sometimes a mirrored inset, glove box, and shelf, or perhaps including a lidded seat compartment to hold rubbers and overshoes, it had become the traditional receptacle for sundry household paraphernalia. Newspapers and mail would pile up on its shelves; coats, hats, umbrellas, and walking sticks hung from its sides. Hall trees were available in every style imaginable, from cast iron to oversize pier mirrors, from the simplest of designs to the most ornate. One ambitious nineteenth-century furniture maker advertised nine different mail-order selections. For only $4.60, a fifty-pound hall tree could be had in what was described as "richly pol-

Another view of the Mainstay Inn hallway— walls lined with oversized and generously filled pieces of carved furniture, create a properly substantial effect. During the nineteenth-century, the simple runner lining the stairs would have been held in place with brass carpet rods or twisted cords of braid, tacked into place with porcelain nail heads.

The hallway in this duplex apartment is treated in a lavish, ornamental way with painted moldings, a reproduction Victorian wallcovering, and plenty of pictures and art objects to create eye appeal in a relatively insignificant place. Animal portraits and prints such as these were a special favorite of the Victorians.

ished and neatly carved golden oak," complete with three double hat hooks and a beveled mirror.

Because not every hallway had space for a full-blown hall tree, decorative concessions were often made. In city townhouses, for instance, where halls tended to be narrow, a wall-mounted hat rack and shelf stand were frequently substituted. If space was truly at a premium, one could hang several pairs of antlers on the wall, in graduated sizes one above the other, to hold hats, umbrellas, and canes, and still be in good taste according to the strictures of the times.

In most Victorian homes, though, the hall tree remained fixed—the "signature" piece for the hall, much as the center table or étagère stood for the mid-century Victorian parlor, or the monumental china-filled sideboard, for the dining room. The presence of the hall tree was more than merely a practical cliché, however, for it also served as a social "telegraph," the answering machine of its day, indicating who had "called." For example, in Edith Wharton's *Age of Innocence*, a chronicle of 1870s New York life and mores, a rather ostentatious sable-lined overcoat and a monogrammed silk top hat resting in the hallway reveal not only the presence of a rival, but also his identity. In this scene, a slightly scandalous impropriety is communicated through the hall tree; obvious to the Victorian reader, it might easily be overlooked by readers today. At this time, etiquette dictated just what one left on view in the hallway. According to *Sensible Etiquette of the Best Society* (1878), gentlemen always left their coats and overshoes in the hall, but, unless they were calling on particularly close friends, they carried their hats and walking sticks with them to the drawing room. The implication of leaving one's hat and stick in the hall was that one intended to stay more than the discreet fifteen minutes that society sanctioned, thereby flaunting the prescribed social code.

The type of artwork proper to the hallway was another case in which taste mingled with etiquette to make up Victorian style. Generally, the hall space was felt to be best enhanced with sculptures and busts displayed on pedestals or in recessed wall niches. Also acceptable was a display of armor, antlers, stuffed trophy heads, tapestry, and heraldic glass. Oscar Wilde, echoing the educated sentiments of the day, felt that pictures didn't belong in the hallway at all, but should instead be hung where one could take the time to examine and enjoy them. If used—and small paintings and etchings were often preferred to an "offensive" bareness—they should be

hung at eye level, he said. "The habit in America of hanging them [paintings] up near the cornice struck me as irrational at first. It was not until I saw how bad the pictures were that I realized the advantage of the custom."

Other suitable supplementary pieces for the Victorian hallway were mirrors, carved oak "ancestral" chests (chosen to suggest an enviable background and heritage, especially when there was none), and wooden chairs or benches, often bearing a medieval motif. Originally, the seats of hall chairs and benches were left bare or were upholstered in leather to prevent waiting messengers from staining more elaborate or expensive seat coverings with their long, muddy coats. They also served to dissuade uninvited visitors too unsavory to be admitted to the parlor from making themselves too much at home. A hall table of some kind would also typically be found in the Victorian hallway. These varied in style and design, but generally were not especially ornate. According to *Nicholson's Home Companion of 1870*, a hall table should be in good taste, but not so overly elaborate as to draw attention from the overall "architectural effect" of the hallway.

The hall table was more than simply another surface on which to deposit parcels, mail, or gloves, however. Most often it held the all-important calling card tray—the silver, silverplate, or porcelain receptacle for calling cards, the pass to civilized social life during most of the nineteenth century. While the purpose of the calling card tray was simple enough (so that the card might be carried to the lady of the house free of fingerprints), so complex were the nuances of this highly ritualized social game that its rules were meticulously articulated in dozens of etiquette books to enable the aspiring participant to fully understand.

All of the social concerns of the nineteenth-century world were reflected in the highly prescribed space of the hallway. Its intimations of luxury and proclamations of status were promises that the rest of the home was designated to fulfill. As the preface to the Victorian home, the hallway set up expectations of what was to come, coaxing one to explore further, beckoning the visitor onward to even greater splendor within. That invitation would first be realized in the Victorian drawing room or parlor, the most public, most significant room in the house, the central focus of nineteenth-century prestige, ambition, and taste.

Above: *A quaint wallpocket served as a handy catch-all in the nineteenth-century home. Placed at the end of a long hallway, it served to hold mail, keys, or copies of the latest magazines.*

Opposite: *Woodwork and paneling, beautifully preserved, and a delicate fretwork arch highlight the grand hall of this historic South Dakota home, once a private residence. With its rugs, fireplace, oversized mantel, and furnishings, the room almost takes on the appearance of a reception area.* (© *John Burrows*)

Chapter 5

The Victorian Drawing Room

For it [the living room] has a serious relation to education, and plays an important part in life, and, therefore, deserves to be thought about a great deal more than it is. It is no trifling matter, whether we hang poor pictures on our walls or good ones, whether we select a fine cast or a second-rate one. We might almost as well say it makes no difference whether the people we live with are first-rate or second-rate.

Clarence Cook, *The House Beautiful* (1878)

Color enriches the parlor in a Boston rowhouse (ca. 1858) being restored by its architect-owner. The furniture is arranged in a classic mid-Victorian way—elegantly grouped around the marble-topped center table. Colors, fabrics, carpets, and wallpaper, although new, are based on original or period styles, but the furniture and accessories all date from 1840 to 1875.

hen escorted into the Victorian drawing room,* one beheld the most lavishly and carefully appointed room in the home, the reflection of Victorian pride at its height. It was here that Americans of the nineteenth century most blatantly flaunted their wealth and status for all to see; here the all-important qualities of comfort, ornamentation, and abundance were permitted to reach their fullest expression. As one entered the room, one would have, in fact, experienced the almost physical assault of its decoration: the warm, layered explosion of pattern, color, texture, and ornaments.

Despite the apparent nonchalance of its arrangement—the casual disorder of drapery and throws and the seemingly haphazard clusterings of objects and furniture—nothing was bought, set, or displayed at random. There wasn't a thing that didn't have meaning, as *Harper's Bazar* frankly admitted. A

*For purposes of simplicity, the terms "drawing room" and "parlor" will be used interchangeably. Generally, both refer to areas we now designate as the living room, although the term "drawing room" (in its antebellum derivation) usually refers to a more formal, elegant space.

The cool silhouettes of 1870s furniture create a restrained and beautiful still life in the front parlor of this Brooklyn brownstone (ca. 1882), a setting that strongly recalls the nineteenth century, without slavishly reproducing it. The furniture includes Renaissance and Egyptian Revivals and Eastlake styles, while the magnificent woodwork, restored by the owners, is original to the house.

few moments of observation in the drawing room would have provided all the information needed regarding the owners' level of culture. Something as insignificant as the "character of bric-a-brac" in the room, the magazine informs us, was very revealing. Further, the *absence* of such trifles was as betraying as the presence of the inferior article. The mere shape of a lamp, for example, was said to show whether people had any taste, individuality, or aesthetic sense, or merely bought what their neighbors bought.

Looking back at the parlor from our vantage point, it becomes immediately apparent that the Victorian world was one divided, and that this room was the domain of a woman. Here, for example, were her dainty porcelains, feminine laces, brocades, and delicate needlework. Men's lives, by and large, transpired outside the home, in the realms of politics, commerce, or the law. Even masculine leisure activities like smoking, cards, chess, and billiards were often more congenially pursued at the private clubs that were popular, rather than in the confines of the home. Victorian women, on the other hand, were born, bred, and lived out their lives in their homes, and so claimed them as their decorative turf. The very concept of the Victorian hearth and home, in

fact, was symbolic of the female sphere, with its domesticity and family life.

In every way, the parlor was the most significant room in the Victorian home, and it shaped itself around feminine activities, feminine models, and the tasks that filled up feminine hours. The overstuffed, over-upholstered parlor, its windows seldom opened, can even be interpreted as an overt symbol of the Victorian woman's own rather upholstered existence: *her* windows never opened, in effect. The rounded, cushiony shapes that filled the room mirrored the womanly Victorian ideal. One can see the female shape re-created in the curves of "bosomy" upholstered sofas, in the overstuffed chairs with "shoulders" draped in fringed paisley shawls. The shape of the low-armed, curved-back side chairs, in fact, very obviously evoke the Victorian fashion plates of the 1840s. Even Persian carpets were considered particularly appropriate for the parlor because of their sinuous designs.

The Victorian woman was fully a part of the decor, and it expressed her explicitly. The typical middle-class parlor's masses of needlework, for instance, can be directly attributed to her hand, to her perception of her place in the world. Home-bound and basically sedentary, she relentlessly sought to beautify her surroundings with evidence of her existence. Embroidery and tatting worked in the long hours of wintry afternoons, hand-painted ribbons made from bits of discarded finery, Berlin stitchery (needlepoint and petit point), beadwork, crocheted doilies, and footmuffs filled all the rooms, but the parlor most of all.

The desired effect of the needlework and other bits of decoration was to emphasize comfort and coziness, while the grand, elegant aspects were left to the furniture and architectural details. It was exactly this decorative seesaw, this balance between luxury and comfort, that characterized the most impressive and appealing drawing rooms of the later part of the century. The luxury of a Vanderbilt home, for example—where the drawing room was swathed in red velvet, and the lacquer and gold brocade of the Japanese parlor subtly glimmered—was always punctuated by evidence of comfort and the consistent presence of family life, children, dogs, birds, and so on. Parlors became far more accessible than their stiff little sitting room counterparts had been a mere generation earlier, and they were certainly distanced from early-nineteenth-century severity and the relentless regularity of arrangement that prevailed in the spacious but cold reception rooms of the eighteenth century. The Victorians cre-

ated a unique blend in these new parlors: a room that managed to be a personalized monument to both luxury and domestic life.

The typical Victorian drawing room was located on the main floor of the home, usually to the right of the front door. Whatever the social or financial standing of its owners, it consistently occupied the choice position: its space was generally larger, its ceilings higher, its fireplace more sumptuously ornamented. To complement the generosity of space, the room's other architectural features also expanded in scale and importance. Cornices and ceiling medallions, for example, spread in size and grew bolder in detail. In the later part of the century, both these elements frequently were highlighted in a rainbow of rich colors. This was in part because of the soaring heights of Victorian ceilings; as the distance grew between medallion and viewer, colors, gilding, and more emphatic detail became necessary to see it clearly.

A common configuration of space in many Victorian homes was one with both a front and a back parlor, which were separated either by heavy, sliding pocket doors—so called because they slipped into a "pocket" in the walls when opened—or by doors with ground-glass panels. This was a convenient

This elegant fringed silk lampshade is a contemporary creation, but its delicate style is typical of nineteenth-century parlor decoration. (© Dennis Wonn, courtesy Shades of the Past)

Overleaf: *The generous proportions of the drawing room in the Mainstay Inn are contained by the room's lavish ornamentation—with unusual wall, ceiling, and border treatments in a reproduction Victorian Neo-Grec pattern (based on an 1887 design), multi-patterned rugs, and splendid lambrequins on the windows. The bold, rather fanciful shapes of the Victorian furniture and the glossy brocade upholstery suggest the dramatic, faintly risqué character of the room's former life—a fashionable nineteenth-century gambling parlor.*

A shimmering nineteenth-century beadwork pillow with original Victorian tassels would have been a much-prized bit of handiwork. Here it is displayed on a nineteenth-century Turkish chair, shirred and tufted to emphasize its rounded contours.

arrangement, especially to accommodate the amateur theatricals or charades that were popular during the era. The back parlor served as stage, and the audience sat in the front parlor, with the sliding doors serving as a "curtain."

The front and back parlors also had separate functions. Frequently, the front parlor was the more sedate and dignified space, decorated in a darker manner and used as a reception room for visitors. This arrangement is evident in Newark's historic Ballantine House, where the larger back parlor displays the decorative, more frivolous qualities of a "French" drawing room. *Godey's* noted that in a house with front and back parlors, "many prefer to use the back room as a library [while] others again, station a piano back there and call it a music room on that solitary claim." Sometimes, too, the back parlor assumed the more intimate air of a sitting room or library, suitable for family recreations, and the front room became the one for formal and picturesque display. Still another variation on the double-parlor scheme can be seen in New York's Old Merchant House, built in 1837. In 1865, at a time when dining rooms were commonly being moved up to the main floor from their original basement level, its rear parlor was made into a dining room.

Occasionally, homes had triple parlors, with the parlor farthest from the front of the home usually being the most intimate and informal. The spaciousness acquired when the doors between the successive parlors were flung open was especially admired, for it provided a full floor for large-scale entertainment, such as a dance. Divisions between the parlors also offered opportunities for additional touches of embellishment. The double doorways between the parlors and the library in the Beckwith House in Mitchell, South Dakota, for example, show a touch of Victorian enrichment in the Aesthetic manner, with handmade Japanese transom screens over the doors, an effect typical of the 1880s.

Whatever its arrangement, the parlor was the room where the Victorian family displayed its most costly and treasured possessions. In more modest homes, where the room was not only a place for entertaining, but the family's actual living area as well, a piano or an organ might have been present. Too, if there was no separate library, a filled bookcase testified to the fact that this was a family that appreciated culture and refinement.

The middle-class Victorian parlor was also where the family Bible had its place on the center table, the father read aloud to his gathered family from "improving" tracts, the wife sewed, and the children played on the floor. Magazines, in fact, encouraged such parlor use among the middle classes in an attempt to subvert the mid-century tendency to leave it as a carefully dusted, but stiff little cloister with curtains drawn to prevent the upholstery and wallpapers from fading, and opened only on special occasions. "By all means use that idle parlor," urged *Demorest's*. "What good are parlors whose seats are covered with pale satin, wrought with silken roses and trailing foliage. The children should play freely. Everyone should enjoy it."

In grander homes, of course, such family recreational activities would have taken place in the sitting room or other specially designated areas—music in the music room, sewing in the sewing room—while the formal drawing room was seldom used but for parties and entertaining callers. In the earlier Victorian decades, such a room was decorated in a feminine and frivolous way, underscoring its purpose as a room for festive gatherings, parties, gossiping, and lighthearted amusements. The walls were covered in an almost dainty manner: a light-cream damask, for example, and painted woodwork in tones of ivory picked out in gold would have been fairly typical. Other parlor wallcoverings were wallpapers in

tints of pearl gray, light green, blue, or lavender, with small scrolled patterns, birds, vines, and gilded traceries, while Axminster carpets were favored for floor coverings.

Furniture in the drawing rooms of this period through the 1860s followed what was called the French fashion, the feminine Rococo Revival and Louis styles predominating. The emerald greens and soft gold hues of the brocatelle drapery and upholstery in the White House's Green Room, for example, which set the tone for this rather formal family parlor during Andrew Johnson's administration in the 1860s, were complemented with delicate rosewood Rococo Revival furniture. An even more classic example of such a drawing room was found at the Marmillion Plantation in Louisiana. Also decorated in the 1860s, its pale lavender walls and ceilings, and its frieze of painted flowers, birds, jewels, and scrolls, were also set off with richly carved rosewood pieces and a blue marbleized fireplace, all of which were considered the very height of fashion at the time.

As the century progressed, Victorian parlor decor changed. While the light-colored "French" drawing room remained popular, it was joined by a heavier style that also brought elements of the exotic and the eclectic into play. The Red Room of the White House, redeco-

Above: Classic Victorian parlor motifs—an unframed portrait on an easel (a common Victorian convention, hinting that someone at home "dabbled"), a fan, a Rogers group (The First Ride), and an embroidered velvet crazy quilt—make this corner vignette just what one would have found a hundred years ago in a similar parlor. The children in the portrait have idealized angelic faces, in accordance with the Victorians' sentimentalized view of childhood; the antique wallpaper dates from the 1890s.

Opposite: A charming tangle of now-rare rope portieres frames this parlor in a family's 1894 Queen Anne home in Alameda, beautifully restored to period-perfect accuracy in a homey, domestic theme. Such portieres were available from the Montgomery Ward catalog in the 1890s, and the room's coved ceiling, also typical of the 1890s, is hand painted and set off with a polychromed ceiling medallion. Objects on the Eastlake/Renaissance Revival center table include a mechanical bird in a gilded cage, a typical Victorian bridal gift.

rated as a family parlor in the 1890s, illustrates this change perfectly. Described by one historian as being a "symphony of reds," this was where the very social Grover Clevelands held court amid such lavish decoration as an elegant Moorish ceiling, Pompeiian-red walls, carved cherry woodwork, and an exotic tiled hearth. In homes across the country, horsehair had been replaced by plush, satins, and brocades. It was with these changes in public taste that the drawing room acquired its late-Victorian grandeur, mingled with the comfort that was still the hallmark of its style.

The veritable rhapsody of color created by the new richly patterned wallpapers, "art" borders, and friezes was accompanied by a similar deepening of the tones used for the parlor woodwork, such as the richer tones of cherrywood previously mentioned. Woodwork painted in the colors taken from other elements of the parlor decor, such as plum, rose, sage green, gold, and ochre, and accented with gilding, were also popular. The treatment of the woodwork and ceiling moldings was often designed and colored to add additional height to already high Victorian ceilings. When the molding was painted to match or harmonize with the room's walls and frieze, for example, and contrast with a lighter ceiling, the ceiling re-

ceived an additional visual lift.

To an extent, the deeper tones of the later Victorian drawing room darkened the space, swallowing up the existing light. To counterbalance this, without diminishing its coziness, mirrors were much in favor. These huge, shiny sheets of silvery glass altered the shape and size of the rooms while they brightened them. Sometimes, in fact, mirrors proved nearly as effective as the architecture itself in creating expansive double views, especially in rooms that were small or awkwardly proportioned. For example, when a pier mirror was placed between two windows at the front of the parlor, a very typical Victorian townhouse arrangement, it often gave the effect of being a third window, and thus it provided more light and sparkle. Gilding further enhanced brightness; gilded wallpapers, picture rails, and furniture picked up and reflected small flashes of light. The shimmer of elaborately papered and gilded ceilings further increased the effect.

One of the most definitive characteristics of the Victorian drawing room was the all-encompassing richness created by its sumptuous drapery, upholstery, and trim. In fact, it was in this area that the connection between women's fashions and the Victorian interior was most apparent. *Godey's* mentions in 1880 that since fashion had long accepted the fad of combining fabrics in two or three shades of the same or contrasting colors, it didn't seem strange to see upholsterers adopting the look.

The swagged festooning of window drapery in the parlor, with its abundance of fabric, cords, and fringe, resembled the complicated draped effects that women's skirts took on late in the century, with their underskirtings and overskirtings, their looped and curtainlike effects. Looking at them today, we find it neither inconceivable nor remarkable that Margaret Mitchell's Scarlett O'Hara was able to fashion her famous green velvet dress from her mother's precious portieres, complete with tassels, braid, and trim. What *is* remarkable is that the idea didn't occur to her sooner.

In her memoirs, a young woman named Eleonor Acland recalls that, as a child in the 1880s, she felt fairly smothered in clothes, just as the rooms of the time were smothered in drapery and upholstery. While furniture in the nursery and kitchen might be bare, she remembered every chair or sofa that stood in the parlor was robed down to the carpeting. Why, nice girls would no more show their legs than would nice chairs, she added. One young lady, on being asked why skirts had to have so many yards and yards of fabric, replied that while she couldn't say exactly, she knew it was a necessity. "After all, if they didn't, just think—people would see one's shape showing!"

Heaven forbid that people should see one's shape showing—any more than they should clearly discern the true contours of a room, window, or door at the height of the Gilded Age. In the drawing room, for example, any such indiscreet openings were demurely obscured with yards of overlay. Sound-muffling portieres tied back with braided silk ropes masked doorways; portieres hung on either side of pocket doors. From the 1870s through the 1890s, indeed, portieres had become so much the fashion that they frequently replaced doors entirely, at least on the main floor of the home, just as embroidered spittoon covers decorously concealed cuspidors.

Window drapery, of course, played the major part in this great Victorian cover-up. According to *Practical Decorative Upholstery*, a handbook on curtain-making written in the 1880s, "a sense of bareness existed" where no drapery was hung no matter how generously a room was otherwise furnished. In consequence, windows wore what were called lambrequins—small, stiffened canopies of drapery spanning their tops that could be scrolled,

scalloped, or gilded. From them depended flowing skirtlike curtains in velvet, brocade, or silk, often looped over lace and decorated with ribbons, tassels, and festoons.

In addition to the obviously luxurious effects of this and other Victorian window treatments, the sweeping curtains and impressive valences also had a practical purpose. In shielding the room from direct sunlight (which wasn't in fashion), they also kept the costly, and often delicate, fabrics in the room from fading, as frequent replacement would have been expensive, even for the wealthy.

The parlor's rich, rustling mass of fabric also contributed an undercurrent of eroticism, just barely checked by Victorian propriety. One would have experienced an intimate, sensual pleasure upon entering the drawing room from such elements as the sway of the rich hangings bordered with deep fringe, the pneumatic puffiness of the Turkish upholstery, plumped by the recently invented coil spring. Fringe, for example, sewn on curtains, lampshades, and chairs, trembling gently each time someone walked by, served to accentuate the room's inherent sensuality, echoing the sway of fringe on bustles, skirts, and slithering trains. This nearly audible chorus was further enhanced by the subtle rustling of women's ruffled

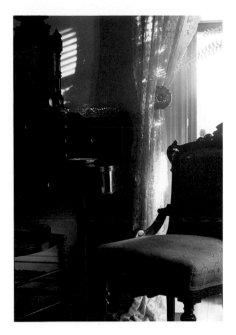

Nineteenth-century drawing rooms were seldom flooded with direct sunlight. Here, drifts of lace, cascading on the floor, help filter the flow of light into this room, softening and shading the contours of the furniture.

Above: *The artful contrast of color, ornament, and texture in pleated Victorian pillows and a colorful collection of late-nineteenth-century British tiles infuses this room with Victorian vitality.*

Opposite: *The Victorian Revival in a New York high-rise makes a gallant bow to the past without excluding the present. The personal collections reflect the owners' taste for dramatic one-of-a-kind textile art: a hand-crocheted contemporary kimono peacefully coexists with the nineteenth-century velvet-covered couch, the antique portieres draping the windows, and an Art Nouveau cabinet. The steel rocking chair is actually the oldest piece in the room, dating from the 1850s.*

silk petticoats, a sound that created a tantalizing awareness of a woman's undergarments. (Later in the century, Victorian women even chose to emphasize the effect by wearing the taffeta "rustle" petticoat.) In short, upon examination, we find the Victorian interior to have been far too emblazoned with frippery ever to be considered strictly chaste. With its explosion of color, ornament, sound, and texture, its overbearing romantic illusion, the message of the room was decidedly libertine.

The more important a room was, the more furniture it contained, and the drawing room was by far the most important space in the Victorian home. The multitude of furnishings that it held produced a richly romantic effect; its cushiony upholstery was inherently more comfortable than any other furniture style up to that point.

The most typical drawing room pieces included medallion- and serpentine-back sofas, love seats, and settees, while Turkish-style pieces, including circular ottomans upholstered around a padded center post, were popular in the 1880s and 1890s. There were also dozens of parlor chairs—corner chairs, side chairs, armchairs, folding chairs, and more. Rocking chairs were a feature of the room as well. Sometimes the front portion of the rocking tread

was shortened to prevent it from tearing ladies' petticoats, while other versions were mounted on platforms, which also kept the treads from cutting into the new and costly carpets. These items were all arranged amid pier tables, occasional tables, credenzas, consoles, rolling tea carts, étagères, ladies' desks, screens, and easels, in any of the five or more revival and reform styles that were simultaneously available. Some forms are familiar to us today; others, less so. A canterbury, for instance, was a low, carved stand mounted on castors, with several filelike vertical partitions for storing magazines and sheet music. A pier table was made to be placed against the wall (or pier) between two windows. A tête-à-tête, or "conversational," consisted of two joined chairs, usually facing in opposite directions.

From mid-century and for the next twenty-five or thirty years, matching parlor suites or sets, usually consisting of a sofa, a center table, an étagère, and assorted parlor chairs, were a standard feature of the room. Such sets ranged from hand-carved Belter masterpieces in gleaming rosewood like the one at Terrace Hill (today the Iowa Governor's Mansion), to a seven-piece cherry set in the Eastlake style, to less impressive mail-order acquisitions. Upholstered or needlepoint

footstools and footrests, in all shapes and sizes, were frequently included as part of the parlor suite and, in fact, were a key feature of the drawing room. (When the Turkish style came into vogue, footstools were even supplemented by soft, puffy, fringed Turkish ottomans.) Footstools, hassocks, and ottomans were usually placed within reach of every chair, not only in the just cause of Victorian comfort but also because, then as now, Victorian homes are subject to low gusting drafts that send their chill across the floors. To help combat those drafts, the Victorians often stitched up long, tubular "snakes" of red flannel, then filled them with sawdust, and placed them on the window sashes and between the door jambs and floors.

Beginning in the mid-1870s, although less sophisticated families continued to laud the parlor suite, it became more fashionable to vary its arrangement, displaying unmatched pieces in one's drawing room, as well as incorporating some element representing the exotic or the aesthetic. On entering the fashionable nineteenth-century drawing room, for example, one might have found a curious "Egyptian" table, a bearskin rug, an eccentric old commode used as a table, and a voluptuous, comfortable chair. This was regarded as a more original, more personal, and rather more sophisticated way of decorating. The idea of arrangements in pairs had come to be scorned as unimaginative, while a delightful asymmetry gained favor. The root of this preference can perhaps be found in the asymmetry of architecture in the Victorian house itself, a rebellion against classicism that quite naturally spread to the interior.

Despite the abundance in the late-Victorian drawing room (or perhaps because of it), there also evolved a special order and art to its arrangement. Filled as it was with sofas and chairs, ottomans and rugs, table tops groaning under cornucopias of collectibles, it still had to allow for the graceful passage of Victorian women in their spreading skirts, trains, and wide sleeves. Wall-mounted hanging cabinets, for instance, were recommended for smaller drawing rooms, as they left floor space free for walking, not to mention easy sweeping and rug shaking. Hassocks and footstools were placed with care in order not to impede movement. Furniture was purposely arranged to encourage circulation and help guests look their best, while photographs, engravings, and souvenirs were props to stimulate lively conversation.

As a result, Victorian furniture was often divided in several separate groupings, much like small scenic vignettes, a system that was unusu-

Above and opposite: *A treasury of collecting—Victorian tiles, a splendid Voysey rug, antique wall tapestries, an inlaid sideboard designed by Bruce J. Talbert filled with Art Nouveau silver—makes this room a strikingly personal, livable retreat.*

Classical statues, suggestive of ancient cultures, were frequently placed in built-in wall niches and could be found in the parlor as well as in hallways, stairwells, and dining rooms.

ally amenable to conversation. In rooms arranged in this traditional Victorian manner, chairs and tables could all be shifted slightly to suit the proclivities and postures of the individuals occupying them, without upsetting the basic order of the room. Within these groupings, the Victorians paid particular attention to what was known as the "massing" of objects, in order to create a sense of visual harmony. Furniture, paintings, plants, all of varying heights, shapes, and colors, were arranged to blend into a single unified pattern, so that the unit could be visually embraced as a whole, rather than in part. In fact, if one item stood out, striking the eye before any of the others, its placement was emphatically wrong. In the case of a boldly patterned chair and an equally patterned rug, for example, neither should "fight" the other for dominance, but rather combine into a harmonious blend. According to an article in *Harper's Bazar* entitled "The Art of Furnishing," the massing of objects in this way helped prevent a spotty and "speckled" appearance within the room, something always to be avoided when dealing with a full, rather than spare, space.*

Nineteenth-century taste further

dictated that an abundance of furniture, rather than diminishing a room, actually enhanced its size. Furniture broke the monotony of space within the room, catching the eye with interest and carrying it smoothly from one object to the next. This created a feeling of distance as the eye traveled on and on, taking in all that was presented, thereby creating an illusion of size. Harriet P. Spofford, in her *Art Decoration Applied to Furniture* (1878), added a confident footnote when she mentioned that "provided there is enough space to move about without walking over the furniture, there is hardly likely to be too much [furniture] within the room."

With so much furniture in so many styles to choose from, the Victorian parlor was, quite naturally, a highly personalized statement. At the same time, there were certain decorative motifs that emerged in home after home. Just as the hall tree was the "key" to the Victorian hallway, the center table and, to a less extent, the étagère were the pieces of importance in the parlor.

As its name would suggest, the center table, often made of mahogany and equally often topped with white marble, occupied the very center of the room. Especially after

* The Victorian art of arrangement into vignettes is also said to have emerged with the advent of gaslight, which cast its welcome illumination about the room in small, distinct circles, each one becoming the center for a conversational grouping. It was the advent of electricity, by replacing gaslight, that some

say even caused the demise of Victorian style. By casting its uncompromising glare, it harshened the previously gentle romantic corners, turned the muted colors garish, and defined shapes that were meant to be submerged in shadow.

mid-century, it was the accepted magnet for family life—the place where family members would gather to talk, read, sew, or pray, thanks to the usual presence of the tall lamp on its surface. Years later, the center table became a more decorative than functional focal point, a "stage" on which to display one's finest objects testifying to one's taste: a stereoscope for amusement, a few morally instructive books, a domed arrangement of wax flowers or fruit. After the 1860s, when photography ceased to be merely an expensive novelty and was more accessible to the average American family, a treasured family photo album, usually covered in crimson plush, also had its place here.

Unfortunately, it was this convention that became stereotypical of the pedestrian middle-class Victorian parlor, which Mark Twain disparaged in *Life on the Mississippi*. He sarcastically described the homes of prominent small-town citizens whose parlors—and most notably parlor tables—all exhibited the same depressing assortment. The particulars of such decor must have been especially distasteful to Twain, who preferred a more innovative style and who, in decorating his own home, enlisted Louis Comfort Tiffany and Associated Artists, the leading designers of their time, to create a look of homey magnificence.

Before it descended into cliché, however, the center table could be quite elegant, and many extraordinary versions were created with remarkable inlaid tops and intricate, unusual carvings. If one's center table was exceptionally fine, in the earlier decades it was permissible to leave the top bare, but as the Victorian home became enveloped in layers of fabric, the table too was submerged under a fringed covering. This decorative device actually provided a decided advantage to poorer nineteenth-century families, who longed for the gentility of a center table in their homes. Catherine Beecher and Harriet Beecher Stowe, for example, suggested that an inexpensive pine table with a broad top could easily be disguised by an ample green cloth with a patterned border, and no one would be the wiser. The universality of the center table in the parlor was further confirmed by *Godey's* when it dubbed one of its popular household columns "Center Table Gossip." The table's diminished decorative cachet can be detected in the 1880s when, as the center table became old fashioned, the column became "Our Armchair."

The Victorian étagère, a large, tiered piece of parlor furniture designed to be placed flat against a wall, was the primary means of displaying the family's burgeoning col-

Two English Arts & Crafts chairs flank the marble fireplace, all set against a backdrop of antique portieres in this Victorian-style drawing room.

lection of treasures, and it too was something of a standard parlor piece. In simpler homes, the humbler whatnot, a triangular corner piece, either freestanding or made to hang on the wall, served the same purpose in contributing to a more cultured atmosphere. It was often adorned with bits of ornamental fretwork, its shelves covered with inexpensive colored paper, such as leftover wallpaper scraps, before being filled with the kind of homey bric-a-brac that labeled the family well educated, well traveled, or well read.

Other articles of parlor furniture were also provided with an abundance of shelves, niches, and other surfaces for display. These included curio cabinets and hanging glass-doored cases, wall-brackets with small shelves, and even bookcases with a top shelf for ornaments and a lower narrow ledge for plates or tiles.

In observing the unusual amount of shelving in Victorian furniture, however, it is important to realize that, for the first time in history, items to fill those shelves were readily available. Souvenirs from any of the great expositions and fairs, and items of foreign origin, were particularly prized.

The parlor fireplace and mantel, while having been replaced by the center table as the family's focus, which they had been in the eighteenth century, were still of considerable importance in the decoration of the room. One Victorian tastemaker called the hearth "the sacred family altar—the place that first catches one's eye on entering the room, and the place where it lingers longest." The venerable Mrs. Lucy Orrinsmith, author of *The Drawing Room, Its Decoration and Furniture* (1877), considered the hearth a "rallying spot, to collect around it the richest rugs, the softest sofas, the cosiest chairs, the prettiest treasures," while *Harper's Bazar* said that a room without a mantel had but the dignity of a tent.

For mantel decoration, a draped lambrequin was among the items necessary for a proper parlor fireplace. These were usually made of velvet, serge, satin, plush, or even lace, then ornamented and embroidered, and were contrived to disguise the blatant bareness of the mantel top. A firescreen was yet another necessity. Although these sometimes seem more decorative than functional (they were painted, needlepointed, embroidered, inlaid with marquetry work, or even made of papier-mâché), they were popularly believed to protect delicate feminine complexions from the heat of the fire. In a less romantic but rather more practical vein, fire-

screens also protected the rest of the room, copious drapery and all, from a sudden burst of sparks caused by a downdraft or by wood or coals crackling or popping. A hearth rug was usually added to shield the edge of the parlor carpet, and a brass fender placed around the fireplace kept coals from tumbling out of the hearth. One of the more creative efforts of the day produced a "rustic" fender, which was made by joining knotty tree branches, then painting them white. Fenders, rustic or otherwise, were also useful to keep women's long dresses from accidentally igniting as they passed, but even with that safeguard, many young women still managed to carelessly scorch the backs of their gowns while warming themselves by the parlor fire.

Other novelties for the parlor fireplace were available. The January 1883 issue of *Arthur's Home Magazine*, for example, mentions that an embroidered and painted bellows was the latest thing in London homes. No artistic fireplace, it said, is without one. Fireboards were still another accessory, usually used in country homes to fill in the bare, unused hearth openings during the months of summer. These, too, were painted, often with scenic pictures or fruit and floral motifs. In the city, the summer fireplace would also have been covered, but

with fans, parasols, arrangements of pine cones, ferns, mosses, and bouquets of artificial flowers.

Within all this, the Victorian passion for accumulation flourished. It was the drawing room, more than any other room, that testified to the nineteenth-century commitment to ornament, particularly as the era wore on. During the 1870s, for example, despite their well-appointed parlor—with its deep-chocolate woodwork, wine-colored draperies, gilded mirrors, bronzes, and new rosewood furniture from the Herter Brothers—the four daughters of New York's Dr. John Frederick May were less than satisfied with its appearance. Compared with the abundance of objects in the homes of the prominent Astors and Lorillards, the few empty spaces on the Mays' walls and marble tables were uncomfortable sore points. While accessories and ornaments were, in part, present to provide a stimulus to conversation and to create the most personalized decorating statement possible, they also served as innocent tributes to the glories of acquisition. "What keen pleasure there is in the possession of one new treasure," maintained one wonderfully Victorian opinion. "Where to place it for the best [effect] is a fertile topic of conversation." Homey knick-knacks and examples of ladies'

Above and opposite: *A matched set of ebonized satin-and-fruitwood parlor furniture, Eastlake-style, can be seen in the drawing room of The Abbey, an 1869 Gothic Revival summer villa in Cape May. The glass dome on the table, protecting the dried flower arrangement from dust or disarray, was a familiar sight in the nineteenth-century parlor, as were fans, which were exchanged by nineteenth-century ladies as tokens of friendship or on special occasions, much as we exchange greeting cards today. During the 1870s and 1880s, at the height of the craze for things Japanese, fans of Japanese paper or silk were especially prized.*

Above and opposite: *The essence of a feminine, Victorian-inspired drawing room is perfect for a romantic nineteenth-century country estate. The ornamental lacquered table (opened, above) is actually a Victorian sewing table with compartments inside; the piano, draped with an embroidered antique Chinese shawl, is covered with family photographs in Victorian silver frames. The lamp on the piano was originally a gas lamp.*

fancywork were, of course, more in the realm of the middle-class parlor than that of the more sophisticated formal drawing rooms of the day. These more domestic decorations would instead have been consigned to a personal sitting room, a family room, or even the lady's boudoir of the soignée home. But a lavish candelabrum, bronzes, china, glassware, lacquer boxes, and interesting bits of more elegant embroideries, feather bouquets, painted fans, and brass jardinieres of leafy palms and pampas grasses kept the corners of these richer spaces amply filled.

While the parlor étagère housed the smaller and perhaps more precious bits of china and porcelain, it was on the parlor mantel that many of the family's larger and more impressive ornaments found their home. For example, such a mantel display might have included a French clock, lustres, porcelain vases, or photographs.

Many of the items interspersed throughout the Victorian parlor were arranged singly rather than in pairs, again reflecting a disdain for what was felt to be the dull predictability of symmetry. Objects of civilized taste, such as porcelains, statues, and crystal, were even juxtaposed at random with objects from nature, such as seashells, stuffed birds, vials of holy water brought back from Jerusalem, and

Above: Brackets and shelves with incised gilded lines were another popular site for proud display of a family's bric-a-brac. Found throughout the Victorian home, they were especially favored in the parlor.

Opposite: *The ornately carved, round white-marble mantel is a nineteenth-century motif indigenous to homes built in the 1850s and 1860s. The lavish gilded overmantel mirror, fairly dripping with garlands, ribbons, and flowers, is a delightful example of true Victorian bravado.*

four-pawed animal-skin rugs. One of the more unusual items in William Jennings Bryan's parlor, for example, was a decorated ostrich egg—a gift from his 1896 presidential campaign—which was suspended from the front parlor chandelier. It was this general mix, in fact, that kept the late-Victorian drawing room from becoming too effete. A further wordly-wise quality could occasionally be imparted by the display of related archaeological objects, such as fragile fossilized bones and fragments of ancient pottery, which testified to the Victorian fascination with the cultures of the past, although these really had a more proper place in the library. A bow to aestheticism could be subtly conveyed by an interesting decorative tile on a stand, Oriental fans, or, more emphatically, a full-sized stuffed peacock with floor-sweeping tail feathers.

Feminine fashion, not surprisingly, also had its influence on parlor accessories, and in some Victorian parlors, the same stylish flower and fruit arrangements or top-heavy clusters of feathers that adorned women's hats were equally at home on the mantel and marble-topped tables. In the 1870s, the passion for taxidermy had invaded millinery, and bonnets were inhabited by stuffed owls, chenille spiders, velvet mice, and plush toads. Subsequent-

ly, the parlor was host to the same infestation.

Another fad in the nineteenth-century parlor was the display of seemingly innocuous china and glass ornaments molded in the shape of women's shoes and high-topped boots. What made them so appealing in the Victorian scheme of things was their slightly risqué quality, for this was an era when a glimpse of a woman's boot as she was helped into her carriage, or the flashing tease of an ankle during a skating party, was considered to be arousing. Victorian photographers often went so far as to delicately erase women's feet from the negatives of their photographs so that their subjects sometimes appeared to be floating supernaturally in the air. It thus becomes apparent that the display of shoe and boot souvenirs in the parlor definitely had something of a daring quality.

In addition to all of the above, the ladylike presence of sturdy white antimacassars gave a homey air and a touch of domestic intimacy to even the grandest of parlors. These crocheted or knitted doilies were draped like giant snowflakes over the arms and backs of all upholstered furniture, making them among the few useful objects in the room. Antimacassars were the Victorians' practical, but decorative, solution for the protection of their

Hairwork, a form of Victorian parlor art, was fashionable during the second half of the century. Pictures, wreathes, and bouquets, patiently crafted from one's own hair or that of a loved one, were set into shadow-box frames and proudly displayed in the parlor. Sentimental jewelry, especially mourning jewelry, was also crafted from hair.

furniture from the greasy stains of Macassar oil, the leading men's hair balm. During the 1870s, however, antimacassars, also aptly called tidies, began to be considered old-fashioned and were replaced by draped and patterned chair scarves, which served essentially the same purpose.

Books were generally considered unsuitable for a formal drawing room, much as a television set might be in a contemporary living room. "People are not supposed to be in the mood for reading when the hour comes for retiring to the withdrawing room," was one explanation. More sociable activities, such as music or conversation, were considered proper. Others argued that a few judiciously chosen titles lying about the room could be just the thing to provoke discussion as well as provide a positive impression, especially if the books were well bound and costly looking. (One bit of Victorian propriety strains contemporary credulity, and it seems doubtful that even the most fastidious Victorians could have carried surface refinement to such a degree. Certainly only the most unimpeachable of hostesses would have thought to check the parlor bookcase to ensure that books by female writers weren't placed back-to-back with those by male writers, something permitted only if the parties were married.)

Artwork played an important part in the decoration and impact of the Victorian parlor, especially since the upwardly mobile Victorians were eager to prove that they were people who could afford not only the necessities of life, but also its luxuries and embellishments. The love of art during the nineteenth century, however, was unique in that, for the first time, it was shared by all classes and income levels. Anyone could own an "Old Master," whether one cut a reproduction from the back of *Demorest's* magazine or brought the real thing back from Europe. Both showed an appreciation and a knowledge of the finer things in life. As a result, no parlor was considered decorated without pictures on its walls.

Sculpture, statuary, and busts also found their way into the Victorian parlor, especially those portraying classically inspired subjects, such as reproductions of Hiram Powers's *Greek Slave* (which had been the sensation of London's Crystal Palace exhibition in 1851), or such sentimental subjects as godlike young lovers. Nudes were generally acceptable in Victorian homes if their faces remained vacant and expressionless, as if purity of mind kept them unaware of the prurient possibilities of their nakedness. To the Victorian mind, the blank-eyed detachment isolated the nude from reality, elevating it to the higher realm of art, beyond human ardor. Although one could gaze on such an object with complete innocence of intention, occasionally, as if to emphasize the point, strategic areas were wrapped with a bit of gauze, a practice that supposedly amused the more sophisticated European visitors to American homes.

Plaster-cast statues by John Rogers, mass-produced between 1859 and 1892, were as much a fixture in the traditional Victorian parlor as was the whatnot or parlor suite, and no discussion of the room would be complete without them. These storytelling sculptures have most often been called the nineteenth-century equivalent of Norman Rockwell illustrations, depicting down-to-earth moments in everyday life with which middle-class Victorians could identify. Rogers groups were collected for their humor and liveliness and much admired for their realism, down to vest-pocket and watch-fob detail. Although much of their heart-tugging sentimentality is lost to us today, they do provide an interesting look at the Victorians as they liked to see themselves.

An overview of the Victorian drawing room makes it abundantly clear that it was the pride of the Victorian heart, a treasure room filled to overflowing, a fantasy of color, pattern,

and design. It is in this decorative bravado, in fact, that the drawing room reveals its true colors: not an adult or a civilized style at all—sober, restrained, and discreet like its predecessors—but appealingly young, with youth's delight in color, pattern, and richness, appreciation of excitement and excess, and acceptance of humor and novelty. It is just this youthful demeanor, with its innocent vanity, its out-and-out competitive spirit, even its tendency to go a bit overboard at times, that makes it so endearing despite its nonsense.

That the Victorian drawing room should exhibit such qualities is, in retrospect, not surprising. Their beards and sober expressions notwithstanding, the Victorians were a young people. The century itself was propelled forth by the ideas, inventions, and visions of young men and women. Teddy Roosevelt, perhaps the quintessential Victorian, was only forty-two years old when he became President—the youngest man to hold that office before or since. What could be more natural, then, than that the Victorian drawing room, the most important room in the Victorian home, became the interior expression of that youthful spirit, combining its swagger and ostentatious vitality with the more mature powers of beauty, imagination, and harmony.

Heavy turn-of-the-century portieres masking the parlor doorway is one of the Victorian decorative practices revived by the owners of The Abbey. These hang from rings hung on a wooden pole, although more elaborately draped and valanced versions were also popular. Through the doorway, a glimpse of the etched, ruby glass transom over the front door is visible.

Chapter 6

The Victorian Dining Room

It is the fad of the moment with rich, smart Americans to prize above all things the luxurious beauty of apartments in which they dine. Stately drawing rooms, dainty boudoirs, even the fashionable English hall, are of minor importance compared to the imposing elegance of the salle à manger. *Naturally, this costly whim has resulted in the furnishing of some superlatively handsome rooms in and about New York city, rooms designed to treble the attractions of feminine guests and offer them backgrounds of unexampled harmony.*

Vogue (Society Supplement) (1893)

A brass and crystal chandelier with etched-glass globes presides over this comfortably furnished room, done in the solid tradition of the 1880s. The oversized Victorian sideboard displays a collection of nineteenth-century crystal and china, while the scrapbook on the table documents the family's step-by-step restoration. The room's dado is covered in an embossed wallpaper, typical in a dining room of this vintage.

One of the dining rooms that met with the near-rapturous approval of the correspondent from *Vogue* was the candlelit red salon of Mrs. Van Rensselaer Cruger, one of the leading lights of Gay Nineties high society. The *"salle à manger"* of her summer home at Idlesse Farm, Long Island, though large and lofty, was "cunningly contrived to enhance the loveliness of every woman who enters it." Today, we can easily imagine its walls hung in dark crimson satin brocade and the clustering white and gold candelabra, each holding a pyramid of candles. Our *Vogue* tour guide tells us:

Ample red silk draperies fall over lace curtains at the windows through which sea breezes blow and shifting marine views delight the eye. The floor is carpeted in crimson; the richly carved furniture is black with age; on the tall buffets glitter much splendid silverplate, most of it in antique pattern, a heritage from Knickerbocker ancestors.

Accessories included stately portraits of dignified old Dutchmen and their wives, gravely observing the flamboyant doings of their descendants, and extravagant life-size bronze figures which supported lamps, their shades probably lined in crimson silk. Oversized silver jardinieres bloomed with wild greenery and field flowers. It was indeed an imposing room in every way.

The actual furnishings of the American dining room have changed very little since Mrs. Van Rensselaer Cruger and her Victorian guests sat back in their high-backed carved chairs for one of their leisurely three-hour dinners, but the look and feel and the social implications of the Victorian dining room were overwhelmingly different from today's counterpart. The Victorian dining room was more than just a pleasant place in which to take meals; it was one of the most potent symbols of security and comfort that the home had to offer. *Art Decoration Applied to Furniture*, one of the era's foremost household guides, sets forth its decorative principle succinctly: "The first impression... which the dining room should make is that of solid comfort. There is to be no airy trifling with either color or fabric."

Great effort was expended by the Victorians in creating a dining room that exemplified these qualities. Clearly, though, it was the shell of the room—its walls and ceiling treatments, the dressing of its windows and floors—not its furniture, that contributed most to its effect. The 1890s dining room of one-time New York mayor Abram Hewitt was one that was said to dispense just the kind of "dignified hospitality" desired, according to one of the magazines of the day. Decorated in the appropriately solid and weighty Renaissance Revival style, its highlights included walls and ceilings paneled in natural wood, heavily carved cornices, and a deep, mullioned window in a broad recess. Ringing the room, a wide painted frieze, said to be the work of some old Italian master, "for the figures, though somewhat dimmed with age, show a warmth and richness of color seldom seen in modern canvases," was hung.

In its purposely heightened atmosphere of security, the Victorian dining room was most of all a rich inner chamber which, if a bit heavy at times, was nonetheless mellow, comfortable, and convenient. The room reverberated with a sense of satisfaction and full-bodied prosperity; undoubtedly sober, it was seldom somber, and therein lies the key.

The dining room as a separate room reserved for the sole purpose of dining was very much an invention of the nineteenth century. In pre-Revolutionary America, it was common for rooms to serve more than one purpose, and, except for the very wealthy, families generally ate wherever it was most convenient. This flexibility depended on

the formality of the meal, the time of day, and even the season. During the winter months, for example, the kitchen would have been a likely choice, as it was warmed by the crackling log fire. In summer, the dining table might have been set up in the sitting room or even in the hallway to catch the cooling early-evening breezes as they blew in through the open front door. The colonial custom of multipurpose rooms survived well into the nineteenth century, especially in rural areas, in smaller homes, or in houses where large, extended families filled all the rooms. Such situations would have had better uses for the sizable space set aside for the dining room, which was used only two or three times a day.

When the dining room was called on to double as sitting room, study, or even schoolroom, the Victorians thought it important to accomplish the partitioning gracefully. Mrs. Spofford, who stressed that "when the dining room would have to be used as a sitting room . . . its feeding uses ought to be kept as much as possible in the background," recommended a unique Victorian room divider: a ceiling-high bookcase with cabinets and its own portiered doorway that, only slightly modified, could easily be used today to divide the space in an apartment or loft. Because it was mounted on large

The simplicity of this Arts & Crafts style dining room in Cape May's Queen Victoria Inn is highlighted by the long antique table and chairs, an Arts & Crafts light fixture, and gilded reproduction nineteenth-century wallpaper. Over the fireplace, a portrait of Queen Victoria surveys the scene.

rolling casters, it could easily be moved when not in use.

By the later nineteenth century, however, the possession of a separate and proper dining room had become a source of pride to the up-and-coming Victorians. The substantiality of the room's appearance was in keeping with the new, purse-proud style of entertaining. Like those of the hallway and the drawing room, its elements were scrupulously arranged to indicate that people of consequence lived here. It is significant to note the social implications of the language of color in decoration. Colors that "hold their own" were repeatedly recommended, such as rich crimsons, dark blues, dull Pompeiian reds, olives, or "any of the kindred tints that do not look faded or *suggest economy.*"

The dining room evoked warmth, a quality of Victorian design produced when darkened spaces were filled with pattern, texture, and objects, one which denied the chill of a dark room left barren and empty. On entering the Victorian dining room, one felt the warmth from that visual impact, from the embossed leather wrapping the room like a rich velvet ribbon, to the changing shadows stippling the walls and the radiant gaslit chandelier swaying slightly overhead. The furniture of the room would have also been

large, like that of the hallway, and purposely impressive. The sprawling dining table would have been blanketed in damask, lace, or even velvet, and flanked by its regiment of straight-backed chairs; the heavily carved sideboard nearby spilled over with silver, crystal, and porcelain.

By twentieth-century standards, what the Victorians considered warmth could be seen as creating a dark, almost baronial, environment. Some reformists of the 1890s tried to reverse this convention by advocating furnishings of a more cheerful nature. "Must the dining room always be a dark and dingy space?" one of them asked. Seen in retrospect, however, the traditional tones of the dining room were appropriate not only to the room's often oversize dimensions—toned lighter, the dining room might have seemed more barnlike than bountiful—but also to its location and the quality of its light. Used only during meals, and generally only the evening meal at that (weekday breakfasts were often served in a morning room or in one's private chamber), the dining room was frequently located on the northern, or darkest, side of the house, making artificial illumination, rather than natural sunlight, the primary source of light. Basement dining rooms were also common, as at Fairview, the country home of William Jennings Bryan, and ground

Above: *Details showing the carved wolf's head and fish-and-fowl sideboard decoration, traditional nineteenth-century dining room motifs.*

Opposite: *Traditional High-Victorian decoration is celebrated in the dining room of The Abbey, ca. 1869, with flamboyant crimson lambrequins, a 12-foot-long antique walnut dining table, the richly gilded Anglo-Japanese wall frieze and dado, polished copper and brass gasolier, and, of course, an oversized oak sideboard.*

Deep crimson reds, traditional in a late-century Victorian dining room, play a major role in infusing this dining room with an authentic period feeling. The depth of color is set off by equally authentic accents: family portraits in heavy gold frames (a type of art thought suitably solemn and uplifting for the dining room) suspended on a gilded picture rail and massive, polished Renaissance Revival furnishings. Through the door, one can catch a glimpse of the hallway, with its antique wallpaper and hand-painted and decoupage ceiling.

floor dining rooms were the rule in city rowhouses, especially in early- to mid-Victorian days.

In addition, the heightened romanticism of the Victorian temperament tended to admire, rather than shun, the velvety comfort of shadows, especially as they seemed to enhance all the new, rich-looking colors that were coming into vogue. Just as the opulent ornamentation of Victorian furniture represented the burgeoning pride in what could be, for the first time, both technically accomplished and financially obtained, so the duskiness of the dining room produced a statement of grandeur, not gloom.

The dining room was also intended to be a calm and restful space. Even after stronger forms of lighting supplanted candles and kerosene, the Victorians continued to cling to these traditional forms of low-level illumination. Some exponents claimed that the powers of digestion were improved in a darkened dining room. Others argued that not only did darkness enhance digestive abilities, but silence helped as well, a belief which perhaps suggests why Victorian children were admonished to be seen and not heard, especially at the dinner table. While not advocating absolute silence during dinner, *Vogue*, in 1894, did declare a "horror" of people who play "mental catch-ball at the table." Dinner

conversation, they said, "must be light and of a character which can easily be shifted from particulars into general. It must aid, not deter, digestion."

Theme rooms or exotic rooms were also created in the dining room. One of the more unusual was the "Dutch" dining room of Mrs. Le Grand Benedict of Newport. Some of its more outstanding features included windows of heavily leaded panes setting off a single central stained-glass brilliant of a knight's crest with flowing plume, panels of Dutch marquetry wainscoting, a wide frieze illuminated with German frescoing, "and, cunningly concealed in the guise of an antique Dutch warming-pan, the register . . . set low in the wall, nearby a chimney piece that is elaborately set with old blue tiles."

The decorative features that contributed most to the opulent shell of more traditional Victorian dining rooms were the dado and the wallcoverings. The dado (or its alternative, the wainscot), in fact, was usually the room's most consistent decorative characteristic. In embracing the lower perimeter of the room, the dado served to impart qualities of warmth and formality, at the same time that it cleverly interrupted what could have become the monotony of bare wall in this rather

large space. The most modest dado treatment might have been a simple, wide band of maroon paint, while probably one of the most opulent was the red marble found in the Newport home of Mrs. W. K. Vanderbilt, setting off to perfection her vast dining room of red mahogany.

Another variation on the dining room dado was the use of wallpaper in a tone or pattern considerably deeper and heavier than that on the upper portion of the wall, topped by a polished chair rail, which kept chairs from scraping the fragile wallpaper's surface. A wood-paneled wainscot in chestnut, oak, walnut, or maple, either plain or carved with fruits, flowers, or emblems of the chase, was another choice, especially in more opulent homes, as was a tooled-leather or faux-leather covering like Lincrusta-Walton, Anaglypta, or the lesser known Tynecastle brands, stained or painted and then varnished to a deep bronze or leather tone. Embossed surfaces in particular were greatly admired for the air of substance and "grounding" they imparted to the lower portion of the wall.

In addition to the practicality of the dado or wainscot (both could be damp-wiped clean with a soft cloth), they also fulfilled a basic Victorian design tenet by preventing the dining room furniture from standing out in harsh relief against a pale, plain-surfaced wall, an effect the Victorians would have found disturbing. With the muted background of a dado or a wainscot, sharp outlining would have been avoided, and furniture blended harmoniously with the walls. In the dining room, the dado would have been either of traditional chair-level height or higher, approaching eye level. Occasionally, however, the dado extended up to cover nearly the entire wall, adjoining the ceiling frieze and borders. When it accompanied a plainer, painted wall, the dado was sometimes further crowned with a stenciled border, the kind of extra ornamental touch the Victorians delighted in.

The woodwork in the dining room, like the woodwork throughout most of the house, was generally dark, complementing the color of the furniture in depth and substantiality. Mahogany tones or cherry red were especially suitable. When oak was used, it was often stained a shade or two deeper than its natural golden hue. The theory was "to avoid all violent contrasts, which are contrary to good taste, and to choose shades that blend together and produce a harmonious whole," according to *The Household*. A too-dark cornice and wainscot, for instance, would have created "a singularly bad effect" against lighter walls, and vice versa.

The love of ornamentation was carried out in many ways in the Victorian dining room, from carved angels on a sideboard, to lace elegantly edging the snowy table linens. The handmade "safe" on the table, made on a wire frame, protected the food from flies.

Occasionally, in well-to-do homes, the dining room woodwork would have been stenciled in gold, as it was in the dining room of Mark Twain's lavish Hartford home, completed in 1874. The house featured the gilded geometric designs of Associated Artists, of which Louis Comfort Tiffany was a principal. The dining room, where Twain expansively entertained such nineteenth-century literary notables as Bret Harte and Matthew Arnold, was located at the rear, on the north side of the house. Its walnut paneling and doors were covered with gilded stenciling, and its walls were patterned with a rich embossed lily pattern in red and gold.

The growing abundance of gilded designs on the dining room walls and ceilings, as well as on much Victorian furniture, can be regarded as a response to the essentially darker quality of the Victorian home in the later years of the century. Gilding was appreciated not only in the service of what design books called "the desired idea of richness" but also as a light source providing a subtle glimmer that complemented the room's rich shadows. Chandeliers, banquet lamps, sconces, and candles reflected off this gilding, creating flashes bouncing around the boundaries of the room. A gilded picture rail was still another popular conceit. The effect was further enhanced by the presence of the large, silvery Victorian mirrors, carefully positioned to double the glow. In the dining room, and throughout the other rooms in the Victorian home, large mirrors, gilding, and silvering were used to add a luminous quality to relatively deep-toned interiors without sacrificing their ambience of dignity.

Except for those most advanced interiors that were precursors of twentieth-century designs, dining room walls matched their woodwork in warmth and darkness of tone (maroon, bronze, old gold, and moss green were among the often suggested colors). The walls would have been either painted and then stenciled with gilded chevrons and traceries or, more often, papered with a luxurious overall patterning that suggested opulence, like Mark Twain's tooled-leather look. The Victorians realized that white tones diminished the size and importance of their rooms and visually lowered the high ceilings they were so proud of, while deeper tones enhanced them, promoting an impression of grandness. Popular patterns were those of William Morris, typified by mazes of tangled vines, lilies, and intricate brambles, as well as those imitating old tapestries and scenic designs. Fabrics like damask, with a sense of "body" to them, were also used. The colors most pleasing to

A simple golden-oak buffet in the dining room of this restored turn-of-the-century New York rowhouse serves the same purpose as do heavier, more massive, versions in more traditional dining rooms. The chairs are carved turn-of-the-century oak, as well.

the Victorian eye and most responsive to their room dimensions were neither too light nor too dark: wallcoverings were found to absorb too much of the precious light when too dark, and over-light tones resulted in a "crude contrast" with the woodwork and the furniture. The effects of various colorings and coverings as a background for pictures were also widely debated, with maroon and olive tones again receiving high marks for being complementary.

Above the foundation supplied by the dado and the body of the wall, the frieze and ceiling formed a focal point for dining room decoration. Stenciled friezes and imaginative wallpaper borders provided the dining room with a sense of excitement and drama, surrounding its upper reaches with everything from flowers, palm leaves, and fruit clusters to Grecian vases, prancing deer, and rabbits.

The Victorians treated the dining room ceiling as yet another canvas for inspiration. It might have been a richly carved heavy walnut or frescoed (the Victorian term for any painted murallike design). Dining room ceilings were also coffered, a treatment considered particularly appropriate in view of the era's fascination with medieval motifs for the dining room and its frequent use of Gothic, Elizabethan, or Jacobean Revival styles. When coffering wasn't possible, sometimes stamped relief papers were gilded, then spliced into geometric sections in imitation of such an effect. Molly and J. J. Brown's dining room ceiling, however, was unique even for the times. Because their Denver home didn't have a then fashionable conservatory, they had one painted

on their dining room ceiling. Even in simpler homes, the dining room ceiling was seldom left plain. A very basic treatment might have included painting it in a stone color, then adding simple stenciled designs in the corners to relieve the bareness.

Filling out the shell of the Victorian dining room were inlaid parquet floors or flooring arranged in contrasting-color wood strips, such as oak against walnut or cherry against Southern pine. Floors, like the rest of the woodwork in the home, would have been stained in dark, rich tones. Particular attention was paid to the borders of these floors, which were carefully designed to create an attractive perimeter for the dining room rugs. When the dining room of Cottage Lawn, in Oneida, New York, was remodeled in the 1880s, floor borders were one of the main considerations. A trim of polished hardwood flooring was laid to surround the large dining room rug and complement the grained wood trim at the windows and doors and the house's original marbleized mantelpiece.

Although carpeting with large, overall geometric patterns predominated in early- and mid-Victorian dining rooms, rugs eventually became the preferred style, since they proved easier to keep clean. Patterned rugs were thought to produce the most pleasing effect,

particularly when they picked up the tones of the room's wallpaper. Often a crumb cloth of woven cotton was placed over the rug and under the dining table during meals and removed for easier cleaning afterward, a custom that dates back to colonial times.

Window treatments in the dining room carried out the same theme of opulent patterning, and the fabrics and opulence were most often comparable with the layered windows of the drawing room. Heavily draped crimson velvets, puddling to the floor and then looped back with gold tassels or a wide embroided border, were a popular choice to set off the sage, terra-cotta, or Pompeiian-red dining rooms. Other colors thought suitable were pomegranate, dark blue, or soft olive and gold. In addition, the tops of the dining room windows were frequently crowned with carved and gilded lambrequins or heavy cornices.

Some Victorian decorating experts, however, regarded the use of heavy dining room draperies with disfavor, for, they claimed—and rightly so—that they tended to retain food odors. They advocated simpler treatments, such as swagged cretonne or even wooden Venetian blinds. Screens of brilliantly colored stained glass were also used in the dining room. According to *Treasures*

The haunting, visual quiet of this Victorian Revival dining room is created with the golden glow of the Tiffany light fixture and the abundance of textures—the rich Voysey rug, the swirl of the hand-printed William Morris wallpaper, and the nineteenth-century tapestry screen and draperies—add a special dimension to the room. Victorian chairs, dressed in crimson velvet and fringe—fulfilling the Victorian need for comfort—surround a table of an earlier vintage, while the antique stained-glass wall hanging takes on a new vitality against a patterned wall.

of Use and Beauty, a late-nineteenth-century home guide, these glass mosaics "excluded the strong rays of the sun and the light filtering through them beautifies the room with its mellow tones."

Stained-glass windows were also popular. One wealthy Victorian woman, for example, was reported to have been so enamored of the long, stained-glass scenes of Calvary in New York's Calvary Church that she attempted to purchase them. Nothing else, it seemed, could complete the decor of the Renaissance Revival dining room in her marble Fifth Avenue palace. The church fathers, however, refused to sell. The Ballantines of Newark fared better with their medieval dining room windows, having them custom-made in blue, gold, and brown for $154. Because the room had a southern exposure, though, the colors proved too strong, so that eventually, Mr. and Mrs. Ballantine had to change their dinner seating from north and south to east and west.

The dining room typically would have been shuttered as well as curtained. The daily ritual was to open the shutters and draperies in the morning to admit the cheer of the early morning sun, draw them both again at noon against the harsh glare of midday, thereby keeping the room cool and preventing the fine fabrics and wallpaper colors from fading, and then to close them in the evening to keep out the night.

Within this environment of dense textures and lighting effects, prescribed decorating formulas evolved whose first consideration was furniture style. In general, any of the styles considered "masculine" were acceptable: solid and bulky Empire in its day, Gothic Revival, flamboyant Renaissance Revival, even the rectilinear Eastlake qualified by virtue of its strong and "honest" construction. Rococo Revival, on the other hand, as an unabashedly feminine style—a drawing room style—seldom was used in the dining room (one of the reasons why the few existing Rococo Revival sideboards are so valued). Within these strictures, however, the selection of Victorian dining room furniture was approached eclectically. The dining room in the Ballantine house, for example, contained Renaissance Revival chairs covered with fringed tapestry fabric, a vaguely Italianate cupboard, Chinese rugs, an Empire sideboard, and the medieval-style stained-glass windows mentioned earlier—a lavish, lively combination that kept the room from appearing too grave.

Perhaps the most significant piece of furniture in the typical Victorian dining room was the large, elaborately carved sideboard. Nearly every Victorian home boasted such a piece, buttressed almost immoveably against one of the walls or contained in a specially built recess. The variety and ingenuity of styling was endless, from machine-made oak servers with basic shelves and quaint niches to uncompromisingly angular Eastlake versions, to those that stretched to lengths of nine or ten feet, their marble-topped black walnut or mahogany groaning with pediments and swags, cabochons, and carved deer heads.

Whatever the style, the sideboard was as native to the Victorian dining room as the center table and étagère were to the mid-century parlor or the hall tree was to the entryway. Its heyday, though, was in the 1880s. Chester A. Arthur, one of the more modish and society-loving of United States Presidents, like any fashionable man of his times, was particularly well versed in the dictates of interior decoration. He impressed his proper Victorian taste on the White House with a massive redecoration, the dining room in particular emerging as a model of 1880s taste, with heavy gold wallpaper, the windows and mantel hung with pomegranate-colored plush, and, of course, an elaborate sideboard displaying Limoges and azaleas in full bloom. When Iowa's Terrace Hill, the "prairie palace of the West" (today the Iowa Governor's Mansion),

was remodeled by its second owner in 1883, the dining room received a fine oak wainscot and an elegant built-in sideboard of unusual beauty, with drawers and cubbies, niches and plate rails for display, and carvings of wheat, sunflowers, and grape leaves as well as the traditional egg and dart.

One of the more characteristic and memorable kinds of Victorian sideboard ornamentation was the decorative carving of fruit, fish, fowl, or game, a practice that may strike some observers today as one of the more unusual manifestations of Victorian taste—and which in its own day incited the wrath of the reformists. Those who displayed such sideboards, however, considered the carving perfectly apropos, as it represented many of the items meant to be placed on the sideboard's surface, and thus fit with the eating theme of the room.

The sideboard cabinet housed the silverware, napery, plates, and additional serving pieces, while its surface held the platters of meats, decanters of wine, and other items that might be called into service during the prolonged and leisurely Victorian dinner. The sideboard's true purpose was, however, as openly symbolic as it was practical. It was there for frank display; the array of silver and silver plate that gleamed on its surface seldom saw actual use.

Instead, it was meant to broadcast a message of prosperity and means as obviously as a movie marquee. This was a world in which wealth equaled moral goodness; an abundance of silver plate on the sideboard was therefore the mark of a venerable citizen.

The nineteenth century's innocent materialism, however, and its visible realization in the home were defused to a large extent by the fact that more families than ever were in a position to adorn their dining rooms with at least a semblance of what had become badges of respectability. While silver plate might have substituted for sterling and ceramics for Sèvres, the honest pride of possession and the messages of taste and civilization they carried with them were the same. The women's periodicals reinforced this message month after month; both the homesteading wife living on a land grant and the frontier bride looking forward to her next *Godey's* well knew that the sideboard was for "the handsome display of china and glass" *when*, not *if*, she acquired them. Victorian optimism and upward mobility reigned.

The more lavish the display on the sideboard, the greater the perception of the family's position. To this end, in the grander homes, the sideboard (like the étagère) was often mirrored to magnify the effect of

its contents. When tall, pale wax tapers were placed on its surface, they, too, were reflected, their light further illuminating the family treasures, creating the illusion of a domestic "altar." Decorating guides even found that altar "much enlivened" by the addition of an "altar cloth": a "heavy rich looking cloth worked in colors and dropping low over the sides with heavy fringes showing handsomely against the dark woods" was proclaimed by *The Household* to be a very attractive effect for the home of the 1880s.

The Victorian dining room table, positioned in the center of the room, could have been circular, oval, square, or rectangular, and was often heavily carved. When not in use, it would have been covered with a cloth similar in coloring to the room's draperies. Extension tables, which were introduced in the early 1800s, were popular. Their leaves sometimes extended the table to a length of twelve feet or more. Another type of dining table was the pedestal style, which appeared either in what was called the frame-and-leg style or in the simpler pillar-and-claw variety, each with its own advantages. Those with legs were considered sturdy and easily extended, while the pillar-and-claw types were less bothersome to seated guests because they avoided the intrusion of table legs.

The main objectives in choosing dining room chairs were comfort and steadiness—that they be "sufficiently comfortable to support a diner in an upright position without fatigue." The actual fashions in chairs varied with each successive decade, however. "The fashion in chairs varies with the fashion in ladies dresses," Mrs. Spofford wrote in the late 1870s. "The wide spreading skirts which were supported by crinolines needed a different kind of chair from that on which the well 'tied-back' lady of the present day can sit comfortably."

Although the balloon-backed upholstered side chair survived well past its initial period of popularity in the 1850s and 1860s, the most typical Victorian dining chair was straight backed and sturdy, upholstered in rush, leather, or woven tapestry, with brass or silver nail heads adding to its solid appearance. It was, of course, coordinated with the room's other furnishings. The dining room chairs at Château-sur-Mer in Newport, Rhode Island, for example, were covered with the same tooled, gilded, and flower-painted leather that scaled the room's walls, as were the low, matching footstools tucked under the dining table—another thoughtful consideration for the Victorian diner's comfort.

Other major furnishings for the dining room included a tea cart or dinner wagon and additional serving or storage pieces like glass-doored buffets and servers, all more obviously functional than the sacred sideboard. A small mahogany serving table, for instance, might be placed like a pier table between two windows and used to hold additional platters or the coffee or tea service, while its drawers stored flatware and linen. If the dining room was large, one also might have found a sofa or two, a locked cabinet for whiskey, sherry, or Madeira, and perhaps even an unobtrusive writing desk. The sofa, desk, and sometimes even a piano would have been typical in homes where the only parlor was a formal one and the dining room served as a family gathering place.

Fireplaces in the dining room were frequently lined in bright, glazed ornamental tiles which radiated warmth back into the room. Since the dining table would have occupied the very central position in the room, someone would inevitably have been seated with his or her back to the fire, making a firescreen a necessity. In a very narrow dining room, for example, the heat from the fire could be so intense that without a firescreen one side of the table would have been virtually unusable.

Because the dining room was

Above and opposite: *A charming Victorian dollhouse roosts on an old-fashioned wicker teacart in the dining room of the Queen Victoria Inn. The gilded wallpaper is printed with the Queen's royal monogram; the windows are hung with white lace.*

A grand Victorian banquet would have taken place in this room a hundred years ago, and today, the owner still uses it for lavish entertaining. Here, the table is a mass of antique linen, Irish crystal, bone china and silver; the tall epergne in the center of the table is gilded sterling, lit with candles and flowers. The fireplace is draped in lamé and lace; the ruby-rimmed crystal bowl on the table is a Victorian grape-washer. The mirror over the mantel, its niches filled with nineteenth-century ginger jars is original to the house. On the walls, are tapestries and traditional Victorian dining room engravings of game birds.

such a grand and imposing space, many Victorians with houses of some size and articulation took their morning coffee or tea in what they called the morning room, which was something of a combination of breakfast room and sitting room for the early hours of the day. The morning room was usually located in the back portion of the house, not too far from the kitchen area, so that it would catch the first burst of morning sunlight and therefore be a warm, bright, and pleasant place to have breakfast.

As in other rooms of the Victorian home, the dining room had its full complement of art and accessories. While those in the dining room were chosen without the unchecked fervor shown for ornament in the parlor, and while the personal, homey qualities were left in the sitting room, the dining room accessories were nevertheless selected with a theme in mind; more soberly, on the whole, to avoid distraction or the disruption of the delicate process of digestion. On the mantel above the fireplace one would have found vases and busts, a clock, candelabra, or, especially, an arrangement of "picturesque" shelving framing a beveled overmantel mirror. This would have held such items as pedigreed bits of "long descended" china (too special for daily use), as well as other objects bearing some ten-

uous connection to the dining room area: mugs, quaint bits of porcelain, pepper boxes, old-fashioned pitchers or decanters. The Victorian attention to detail is evident in the specification of mirrors with beveling to enable the jewellike cutwork to add greater brilliance to the display. Cases of stuffed birds and trophy heads were also in keeping with dining room decor.

Plants and greenery had a substantial place in the decoration of the dining room, whether manifested by a plant or two on corner pedestals near the window, a fernery, large pots of tropicals, or just a few leaves arranged in decorative patterns on the tablecloth. More often, however, the effects were lavish, as at a spring dinner party in the 1890s described in *Vogue* where "great pomegranate bushes in square boxes of old Sèvres porcelain raised their crimson blossoms against the somber magnificence of the walls, and the chandelier above the square dinner table was swathed in drooping wreaths of bright Chinese hibiscus and lustrous Indian ivy."

Traditionally, Victorians preferred cakes, fruits, and other sweet edibles as dining room centerpieces, and when live flowers were used, scentless ones were specified so that the perfume wouldn't interfere with the aroma of the food being served. Floral decorations did reach heights of extravagance during the last part of the era. At the same dinner fête mentioned above, for example, a bank of white roses concealed the tablecloth, while the individual plates were surrounded with a border of rosebuds. According to the magazine, "Nothing can give an idea of the coup d'œil presented by this flowery board and a murmur of admiration escaped the lips of the guests as they took their places."

Parisian table decorations were also described in detail for luxury-hungry Americans to copy. Among the recommendations from across the Atlantic was the use of delicate blue-mauve hyacinth framed in maidenhair-fern sprays and tied with wide bows of saffron-colored ribbon, rose-pink cyclamen set among white lilacs, and silver repoussé bowls of Parma violets, supplemented by crystal vases supporting trails of smilax and mixed with feathery mimosa blossoms. Some critics, however, protested against the over-lavish decoration of the table that had emerged. "The days of mirrors and lakes and pond lilies and all that sort of thing are over," *Vogue* finally decreed in the early 1890s. "They were displays of gross vulgarity at best. Silver and glass with one centerpiece of flowers—this shows good taste. Even candles with pink shades are being discarded, the restaurants and hotels having adopted them."

Outside of such extravagances, which were mainly reserved for special balls or gala parties, the most typical Victorian centerpiece would have been the tall, trumpet-shaped epergne. Spilling over with flowers or fruit, and surrounded by smaller satellites of candles and candelabra, it was usually set above eye level so that it wouldn't impede conversation. In other middle-class homes, a revolving cruet set of metal or silver plate, holding as many as five condiment bottles for sweet oil, vinegar, pepper, and mustard, was the most universally accepted center ornament. Eventually, it was replaced by individual castors placed in front of each setting.

Victorians had curious ideas concerning suitable dining room art. Currier & Ives, for example, issued an entire series of *Art for the Dining Room* consisting of still-life prints and engravings of flowers, fruit cornucopias, and, especially, fish and game scenes and hunt images, such as dogs tracking down unfortunate rabbits or deer. This tradition, along with that of using stuffed birds and trophy heads mounted around the room, had its roots in earlier days, and the Victorians continued it, perhaps to excess. Reformists rejected such use with vigor, however. One wrote: "It has been the custom to

have pictures of still life in the dining room—of game, fish, fruit. But this is hardly a cheerful view, to see representation of the fish and game—that one is soon to eat—in all the agony of death." Alternatives suggested for the dining room included blander pastorals, landscapes, and flower pictures.

Sometimes the artwork in the dining room took on an inspirational tone, as in the use of mottoes, samplers, and "moral" illustrations. Frances Willard, leader of the Women's Christian Temperance Union from 1874 to 1898, recalled that the dining room of her childhood (ca. 1835) was hung with a pretty steel engraving "representing a bright happy temperance home with a sweet woman at the center, and over against it a squalid house with a drunken man staggering, bottle in hand."

Family portraits, especially those from past generations, were also hung in the dining room, like engravings, in hope of good moral influence. When suspended on gold wires from brass rods, they were said to have been impressive. There, from their perch on the walls, they looked down from their frames, "welcoming each meal and the train of life it brings, and exercised, as it were, a mute guardianship over thought and behavior," or so the decorating books suggested.

The Victorian character of the dining room in the Mainstay Inn is established immediately by the massive Renaissance Revival sideboard and its bountiful display and the unusually ornate solid brass gas fixture, with cut-glass shades that the owners cleaned and electrified. Long, lace curtains, topped with simple swags of red taffeta and antique tassels, add to the room's allure.

All the elements of the dining room—its dark massing of shapes, its mixing of heavy textures, its brightening accents of gilding throwing off small pockets of light, its art and portraits—make it very clear that the room was meant to be as much a restorative as a room of luxury and ease. In the decades following the Civil War, when social and economic changes reached an almost bewildering scale, this was particularly evident: the room became darker, deeper, more enclosed, more secure. As new fortunes were made in new ventures—oil, coal, steel, railroads, the new emporiums known as department stores—previously unknown men were catapulted from humble cottages to prominent mansions, and few arrived with a hardened social veneer. The security the dining room promised seemed a reassuring refuge.

In addition, the evolution of the nineteenth-century interior suggests a retreat into the sphere of the home. However enthusiastically Victorians responded to the wonders of novelty and progress, it was not without a twinge of uneasiness, perhaps even regret, about the world that they were creating. The sentimental, almost Arcadian, scenes that Currier & Ives sold by the tens of thousands must have seemed as remote as Camelot to a country nearly torn in two by war and still feeling its bitter aftereffects. There was an undercurrent of longing for the simpler life of the first half of the century, as people retreated into utopian communities and sought solace in cults and the spiritualist movements that thrived throughout the era.

Home decor was enlisted to provide something of an antidote to all these changes. The dining room in particular—designed as a bastion of permanence, exuding solidity and old-fashioned virtues from the stately ceilings overhead to the sound-muffling rugs and runners on the polished wood floors below—was the home's decorative triumph. There, Victorians could seek security of their place in the world in a room that seemed to embody in every way the good spirits of prosperity and the rock-solid values of traditional family life.

Above and opposite: *A traditional Victorian tea, with tea sandwiches, pecan tarts, even bon-bons, is one the nineteenth-century pleasures being revived today. The sunlit alcove of this 1856 dining room is draped in handmade antique lace; the fixture is bronze and Victorian pressed glass.*

Chapter 7

The Victorian Bedroom

India matting covered the floor with a gay rug here and there; the antique andirons shone on the wide hearth where a cheery blaze dispelled the dampness of the long enclosed room. Bamboo lounges and chairs stood about and quaint little tables in cosy corners; one bearing a pretty basket; one a desk, and on the third stood a narrow, white bed with a lovely Madonna hanging over it. The Japanese screen half folded back showed a delicate toilet service of blue and white, set forth on a marble slab, and nearby was a great bath pan with Turkish towels and a sponge as big as Rose's head.

Louisa May Alcott

The Victorians would have felt fully at home in this present-day city apartment, with the delicate textures of its antique lace coverlet threaded with ribbons, its softly draped tables, and its pale, subdued walls. The curls and frills of the ornate photographer's "prop" chair—which would have been used for studio portrait sittings—make it typical of the fanciful turn that Victorian wicker took in the 1880s and 1890s. The book in the foreground is covered in fine nineteenth-century beadwork.

he preceding passage, taken from the popular 1874 girl's novel *Eight Cousins,* gives us a peek into a newly decorated Victorian bedroom that, even today, beckons us into its light-filled sanctuary. Originally "shrouded, still and solitary," the bedroom had become full of "light, warmth and simplicity" by the time of this description, which includes careful mention of many of the major design trends employed by fashionable Victorian society at the time. From the evocation of exotic cultures of the faraway Orient brought to mind by the bamboo lounges and Japanese screen, to the "artistic" touch of a toilet set in blue and white and the pointed reference to the prominent washing facilities (this was the era when Victorians, with increasing medical know-how, were beginning to equate cleanliness with godliness), it seems a perfect "textbook" description for the bedroom of a proper Victorian lady.

The most important aspect of this passage to note, however, is the atmosphere of lightness it imparts—a dramatic difference from the other rooms in the Victorian home, a counter to the bric-a-brac-filled exuberance of the parlor or the rich-ly enclosed dignity of the dining room. But these two rooms, along with the entryway, with their symphony of sculptures, paintings and prints, souvenirs of travel, and gilt-edged books, would already have established the family's social standing and taste. In contrast was the bedroom—or bedchamber as it was more genteely called—which was airier, simpler and, while by no means sparsely decorated, sparer than the more public rooms of the home. Seldom seen by anyone other than family members or servants (except in the case of the wealthiest households, where the grandeur of the bedroom sometimes seemed to equal, if not exceed, that of the reception rooms), it would have hardly been the place for pomp and show.

In further contrast, especially to the parlor, which always boasted furnishings of the newest and latest manufacture, the typical Victorian bedchamber had a faintly old-fashioned air, hinting at hand-stitched lavender sachets tucked away in every drawer. Frequently its furniture was second-best, the kind of comfortably out-of-date pieces no longer fine enough for the other rooms of the house. While certainly not austere—something no Victorian room could ever be—the preferred colors and patterns were of serene, almost feminine, tones, pale as op-

The impressionistic patterning on the walls, the lace throws, and the colorful Victorian needlepoint pillows all contribute nineteenth-century charm to this Victorian Revival bedroom in a present-day city apartment. The elaborately swagged bed draperies, enriched with fringe and adorned with rosettes, would have satisfied the Victorian need for drapery which does not fully enclose the bed (a look that would have pleased the tastemakers of the last century), while the hanging lantern is a reminder of the period's interest in chinoiserie.

posed to rich, creating an effect much like that of a rain-washed spring garden transplanted indoors.

Bedchambers in private homes of the era were reached by ascending the graceful curve of the central staircase, which helped preserve the mysteries of the home's upper rooms, separating them from the more public spaces. In Victorian middle-class apartment houses, bedchambers were necessarily on the same floor as the living rooms, and sometimes they even opened into the parlor or library in the manner of French dwellings of the same time. This type of layout was considered vaguely suggestive and somehow indecent. For visitors in the sitting room to actually catch a glimpse of a lady's bedchamber, as happens in Edith Wharton's *The Age of Innocence*, was considered mildly shocking: "That was how women with lovers lived in wicked old societies in apartments with all the rooms on one floor and all the indecent propinquities that their novels described." American Victorians had very clear ideas about the implications of their private spaces versus those of their public ones, and one of those ideas was that the two should be firmly separated, the bedroom in its own zone of privacy and quiet.

Ground floor bedrooms did exist in private homes as well, however. Judge David Davis occupied the ground floor bedchamber in his home, although he also used it as a study. Often the ground floor chamber was designated as a guest room. When William Dean Howells, novelist and editor of *The Atlantic Monthly*, was visiting Mark Twain in Hartford, he remembers the "royal chamber" he had in the Twains' ground floor room. Sumptuously furnished, it was elegant without being grand, with its bed and dresser handsomely inlaid with English tiles, fireplace tiles inset in gleaming brass, brass and cloisonné enamel lights, and silver-plated hardware. The room had its own bath too, lit by clerestory lighting which provided both light and privacy. Still, a look at the floorplans shows the guestchamber was almost in a wing by itself, well separated from the drawing room by an ample hallway, and situated just off the quiet library.

Still another ground floor bedchamber belonged to Carl Gustav Adolphus Voight of Grand Rapids, Michigan, a German immigrant who came to the United States in 1843 and later became a prosperous store and mill owner. In the retirement house he built in 1895, he and his wife took the ground floor room as their own. Later, because of its proximity to the kitchen (and because it had its own bath), it became a sickroom, another common Victorian use for lower-floor bedrooms. In the manner typical of many other homes of the time, the Voights kept the old 1860s carved walnut bedroom suite from their early married days in this private chamber, even though most of the house was decorated in the spirit of the 1890s, with Tiffany-style wall treatments, stylized Art Nouveau stenciling, and the golden oak that was becoming popular.

Like the other rooms in the Victorian house, the bedchamber was intended to be something of a testament to the domestic creativity of the nineteenth-century woman. The room's essential comfort, and what was called "wholesomeness," was tangible evidence of her skill in the womanly art of making a home. With earnestness and industry, she took to heart the advice of *The Household*, which said that every room should express "some distinctive feature in decoration, an air of individuality which would afford a clue to the designer's and owner's special tastes and fancies."

It was not an investment in major furniture or imported art that made the bedroom special, although that was certainly often true in grander homes where costly Belter slipper chairs nuzzled up against bedroom mantels of hand-carved Carrara marble; it was the attention to small, personal touches. A lacy crocheted bedcover, a cozy throw or hand-embroidered lamp mat, a primly arranged wicker basket of flowers, graceful silhouettes of one's nearest friends, or botanical prints made all the more personal by homemade twig frames—all bespoke this attention. A female houseguest might even be pleased to see a fresh pincushion on her bedroom bureau, especially if the bead-topped pins that studded the sides thoughtfully spelled out her initials in welcome.

The emphasis on the lightness of appearance in the bedroom was due in part to reform influences in the later part of the century, which called for a move away from dark, musty rooms, toward brightened, airy, well-ventilated retreats, filled with "sweetness," the Victorian euphemism for fresh as opposed to stale air. One Lady Barker, writing in 1878, deplores the earlier tendency to make bedrooms and boudoirs (the adjoining sitting room or dressing area) gloomy with heavy colors and weighty draperies. She evokes, for example, a "horrible vision" of a bedroom with spotted robin's egg blue walls and the travesty of *black* furniture "whose owner could not be induced to brighten up her gloom by so much as a gay pin cushion."

The lightened look of the Victori-

Scrolled and hammered silver trinket and pin boxes, often displayed on a bedside table, were produced in great quantities in the nineteenth century and are eagerly sought by collectors today.

Above: *A particularly appropriate treatment for the smaller or the lower-ceilinged bedroom—half-canopied bed draperies—adds a romantic flourish without overpowering the room.*

Opposite: *A table and chair of Victorian papier-mâché are inlaid with mother-of-pearl and would have been greatly admired for their mingling of the romantic and ornamental with the exotic.*

an bedchamber was also a response to the era's higher standards of health and cleanliness, which arose from the first tenuous connections being made between dirt and disease. Regular bathing was beginning to be promoted and young women scrupulously donned "bathing mittens" made from the ends of worn Turkish towels or thick lengths of linen, presumably so they wouldn't accidentally touch themselves when they washed. Some even washed standing up, shivering on the cold rubber or oil cloth matting that many doctors considered more hygienic than the new zinc-lined bathtubs.

Not only was cleanliness of the body avidly promoted, but cleanliness of the home was just as directly championed, especially when applied to the bedchamber. It was discovered, for example, that that innocent room offered one of the greatest potential hazards to health in its accumulation of stale air. As a result of this belief, women were instructed to choose furnishings for the bedroom as much for their hygienic virtues as for their aesthetic appeal. Windows, for example, were supposed to be opened in the mornings for at least half an hour, according to *Beeton's Book of Household Management.* This practice, while it brought in fresh air, also brought in soil and dirt, thereby leading to the

preference for relatively plain bedroom furnishings which were easy to clean. Housemaids were instructed in the methods of shaking and airing blankets, tossing horsehair mattresses high in the air, and rubbing down the bedroom furniture with an old brick encased in a soft flannel wrapping. Part of the reason for this was that people had begun to believe that, during sleep, the body exuded unsanitary "emanations" and "effluvia," which could contaminate the room and everything in it. This "effluvia," according to *Beeton's*, was said to "hang, a viewless vapor in the air, steep linen and reek in blankets." Victorians were even warned not to leave soiled clothes draped over a chair overnight because they also contributed to the dreaded "effluvia."

However bizarre these notions sound today, they were based on an inner core of sense and logic. Bedroom walls and ceilings *did* collect soil and dirt, if not directly from the humors of the sleeping human body, from the oil lamps and from coal and wood fires. The rooms certainly *did* need to be scrubbed down regularly; that, in fact, was what the age-old tradition of spring cleaning was all about. Anything that could make that chore easier—easy-to-clean wooden furniture, wainscoting, simple, painted walls rather than ornate papered ones, all features the Victo-

rians advocated for the bedrooms—was a step in the right direction.

Some Victorian beliefs drifted alarmingly (if delightfully) far afield, however, and it's doubtful that even the most proper Victorian accepted them all. The fear of contamination by nightly vapors, for example, led some American medical experts to advocate the British custom of separate but connected bedrooms for husbands and wives. Victorian men were duly warned that the mysterious "emanations" of the sleeping female were to be especially feared. Even more threatening was the belief that the "vital forces" of each might be unknowingly exchanged as a result of too frequent nightly intimacies—causing the wife to show masculine appetites and the husband to demonstrate effeminate ones. Separate bedrooms, with the all-important key remaining in the safety of the wife's possession, were also touted in order to safeguard women from husbands who couldn't manage to control their amorous proclivities, as well as to provide a means of avoiding undressing in one another's presence. This, too, could inflame "excessive emotion," as it was delicately phrased. Despite much writing and raging about these dangers, even Victorian America apparently found their own strictures hard to take, for separate bedrooms,

except in the case of an invalid spouse, and twin married beds were relatively rare. The twin brass beds in President and Mrs. McKinley's White House bedchamber at the turn of the century were more a comment on Ida McKinley's frail health than anything else.

It was because unwholesome bedchamber vapors were commonly thought to cling to the surrounding walls that appropriate wall treatments became the subject for much discussion. Many people were violently set against the use of wallpapers for sanitary reasons, while rooms in older homes which had managed to retain their old-time oak wainscoting were considered to be ideal sleeping areas. The wainscot, especially when dark and lustrous with age and polishing, was not only handsome and told of "heritage"—a special plus to Victorians during America's Centennial years—but it was also easy to clean and supposedly wouldn't attract any objectionable particles. Housekeepers were advised to polish the old wainscot until it glowed. Resorting to "white washing" as a means of lightening the room was a practice much despised.

"Tinting," or painting the bedchamber in a pale, delicate color, with lines of a contrasting color at the ceiling, creating a sort of simplified frieze, was considered the most

Cozy table-top vignettes abounded in the traditional Victorian bedroom, where cherished photographs and personal memorabilia all had their place. Here, the photographs are in nineteenth-century silver frames, arranged on a long swatch of antique lace. Lace or dresser scarves were usually used to cover the top of a bureau to protect its finish and to alleviate the appearance of bareness.

enlightened approach to decorating bedchamber walls. The look of painted walls also had the additional appeal of being rather novel at the time, thereby appealing to the Victorians' progressive nature. Care had to be taken, however, to avoid too cold and spare a look, since a bedroom, it was felt, should still be warm-looking and comfortable. Tender hues, such as seashell pink, luminous pale greens, soft muted blues, and pearly grays, all got the tastemaker's nod, especially when the tones of the ceiling border were picked up in the draped tabletops, pillows, and curtains. The Presidential bedchamber during the occupancy of Rutherford B. and Lucy Hayes, who were widely admired for their exemplary home activities and proper Victorian family life (she was said to have the most motherly expression imaginable, despite the unusual distinction of being a college graduate), would have met with full approval. Its white marble mantel, marble-topped tables, and low bed were all set off by pale blue walls with panels of light gray and pink and discreet bands of gilt. Even Edith Wharton's not-so-exemplary Undine Spragg, in *The Custom of the Country*, went to bed at the fictional New York "Hotel Stentorian" in a white and gold bedroom with sea green panels and an old rose carpet.

Victorian women were advised that despite the trend to lighten and brighten their bedrooms, light colors must still be chosen with care in order to avoid an effect that was glaring. Pale tones, which tend to reflect light more than darker colors, often seemed harsh to the Victorians who were more attuned to the harmonious blending of dark shades, muted even further by their traditional mix of dense textures. In draperies or curtains, as in women's fashions, a too-harsh pastel, such as an assertive green silk, could be softened by the addition of a muslin or lace overskirting which would obscure the "glare" while still letting the glow of color come through.

The Victorian bedroom's coloring was also determined by the room's view. For instance, one decorating writer of the late 1870s explains how to tone down what must have been the unseemly "dazzle" of a bright sunny room with a southern exposure by using cool gray-greens and sea-blue tones. Deep violets, dark blues, and warm reds, on the other hand, were reserved for taking the chill off a chamber with a northern exposure.

Despite the many warnings and health admonitions, wallpaper, which had become a fairly inexpensive and accessible commodity by the second half of the nineteenth century, continued to be used in bedchambers, particularly those of the middle classes. Care was advised in choosing a pattern that was restful and subdued and that wouldn't "torment" the sleeper with its fanciful designs. One magazine explained that bedroom paper "ought never to have a distinct pattern spotted on it, lest, if you are ill, it should incite you to count the designs or make faces at you." A feature on bedroom furnishings in an 1877 *Harper's Bazar* takes the opposite view, however, citing an authority no less than the revered Florence Nightingale who maintained that "variety of form and brilliancy of color in the objects presented to patients are actual means of recovery." Concurring with her, the magazine concluded that "we had better secure beauty for our healthy moments any way and leave it to work its own special charm on our sick ones."

When wallpapers first became available, the same vivid reds, blues, and greens in the fervid, full-blown patterns that were used in the parlor also found their way into the privacy of bedchambers. By the 1870s, however, that had changed. The discreet vertical floral stripings, vinelike gardens, and other delicate patterns of the wallpapers of the Gilded Age bedchambers were as different from the earlier versions as a circus is from a finishing-school tea. Colors like fawn, pale blue, rose, and light olive predominated, with traceries in contrasting tones. One decidedly romantic and original design, qualified as being "not strictly according to the rules of modern taste," consisted of a satiny white paper, bordered by pink ribbons and trompe l'oeil bows that dropped into the corners of the room as well as encircled the area over the fireplace to prettily surround a portrait or print. Such wallpapers, with their dainty and feminine designs, were also put to use to line and decorate Victorian bandboxes, the round or oval, wood or pasteboard containers used by the Victorians to store hats, handkerchiefs, letters, and other personal treasures. Wallpapers were cleaned in a variety of ways, from brushing them down with a cloth-covered broom to using the soft side of a cut-open loaf of stale bread as a sort of pumice for scrubbing.

Although twelve- and fourteen-foot-high ceilings were a hallmark of many of the more elaborate Victorian town homes and mansions, more modest dwellings, as well as country or rural homes, were low-ceilinged, and care had to be taken to choose a bedroom wallpaper that wouldn't crowd the space. In these cases, a hand-stenciled border was often the solution, most frequently a simplified ceiling border with a line of stenciled ornamentation above the room's dado.

Fabric was another popular wall

Above, below, and opposite: *The bare, gleaming parquet floors in the bedroom of this rowhouse, built by Clarence True, ca. 1890, reflects modern tastes, while the restored oak woodwork, impressive brass bed, and Eastlake-style table in the bay window have definite Victorian antecedents. The pale gray stripe circling the upper portion of the walls integrates the nineteenth-century wall divisions, a subtle twentieth-century salute to the more elaborate Victorian frieze.*

treatment for the bedchamber, and, unlike wallpapers, could be taken off the walls (fabrics were often hung in panels on furring strips) for heavy-duty cleaning. It was also considered fashionable for the same fabric to be used on the windows, pillows, and bedroom lounges and as mantel and table drapery. Chintz was one of the most popular choices, panels of cream-ground chintz bedecked with tendrils of green and brown ivy looped in garlands being especially admired when stretched right above the bedroom dado with all the matching accouterments. Fluted white muslin over pink or blue silk or apple-green batiste were also suitable. Tapestry fabrics, however, were rejected by some experts as being too dark and somber, although on occasion a hunter-green silk damask would be used in a bedroom; especially in a masculine room, its darkness would have been dramatic and appropriate.

Bedroom curtains derived their tone from the rest of the room. In a grand room, for instance, no expense would have been spared, and curtains in bronze or crimson, in rich velvets, antique brocades, twilled silk, satins, and foulards, trimmed with wide panels of appliqué or embroidery, would have been found. "Insertion" curtains were one of the Victorian styles that crossed all income barriers. These were first made of brocade, silk, or satin, and inset with alternating strips of lace. They became popular with the middle classes, however, because they could easily be imitated by using less costly strips of the popular Turkey red fabric with inexpensive lace, or with still cheaper muslin, for the same kind of transparent effect.

More typically, however, advice on bedroom curtains recommended keeping them light in order to permit fresh air and light to flow into the rooms. Housewives in the 1880s, for instance, were instructed to opt for a variety of airy, sheer material for their bedroom curtains, such as cretonnes, floral chintzes, lace, madras (when it was light enough to permit the sun to shine through), white batiste inset with lace strips or finished off with hand-painted borders, and even the better varieties of cheesecloth with an edging of antique lace or floral chintz to "dress it up." Striped, sprigged, or dotted muslins were still other alternatives. Typical trimmings for curtains were lengths of antique lace, often pleated, and gathered flounces, although cretonne curtains were felt to be most attractive when left plain or trimmed with fringe. In general, if one preferred a solid color to a print, pastel tones like blue or rose were thought best, with a layer of muslin under or over it. In addition to curtains, wooden venetian blinds and shutters which folded back into the window frame were used.

Curtain-making itself was one of the time-consuming chores in the Victorian household and the letters of many Victorian women are filled with references to curtain rings and rods, to curtains being made and be-

ing hung. This was especially true in the South, where custom dictated two sets of curtains for each room, one for the summer months and another for the winter.

As for floors, according to *The Household* "most all ladies" preferred rugs and oiled floors to wall-to-wall bedroom carpeting. (Wood floors, at that time, were oiled once or twice before being varnished.) Rugs were generally considered to be more modern, more "picturesque," and more fashionable than carpeting, as well as being easier to care for. Both bedroom carpets and rugs had to be carefully swept daily, after having been strewn with moist tea leaves or, when obtainable, freshly pulled grass, in order to create a pleasant odor. Beneath the rug, it was common to place a layer of matting, which served to double the warmth of the room.

Even if one preferred wall-to-wall carpeting in one's bedroom, a few rugs were always a good idea—in front of the bed, dresser, and fireplace—for the extra warmth and comfort as well as to save wear and tear on the pile. Patterned rugs were largely preferred over solid ones and dark but bright colors were to be placed over lighter ones. Suggested combinations included blue with pink, scarlet and gray, deep red and pale blue, olive or other greens with gold, and light blue with accents of

Above and opposite: *The designer-owner used Gothic Revival arches, strong verticals, and finials to highlight different areas in this sophisticated studio apartment. The use of black lacquer and white pine, however, suggests the Japanese Revival, while the fluted pilasters lend a classical note. Mirrored insets accent the doorways and fireplace.*

Above and opposite: *Even dressing-table accessories—cannisters for creams or pomades, perfume flagons, and the like—reflected the nineteenth-century concern for ornament. These silver-topped crystal containers rest on a bedroom table that opens to reveal a hidden wash set.*

dark red. Despite the light, cheerful look being sought, the Victorians also somehow considered a rug of tiger, bear, or fox skins to be "a charming acquisition" that added an "Oriental touch."

As mentioned before, the furniture in the Victorian bedroom was frequently somewhat old-fashioned; the family's older side chairs which had been replaced by the new parlor set, the slightly battered chest that once graced the hallway, grandfather's old, worn desk—all found their way to those upstairs bedchambers. The old-fashioned wing chairs, with their big, draught-excluding wings, a holdover from the earlier part of the century, are another example. A favorite of elderly members of the nineteenth-century household who would have had trouble keeping warm, these chairs were relegated to the Victorian bedchamber from the parlor, further contributing to the room's vaguely eighteenth-century air.

After the 1840s, when matching bedroom suites began to be advertised, the Victorian bedroom acquired a more unified appearance. These suites consisted typically of a bedstand, a bureau and mirror (called a dressing bureau), a nightstand, a washstand, and an armoire. They were available in ornately carved and gilded fine woods as well

as simpler, machine-manufactured cottage sets. The carved rosewood bedroom suite in the White House's Lincoln bedroom (the only Victorian furniture remaining in the White House today), with its nine-foot-long bed and ornately carved chairs, upholstered in yellow velvet, was purchased in 1862 by Mary Todd Lincoln, and is a typical example of one of the more elegant suites in the Rococo Revival style. So exuberant and detailed is its carving that between the legs of the center table is a carved bird's nest complete with eggs. In general, the use of dark woods like rosewood, black walnut, or mahogany was typical of the times, for they satisfied the Victorian craving for luxury most fully. Lighter woods, like bamboo or faux bamboo, were used in the later part of the century, especially in bedchambers of a Far Eastern or Anglo-Japanese character.

The tall wooden bedstand and brass bed are the two styles most frequently associated with the Victorian era, though neither came into popularity until fairly late in the century. Earlier, Victorian beds were simply the canopied fourposters that had been used throughout the eighteenth century and early part of the nineteenth. They were draped with sweeping bed hangings which served a practical as well as decorative purpose by insulating the

A mix of family heirlooms and eclectic finds—hand-hooked rugs, a child's wicker chair (ca. 1910), the casual pile-up of books and magazines on a Civil War-vintage trunk—makes the bedroom in this 1882 San Francisco home an inviting and romantic retreat. The nine-foot-high Renaissance Revival bed, fashioned in walnut and walnut burl, is set into the alcove of the room, an arrangement common to many Victorian homes. The stenciled frieze is an Egyptian/Eastlake design taken from **The Grammar of Ornament,** *while the walls were painted, and then inset with crimson brocatelle. The night table, actually a sewing/shaving stand, belongs to the original bedroom suite, and the lamp on the Renaissance Revival pedestal dates from 1910. The lounge at the foot of the bed is not Victorian, however, but was rescued from an old movie theater.*

sleeper against cold and draughts. Fourposters remained popular through the mid-Victorian decades, especially in the Southern plantation homes where they were often over-draped with mosquito netting for protection against insects, but by the 1870s they had come to be regarded as old-fashioned.

Another style of bed that was popular in American homes during the 1840s was the Empire-style sleigh bed, with its headboard and footboard of equal height and its curved sides resembling those of a sleigh. The spool-turned, or "Jenny Lind," beds were also frequently used, and half testers and iron bedsteads (one of the latter was shown at the 1853 Crystal Palace exhibition) were just beginning to be seen at this time. The monumental all-wooden bedstead with towering, carved headboard and slightly lower footboard was the preeminent style during the later Victorian decades. Popular versions included both the Rococo Revival and the Renaissance Revival styles as well as the later Eastlake-inspired versions, the relative simplicity of which made them particularly appropriate for the rooms of young people.

The headboard ornamentation of the two "Revival" styles heralded the end of the full-draped and canopied eighteenth-century bed. Clearly, the new styles clamored to be

The enrichment offered by lace of all kinds—embroidered, crocheted, netted—moved from nineteenth-century fashion to interiors, particularly the bedchamber, where the delicate freshness of this lace bedcover would have been especially apropos.

seen and not draped, and the half tester, a half-draped bed—or no drapery at all—seemed to be the solution. An impressive bedstead with a built-up, crested headboard was a style particularly favored by wealthy tycoons who felt it invested their private chambers with a suitable grandeur, especially when inset with fancy portraiture, porcelain plaques, and carved initials.

In contrast to the high, colonial bedsteads with their bed steps, Victorian beds were positioned rather low. One household guide explains that this was because a lower bed was felt to ensure a "better quality of air above the sleeper's face, as well as doing away with the untidy clutter of boxes or carpet bags that might be stored under the bed itself." This factor also contributed to the eventual demise of the old four-poster. Bed valences (what we call dust ruffles today) were also rejected, as it was thought to be healthier if air currents flowed and circulated beneath the bedframe without restriction.

The new theories about bedchamber freshness caused the Victorians to eventually prefer brass beds over wooden ones. Impressive as wooden beds were, not only did their bed hangings tend to retain odors, but often the big wooden bedframes themselves harbored bedbugs, which required that they

be taken apart and aired several times a year. (The method that many housewives used was most elaborate. First they had to soap down the frame with a solution of boiling-hot salt or alum water, then fill in any chinks with putty, and finally revarnish the frame.) New brass beds were beginning to be imported from England during the 1880s, and they presented a modern and attractive alternative to this chore, thereby soon becoming the most typical style of Victorian bed.

Early brass beds were simple and tubular in design and had a heavier, somewhat more solid appearance than later versions, which were embellished with flowers, scrolls, and curlicues. Originally, Victorian beds were made of solid brass, but later many were manufactured out of brass-plated iron.

Other types of beds were also available in the later Victorian years. These included metal beds enameled white with shiny brass trim and day beds which were closed on all but one side and were meant to be placed against a wall (these were often used in sitting rooms, in spare rooms downstairs, or occasionally in the second parlor).

Mattresses for these and other kinds of beds were generally filled with horsehair; the best had thirty-five to forty pounds of pure, curled horsehair, while the more old-fashioned versions were stuffed with the same amount of goose feathers. In some areas, however, mattresses were still filled with straw. The most luxurious kind of mattress had the horsehair sandwiched between layers of wool, a measure that presumably kept the prickly hairs from poking through the ticking. The Victorian version of a "regular full sized mattress" measured slightly smaller than our contemporary queen size.

Mattresses were periodically taken apart, restuffed, and layered. They generally needed three to four pounds of new hair in the middle every few years in order to remain solid and firm. Sheets were made of lengths of unbleached muslin. The most popular form of bed covering was quilts, which might have been one of the heirloom varieties in such sentimental styles as Wedding Ring, Northern Star, or Hearts and Flowers. For summer, lace or muslin, pastel-colored silks, and batiste coverlets were suggested, as were ones in embroidered linen or eiderdown covered with silk or twilled cotton.

Although the heavy, full canopied hangings supported by fourposters declined in use, the high-ceilinged Victorian bedchambers seemed to require a more furnished type of bed, and women were counseled that some form of bed drapery be used lest the bedroom appear bare

and unfinished. Half testers, or half canopies, extending out about three-and-a-half feet over the headboard, appeared with drapery that was decorative rather than practical. Their height depended to a large degree on the height of the room. In high-ceilinged rooms, for example, it was felt that the half canopy shouldn't be allowed to conflict with the room's frieze and was kept to a height of just below the border of the frieze. In a lower-ceilinged room, however, they might fall from the very top of the ceiling to the bottom of the frieze itself. All sorts of materials, including silks, muslins, and cretonnes, were used for these abbreviated canopies, and they were arranged in a draped, swagged, tufted, festooned, ruffled, or pleated manner, making full use of the same imagination that exhibited itself in the draping and designing of Victorian parlor curtains. Sometimes, as in the case of the White House's Lincoln bedroom during the later administration of Benjamin Harrison, they were done with an almost lordly fervor: purple print satin and gold lace bed curtains were gathered up from the sides into a circular corona. Drapery designs were even improvised for the new brass beds, which, women were assured, "could be tasteful pieces of furniture when curtained." These were often accompanied by tufted-back pieces,

The shape of this tile-bordered mantel is decidedly nineteenth century, but the Victorians would have stained the wood rather than painted it. The shapely Rococo Revival ladies' chair also presents a modern touch, with its contemporary, though romantic, upholstery.

falling behind the brass headboard with sweeping half curtains around them.

The most modern Victorian bedrooms were furnished with screens on either side of the bed instead of with bed curtains. Screens of some sort had always been "regulation" for bedchamber decor—a good way to shield unsightly washtable articles and toilet necessities from public view, as well as being decorative additions. In lieu of a separate dressing room, the Victorians sometimes dressed behind tall screens (if of sufficient height to completely conceal the person behind it, we're told). On hot summer days, the screen was also used to conceal a large wet sponge which helped keep the room cool. Screens might be made of stamped leather or Japanese lacquer, of fine stiff paper painted with butterflies or birds, or of fabric resembling fluted muslin or lace. Most popular were those covered with fabric which matched the room's window curtains.

The typical Victorian bedchamber also contained a washstand placed in a small recess or corner or partially hidden behind the bedroom screen. Some of these were marble-topped, others were inset with tiles, and still others were fashioned simply of plain wood with two towel bars on either side. The commode style of washstand was a small cabinet with two doors below opening to reveal shelves used to hold sponges, towels, a painted ceramic pitcher and bowl, or even a matching chamber pot if the house didn't have indoor plumbing yet. A fringed towel was often placed across the marble top of the washstand to politely deaden the unseemly clatter of articles being placed on the hard stone, and a strip of linen was hung behind the washstand to protect the wallpaper from accidental splashes. Even after indoor plumbing and bathrooms were middle-class norms in the private homes of the 1880s, many Victorian bedchambers retained the custom of the washstand by including a corner bedroom sink.

A wardrobe or armoire, often more than six feet high, with tall, mirrored doors, was used for hanging clothes, a step beyond the simple hooks of the early part of the century or from the frontier and prairie cabins where clothing was hung on hooks concealed by a hanging quilt. While some Victorian homes had closets, more didn't, since taxes were levied according to the number of rooms in a home, and closets were counted as rooms. If the armoire didn't have mirrored doors, a cheval, or framed mirror in a standing base (a style first introduced to America around the 1830s), would have stood nearby. Smaller versions of the cheval, small enough to be

The Victorians' love of the sea is expressed in this reproduction nineteenth-century wallpaper, printed with shell motifs, which has been draped with fishnet and studded with old family photographs. Among the bibelots on the table are an old-time wooden collar box and a painted papier-mâché pincushion, shaped like a shoe and hosting a collection of jeweled and filigreed Victorian hatpins.

The strong curves of horn furniture recall the vigorous frontier spirit that was so much a part of the nineteenth century. This unusual horn settee, set off with simple contemporary upholstery, is a striking addition to this Victorian Revival bedroom. Also from the Victorian era are the golden oak dresser, Art Nouveau lamps, and dark woodwork—all played against the more contemporary plain carpeted floors and simple walls.

placed on top of the dresser and known as dressing-case mirrors, were also a frequent sight.

When the bedroom was well furnished, it actually contained quite a variety of furniture, but, because of the large size of the rooms, a crowded look was seldom the result. The bedroom was more than just a sleeping place—it often functioned as a boudoir/sitting room. Often a low couch or lounge, called either a fainting couch or a recamier, was placed in a corner or bay-window area to allow ladies to rest during the day without disturbing the main bed after it had been made up.

Near the curtained bedchamber window, the Victorians would certainly have placed a chair or two, perhaps a rocker or a sewing chair and a workbasket so that they could keep busy while enjoying the outside view. One of the more ingenious and practical ideas for the bedroom was to place one or two oblong boxes, with hinged lids, covered with fabric, and mounted on casters, near the window. These served as ottomans, while their cushioned inside compartments were used to store shoes or bed linen.

Most bedrooms also had a table for writing, a hanging bookshelf, wallpockets, flowers, pictures, and other personal ornamentation, while

avoiding the heavily layered and stacked look that prevailed in the parlor. A footwarmer was a typical comfort, useful if the warmth of the fire failed to extend to all areas of the room. The Victorian bedroom would have also contained assorted footstools and perhaps delicate-looking boudoir chairs made of lacquer or papier-mâché, embellished with mother-of-pearl. Slipper chairs were small, low-bottomed chairs that one sat in while lacing or unlacing one's shoes. Some even had compartments under the seat for the storage of slippers, hence the name.

Victorian dressers came in all shapes, sizes, and styles, from simple machine-made chests of drawers to more elaborate versions with marble tops, inset gas brackets, and even glove boxes, which were built-in cases on top of the dresser, often locked, where one stored gloves, wisps of lace, handkerchiefs, and other trinkets. Dresser drawers were lined with damask and scented with plump little sachets of lilac or lavender tied with ribbons. On the top of the typical dresser, along with other elements of grooming, one might have found a hair receiver, a porcelain or silver receptacle used to store the strands of hair retrieved from one's brush or comb. This hair was saved perhaps to make a hair switch, to augment the sumptuous curled and waterfalled hair styles of

the 1880s, or to provide material for hair art, a popular pastime of Victorian young ladies. A ring holder was another curiosity—an outstretched porcelain, silver, or wooden model of a hand, each finger "wearing" one or more of the lady's rings.

Most nineteenth-century ladies of means also had a vanity table, either in their bedchambers or in the adjoining dressing rooms. Many books and magazines carefully enumerated instructions on how to drape this table in the latest style with filmy skirts of lace, muslin, or silk. The top of the vanity would have been littered with silver-topped crystal jars for homemade face creams, tortoise-shell combs, and containers of powder and pomatum. Small embroidered boxes were used to hold hairpins or crimson silk swatches, which, when moistened and rubbed across the cheek, produced a reasonable facsimile of a blush.

Most of the cosmetics of the time, if indulged in at all, were homemade remedies taken from recipes sandwiched between household hints in the women's journals of the day and were meant to improve and whiten the complexion. For example, Sarah Hale, the editor of *Godey's*, was said to apply brown paper soaked in cider vinegar to her temples at night in order to prevent wrinkles. Mascara was made from

lamp black, and kohl, to enhance the eyes, from powdered chalk. On the whole, though, the preference was for a demure and unmade-up beauty, and the use of any of these treatments was inclined to be more secretive than discreet. In contrast to the women of previous generations, who used cosmetics openly and in abundance, the Victorians felt that soap and water was the best beauty aid.

The gentleman's equivalent of the dressing table was the shaving stand, which occupied another corner of the bedchamber. Typically, it would have had a revolving or adjustable mirror, towel bars, a basin, and a small cabinet drawer. Shaving accessories included the straight razor and strop, shaving cup, brush, and soap (all five from Sears for 75¢ the set in 1897), and such aromatic aftershaves as Cherry Laurel Water. Beauty and grooming aids for men were largely frowned upon, despite the fact that the colonial Founding Fathers were powdered, perfumed, and rouged in the French manner. By the 1870s, the disclosure that Martin Van Buren used Corinthian Oil of Cream, Concentrated Persian Essence, and Double Extract of Queen Victoria was said to have helped finish his political career. The best-known men's hair dressing was Macassar Oil, which led to the design of antimacassars, the lacy

A mix of styles is found in this Victorian Revival bedroom in an alcove of a studio apartment. The richly painted crimson walls, opulently draped curtains, and Victorian wicker rocker all beautifully recall the nineteenth century, as do the plates scaling the wall above the bed. The white bookcases are distinctly modern, however, and the quilt adds a country touch.

doilies placed on the backs of Victorian parlor furniture to protect them from grease stains.

There were, of course, more elaborate Victorian bedchambers than these described, drenched with color and dressed with a lavish hand. In a Portland, Maine, summer house whose grandeur belies its seasonal status, for example, a young woman's bedchamber ceiling was adorned with a mural of the four seasons, while the master bedroom featured a painted landscape motif in each of its corners. Such rooms, grandly romantic in the Victorian tradition—with their marble tops, flamboyant velvet draperies, and inlaid woods—seem a far cry from the spirit of repose and simplicity the Victorians supposedly aimed for in their private chambers. At the same time, in comparison with the density of ornament and the gilded overlay of the nineteenth-century drawing room, they did succeed. The Victorian equivalent of a "lighter touch" in the bedchamber, even with the sometime extravagance of ornamentation, was fully evident.

Chapter 8

Special Victorian Rooms

As with the commander of an army or the leader of any enterprise, so is it with the mistress of the house. Her spirit will be seen through the whole establishment; and just in proportion as she performs her duties, intelligently and thoroughly, so will her domestics follow in her path.

Beeton's Book of Household Management (1861)

A shallow alcove in a back parlor, typical of the nooks and crannies in a Victorian home, is transformed into a study with this nineteenth-century desk, chair, and easel. Paintings and prints, such as this one of Queen Victoria, were often enhanced with an artful flow of drapery. The bust on the desk is, of course, a likeness of Albert, the Prince Consort.

Above and opposite: *A Victorian-inspired sitting room at twilight and set for afternoon tea is couched in a decorative framework pleasing to the contemporary eye. The cozy Rose Cummings chintz, bright rose-colored walls, and intimate gathering of seating around the focal-point fireplace all contribute to the effect. The floral chintz on the Victorian-frame chairs accents their curving shapes and indented "waists," reminiscent of the nineteenth-century feminine ideal.*

It was the rapidly increasing size and scope of many of these "establishments" of the Victorian middle and upper middle classes that dictated the army of domestic servants that the Victorian lady held in her command. The simple homes of simpler times were fast becoming obsolete when Isabella Beeton, a twenty-eight-year-old English housewife, began what turned out to be over a thousand pages of painstakingly detailed advice regarding the care and management of the Victorian home. Houses, quite simply, were expanding. What caused this expansion was in part the magnified Victorian regard for domestic comforts, as well as the century's increasingly complex code of behavior and taste—a code that suddenly banished smoking to the interior recesses of the private smoking room or declared no house a genteel home without its own conservatory. Soon, upper-middle-class Victorian houses were distinguished by veritable mazes of supplementary living spaces beyond that of the formal drawing room—the prestigious masculine retreat of the library, for example, and the sitting room, bright with chintz and a warm fire. In addition, the Victorians felt that forgotten corners in the home could be used to great advantage. Nooks, passages, and vestibules were transformed into someone's cozy corner, by means of a cushiony chair, a table, a candle, a pot of tea.

With every pocket of the home filled—and sometimes over-filled—interiors gained in intimacy, both visually and emotionally; their closeness became a protection, casting a veil of softness and a soothing blur of color and pattern over the rough edges of life. The Victorians attempted to extend those tranquilizing boundaries further, creating spacious porches and verandas—additional "rooms," as it were, annexing and appeasing the frontier of the outside.

As more rooms were added to the home, the individual purposes of each space became more clearly defined. This articulation is one of the primary characteristics of the Victorian interior. The greater the number of rooms in the house, for example, and the more specified their purposes, the higher the status that was implied. The nineteenth-century luxury of having an entire room set aside just for company (the parlor), to ponder or play the works of the great composers (the music room), to contemplate one's collection of pictures (the private gallery), indicated respectability and respect. In addition, such articulation fortified the sense of order that the nineteenth century so admired, pre-

venting the life of the occupants from spilling over from one room to the next. Even the kitchen became party to the partitioning—its butler's pantry, its service rooms all demonstrating how far the home had come from its early-American roots, when a one-room cabin was bedroom, living room, dining room, kitchen, and playroom all at once.

In addition to serving specialized functions, Victorian rooms had special shapes. Seldom simple squares or rectangles, they were made irregular and individual by balconies and towers, bay windows, fireplaces, elaborate door and window frames, transoms, chair rails, cornices, moldings, and medallions. Victorian decorative taste further enhanced the individuality of spatial divisions—lambrequins that extended the grandiosity of windows, screens used all over the house, from parlor to bedchamber, artificially segmented space. The plain, bare-walled, boxy spaces of many contemporary interiors would have looked to the Victorians like the unsightly tenements that were beginning to crop up in the big cities.

The Sitting Room

Today we would consider the nineteenth-century sitting room an informal, or everyday, living room. More "lived-in" than other areas of the house, it reflected the sense of day-to-day life and personal attitudes that its daily use by the family imparted. The need for such a room evolved in tandem with the development of increasing splendor in the Victorian drawing room. As the drawing room became a place for company receptions, parties, ritualized calls, and teas, the more comfortable sitting room became the nucleus of Victorian family life.

The Victorian sitting room was a cozy spot where comfort was more important than style or appearance. Life in the sitting room focused on family, children, close friends, hobbies, and it was designed to stand up well to the rigors of such an existence. For example, rugs were preferred to carpets so they could easily be removed for children's games. Low chairs and lounges of a well-worn and cushiony nature were advised because they could endure the scratches, kicks, and tumbling to which they were inevitably subjected. Even in the greater nineteenth-century homes, where sitting rooms were illuminated by impressive crystal chandeliers and chairs were covered with velvet plush rather than chintz, Victorian grandeur was kept in perspective by the warmth and informality of family life. The time-worn textures and heirlooms harmonized with elegant silks and satins; the throngs of family pictures

Above and opposite: *This relaxed and charming sitting room, called "the Victorian room" by its owners, owes its nineteenth-century character not to essential architecture, but to the furnishings solely, specifically the treasure trove of eye-catching collectibles, from beaded and Berlinwork pillows to valentines, marionettes, parasols, and more.*

A window seat, often found in the sitting room, was a favorite spot for reading. This one's charm is enhanced by the lace window panels, attached to a roller shade, that create the illusion of etched-glass windowpanes.

on the mantel, covering tables, shelves, and walls, were family totems that reinforced the room's status as an exclusively family sanctuary.

To ensure privacy, the Victorian sitting room was often located upstairs, far from any possible intrusion by a guest or visitor who had inadvertently taken a wrong turn down one of the main floor halls. A location near the nurseries would have been particularly ideal if the room also served as a schoolroom, which was a common convention.

The most common function of the sitting room, however, was as the family "den." It was often the place where each family member was given a corner to pursue his or her interests and hobbies, such as reading, sewing, writing, painting, or drawing. This was customary, especially in a home where servants couldn't be spared to light a fire in each of the private bedchambers.

Every effort was made to make the sitting room as comfortable and appealing as possible. The mantel and shelves would be cluttered with photographs, flowers, ferns, sentimental souvenirs, and quaint bits of glassware; its walls lined with favorite prints, with engravings, and with the family's own artistic efforts, such as stitched mottoes, samplers, watercolors, "artwork" made of pine cones, acorns, or feathers, or

crayon portraits. In addition, carved wall brackets might have held pots of ivy, which could be cultivated to gracefully trail down and surround one of the portraits in a living "frame."

The passion for covering things was as evident in the sitting room as it was in the parlor. Its chairs, tables, shelves, mantels, and other surfaces were duly shrouded in embroidered cloths, shawls, and tacked-on antimacassars. Other Victorian decorative conventions, such as overstuffed chairs or the pattern-on-pattern concatenation of wallpapers, fabrics, rugs, and the profusion of objects, were also particularly apropos for disguising the scuffs and signs of wear and tear that were a necessary part of daily life.

Subdued and muted tones were encouraged for the wallcoverings, floors, curtains, and upholstery fabrics, in keeping with the effort to create a mood of familiar coziness. Colors of too bright a hue were regarded as vulgar. Wallcoverings in umber, pale olive, pale rose, fawn, light blue, or gray, with designs in contrasting colors, were associated with taste and quiet harmonies, and therefore were suitable. Such color schemes functioned to pull together the sometimes disparate furnishings that often made up the room.

The Victorian richness in drapery also carried over to the sitting room, although it would have been lighter in tone and fabric than drapery in the parlor. Curtains were made of dotted swiss looped back with colorful ribbons, Indian muslin with gathered flounces, or striped, sprigged, or dotted muslin. The insertion curtains encountered in bedrooms of the time, made of red twill and lace, were also suitable for the sitting room. Slightly dressier sitting room curtains could be made in twilled silks, satin, or foulard, with bandings of appliqué and embroidery and with typical Victorian festoons. While these were more opulent than the lighter muslins, they were less formal than the velvets and brocades of the parlor.

Furniture in the sitting room followed the standard Victorian parlor arrangement of "massing," which led to the familiar and distinctive density of the interior's look. For example, an upholstered chair would stand near a carved and draped table; on the table would be a lamp; behind the lamp, a piano; and above the piano hung a framed picture, thereby drawing the eye from object to object in a leisurely succession, without a decorative jolt or break. The textures, from the embroidery and fringe on the table draping, to the carved legs of the table and the floral patterns of the upholstery, were selected to further engage the eye.

The more activities the Victorian sitting room was host to, the more clutter it contained. If the house lacked a separate music room or library, for instance, both a piano and books would have occupied honored places in the room. One nineteenth-century convention was to place an especially fine picture or portrait above the piano or organ to encourage family members to gather there (or perhaps to make practicing more pleasant). The tops of bookcases provided yet another surface for arrangements of vases, ginger jars, albums of pressed flowers, and so on.

Large and fashionable Victorian homes often had more than one sitting room and might have done up one of those spaces in any of the historical or exotic motifs that were popular—Chinese and Turkish sitting rooms both fashionable possibilities. Such rooms were generally regarded as examples of a family's advanced and "artistic" tastes and can be appreciated as expressions of the century's theatrical flair.

A wholly other type of Victorian sitting room was neither a family den nor an exotic indulgence, but was the exclusive, private, and feminine retreat of the lady of the house. The atmosphere of the sitting room/boudoir would have tended more toward the luxurious, and even mildly erotic, than to the sentimental and cozily domestic. Louise Marmillion

Pillows like these in antique lace and chintz, as well as quilted, embroidered, or tapestry-worked versions, were just one type of handiwork that made Victorian corners so inviting.

An American Victorian sewing basket, with a top enclosure for sewing tools (thimbles, threads, darning needles, and so on) and a lower basket to handily hold yarns or work in progress, graces the corner of this bedroom.

of New Orleans, for example, adorned the ceilings of her exquisite sitting room/boudoir with trellises and leaves enlivened by cherubs with adult heads and Moorish features. *Harper's Bazar*, however, deemed Mrs. Marmillion well within the bounds of Victorian good taste. If a lady wished her boudoir "serene as an oratory, she has the right to order it," it asserted. "And if she prefers to present in it the interior of a wigwam, there should be nobody to gainsay her, for that sole corner of the house is hers."

The Sewing Room

Like the boudoir and the private sitting room, the sewing room was another feminine preserve found in the more substantial Victorian homes.

Although a bit of fancy work or decorative sewing was permitted in the parlor, creating a pretty and appealing picture of Victorian womanhood for all to see, if a room could possibly be spared, one was advised to designate it as sewing room to accommodate the enormous quantities of plain sewing that had to be accomplished. Children's clothes constantly had to be repaired and replaced, as did household linen, curtains, and sheets. And, of course, dresses were made at home, as well.

Proper household management was the method suggested to lighten this burden, thereby making sewing, if not a pleasant pastime, at least a more comfortable one. If even a small room could be spared, such as a hall bedroom or an attic room, where the materials could always be on hand, at least some of the vexations of the task would be relieved. Ideally, the room that was dedicated to sewing was located in a "retired" section of the house, making it an area that was quiet and free from distractions. If it overlooked a green lawn or grove of trees or some other pleasing view, the occupants would be provided with an occasional rest for their tired eyes.

Because the sewing room was a strictly functional workroom, it was furnished plainly with little extraneous adornment. *Good Housekeeping*, which describes the ideal 1885 sewing room in detail, makes a particular point of the fact that plain bare floors of painted or smoothly finished hardwood, with no rugs or carpets, were preferred. "This prevents the accumulation of dust and makes it easy to sweep up the scraps and threads which are allowed to fall freely on it during the day's work. The pins and needles too, that will gravitate to the floor are more easily found," it explained. Often, when there was no spare sewing room and plain sewing had to be done in the parlor, a sheet was spread over the parlor rug to catch threads.

"Furniture in the sewing room should be of the simplest sort," *Good Housekeeping* maintained. In addition to the sewing machine (invented in the 1840s and a standard in American homes by the 1860s), furniture basically consisted of two or three comfortable chairs (no rockers), a table and cutting board, a bureau with large drawers to hold buttons, tape, thread, and lengths of wool, silk, or lining, and a chest for the crinkling tinted tissue paper patterns. A box with a cushioned lid covered with chintz provided some extra storage as well as seating, and a closet (probably an armoire), for hanging half-finished garments or storing boxes holding bits of ribbons or lace, was also mentioned.

Nineteenth-century fiction often makes mention of the ladies' sewing table or workbasket, and most women had some version from the time they were old enough to hold a needle. They varied from those of finely carved rosewood with handsome compartmentalized drawers (which were actually more suitable to the parlor than to the utilitarian sewing room) to charming workbaskets lined with quilted satin and hung with dangling chenille tassels. Most featured a narrow tray on top and a suspended pouch or workbag below for scissors, needles, and other useful paraphernalia.

The sewing box was a smaller, portable version of the worktable, made to be carried into the sitting room or parlor with just the work and necessities of the moment. These were ornamented, inlaid, covered with fabric and trim, as ladies often took some decorative sewing with them while visiting and paying calls. A lady might have also slipped a small bottle of cologne or an egg-shaped Victorian "handcooler" inside her workbox to periodically refresh her hands while working.

The Library

As feminine as the private sitting room, the boudoir, and the sewing room were likely to be, the library was the man's sanctuary within the home. The maid or lady of the house might tiptoe in to empty the ashtrays (called ash receivers) or dust the tall, glass-doored bookcases, but that was the extent of female "intrusion." This was the man's private domain, and here the symbols of his masculinity were assembled: the carved pipes and tins of tobacco, the gleaming decanters of brandy and port, the sporting prints and framed documents, all surrounded by rows of bookshelves. The library was the room where the Victorian gentleman went to escape what he must have fondly regarded as the feminine fussiness of the parlor. Not that his library was any less cluttered—with

Above and opposite: *Walls of a dark, textured fabric, trimmed with twisted-rope borders to conceal unadorned edges, create a hospitable backdrop for this collection of nineteenth-century-inspired exotica: the pile-up of pillows, the inlaid table, and the profusion of artifacts. Details,* **above,** *show the overlay of textures common to the Victorian exotic room, from banquettes outlined in graceful loops of tassel and fringe to the richness of the carved moldings.*

Overleaf: *The panache of this library/sitting room is tempered by its variety of relaxed and informal Victorian furniture in unusual shapes and upholstered in multifarious fabrics, as well as by the paneled wall of well-thumbed books, the leafy ferns, and the layered rugs.*

its minerals, fossils, geodes, obelisks, and antique hunting tools—but the idea that it could be objectively regarded as "cluttered" would probably have escaped his notice. The Victorian gentleman would have regarded his library as a dignified bastion of masculine sobriety, science, and sense, in an otherwise essentially feminine home world.

Because a library was felt to dignify even the smallest of households, it was, along with the sitting room, one of the first of the supplementary rooms to be added to the home. Mabel Osgood Wright, a young New York girl, recalled the joy her whole household felt when their landlord actually decided to add a library across the entire end of their home, which would at last provide "an adequate place for Father's treasures." Mr. Wright, a minister, had formerly used the back parlor as his study, no doubt something of an inconvenience in a house with several children.

Designating the back parlor as a library was, however, a fairly common arrangement in the nineteenth-century home, particularly in city townhouses and brownstones. Floor plans of The Portsmouth (1882), one of New York's first apartment houses, label the first two front rooms in its modified railroad-flat layout as a parlor and a library. It was apparently felt that such a com-

bination would most appeal to the genteel pretenses of its solidly middle-class tenants. Because it usually adjoined the front, or company, parlor, however, when the back parlor was a "library," its decor would often have included elements of the Victorian sitting room, although in a quieter, less personal, and more sober way. Since the library was generally regarded as a place of culture, it was never allowed to become too cluttered with feminine or homey items.

The real prestige of possessing a Victorian library was derived from its grander forms, however. In 1882, around the time of The Portsmouth's construction, journalist James McCabe noted the cachet which the very existence of a home library bestowed on the Fifth Avenue mansions of the city's elite. "Whether the books are read or not," he observed, "it is the correct thing to have." McCabe describes such a spacious room in detail, with its "rows of daintily bound books in elaborate cases, its works of art scattered about in tasteful negligence and its rich and cosy furniture." By the 1880s, it was apparent that the library had become a possession necessary to the advancement of any gentleman's social position, with its strong intimations of culture and refinement.

As different as the sitting room

This High-Victorian mixture of pattern and textures covers every inch of the room. Pictures rest on the shelves of the bookcase reflecting the nineteenth-century tradition of propping paintings against a wall or table leg to create an interesting and casual effect. The paisley shawl draped over the chair also reflects bygone tastes: worn as a fashionable status symbol during the early Victorian years, the shawl had become part of the interior by the later Victorian decades and was loosely draped over sofas, armchairs, and pianos.

The library in this 1880s home evokes the fashionable late-century study, with its Victorian-style wallpaper lit with gilding, inlaid-walnut dado, and comfortable, cushiony chair.

was from the library, the two rooms had their Victorian dedication to comfort in common. The library was comfortable in the warm, dark, dignified manner of Victorian style. Libraries, for example, were often arranged to include at least two separate reading and writing areas: one by the fire and one near the room's tall windows. Other such areas were the small tables and desks placed around the room at convenient intervals. Since reading aloud for an hour or two—especially the serialized stories that appeared in the daily newspapers—was a common evening activity, chairs and footstools were arranged around the room, if the library was also the family room and not an exclusively masculine den. Large layered area rugs, warming the floor, would even have permitted the children to listen, curled up in front of the fire, especially if the tale had a moral aimed at self-betterment, which it frequently did.

For most of the nineteenth century, the basic decor of the library was consistently Gothic, done in the quiet grays and earth tones thought conducive to learned pursuits. The walls might have been painted to simulate marble or stone, while the dado would have been lined with a thick "leather" paper or with oak paneling. Typical furnishings were heavy and solemn, carved in oak or

black walnut, and chairs were upholstered in dark leather or sturdy tapestry fabrics.

Although the Gothic Revival library remained an established standard of good taste through all the Victorian decades, during the 1880s the library, now a "fashionable" room for the family to own, began to be warmed by richer hues, including the deeper, more *au courant* colorings that predominated during those years. Deep purples, violets, crimsons, emerald greens, and other darkened shades, lightened by gilding, were used. One example of such a library can be found in the family home of the wealthy Ballantines of Newark. Their library, redecorated in 1885, was as up-to-date and opulent as possible, with its deep cherry mahogany wainscot, splendidly gilded ceiling panels, gilt-trimmed crimson walls, and matching crimson draperies, pleasing counterpoints to the darker furnishings that filled the room. Its focal point was the elaborately carved Renaissance Revival mantelpiece flanked by comfortable velvet covered chairs, including one of the new Morris chairs covered with dark green cut-velvet upholstery. In addition, this library was located at the front of the house, granting it more light than would the more typical northern or northwestern exposures—which were preferred to prevent sunlight from

damaging the books or disturbing one's reading or writing. The light in the Ballantine library was therefore tempered by tall, dark (but brilliant) stained-glass windows.

Of course, books were the major attraction in any library and the more leatherbound volumes one possessed, the more status was enjoyed. The traditional Victorian method of housing those books was in tall oak, walnut, or mahogany cabinets with glass doors, to protect them from dust or the damaging rays of the sun. As in the sitting room, when cabinets fell short of the ceiling height, their tops were used to display statuary or busts.

Some Victorian home experts, however, found the notion of books locked behind glass an uncomfortable one, somehow making the acquisition of knowledge less accessible than it should be and creating a cold, remote feeling that was at odds with other areas of the home. Further, they felt, glass doors distorted the book titles, making the lettering on the spines difficult to read. (Victorian glass was less perfect than glass today and frequently possessed a flow, or "wave," in its surfaces.) An acceptable alternative to glass-doored cabinets was to cover the bookcases with a curtain, hung on a brass rod, in the manner of a portiere, that could be easily swept aside. One magazine suggested a shielding leather valance around the edges of the bookshelves as sufficient and attractive. It advocated a green, natural calfskin or, especially, a crimson valance stamped with gold designs. None other than the duke of Orleans, it was pointed out, followed a variation of this fashion, by using rich gilt-fringed velvet valances in his library

The Smoking Room

Often, in addition to the sanctuary of his library, the Victorian gentleman of means would have had a smoking room, or "den," in his home. This was a room where women were seldom, if ever, admitted, or for that matter would have cared to go. Although by the mid-1890s, protocol had relaxed somewhat and American women were beginning to take their first public puffs of cigarettes, for most of the nineteenth century, it was considered unthinkable for a gentleman to smoke in the presence of his wife and daughter or, for that matter, any woman he regarded as respectable. In the 1870s and 1880s, in fact, a lady was well within the bounds of etiquette to refuse a proposal of marriage from a man she otherwise "devotedly loves" because of his use of tobacco.

The Victorian custom of men departing the dinner table for brandy

Victorian smoking room motifs, when revived today, can make up a striking room. While these chairs and sofa are modern, a vivid nineteenth-century effect is created with the multi-layered rugs, dark fabric lining the walls, brass candles, artifacts, and textured throws. The original stained-glass transom disperses the light throughout the room.

Above: *The back parlor in this restored brownstone has the quiet charm of a Victorian study—the painting and easel, the bust, and the books all announce nineteenth-century cultural pursuits and interests. The wooden, Victorian-style Venetian blinds, reproduced today, present an authentic alternative to more elaborate Victorian window treatments, and one that would be particularly appropriate for a "smoking room"-style study.*

Opposite: *The picture of Victorian comfort in an 1880s home, where brown velvet portieres divide the sequence of parlor rooms. The front parlor has been turned into a personal sitting room/study, where a vast collection of curios from all over the world evokes a mood of Victorian exotica. The comfortable English "draft" or pub sofa is draped with antique Syrian rugs; the nineteenth-century zebra-skin footstool is set on antlers. On the Victorian tables are such finds as a leopard-skin box and treasures from Tibet, Nepal, and nineteenth-century China. In the corner is an unusual antique grain-painted pie safe, its interior cabinets burnt and scarred from hot pies.*

and cigars while the ladies withdrew to the parlor is well known. Smoking in the dining room was regarded with extreme disgust, as tobacco odors lingered in the room's heavy layered draperies and deep carpets. In the smoking room, however, a man had his smart, padded smoking jacket to slip over his suit, as well as an embroidered smoking cap, which was something like a fez. Both of these, introduced around the 1850s, were worn to prevent his hair and clothes from retaining the offensive odor of tobacco.

The smoking room, like the library, was decorated in an emphatically masculine way. In examining the room, however, it is again important to view the past through its own eyes, realizing that "masculine" in the nineteenth century did not preclude an appreciation of adornment. More than just accepting the inevitability of ornamentation, Victorian men fully enjoyed its presence. The tiles in the room's fireplace, for example, would have been richly decorated, the chairs tasseled and fringed, and the walls covered with patterned and bordered wallpapers or perhaps tooled leather. Cigar cases were shiny with delicate beadwork, tobacco pouches fashioned from crocheted silk, velvet smoking caps embroidered with braid trim and perhaps the added fillip of a swinging gold tassel. In a world

compelled to put a design on everything as evidence of refinement, all these decorative measures were natural.

Most of the furniture in the traditional smoking room was akin to that of the library. A rocking chair, considered to be masculine as well as feminine, would certainly have been present. Smokers' chairs, with a drawer below the seat for a built-in spitoon, became popular in the 1890s. A cabinet on one wall would have been used to hold a private stock of liqueurs and brandies, and, although snuff was no longer in fashion, a collection of old-fashioned snuff boxes made of horn or silver would have made for interesting conversation pieces.

Because the smoking room was more or less private, its look was much less strictly formulated than that of the parlor, hall, or dining room, and a strong sense of individual style could be indulged here. One smoking room, ca. 1893, even featured an imported carved state bed as its centerpiece, with a carved canopy of demons, angels, and goblins peering out of carved vine-covered trellises. Extravagant in style and also too large for the bedroom of an ordinary New York townhouse, when its bedposts were cut down, it became the chief curiosity in this Victorian man-about-town's posh smoking den: it was piled with

Dignified ornament—the sort indigenous to a man's private study or smoking room—sets the tone for this room in a restored Brooklyn brownstone, ca. 1882. Note, for example, the fringed lambrequins draping the fireplace and the discreet touches of ornamental tile work. Also included are a nineteenth-century fire-screen frame and an old-fashioned brass coal hod and spittoon. The restored brass and iron gasolier is original to the house.

Turkish sofa cushions and furnished with Turkish "ash receivers." It was here, we're told, that after dinner, the host would recline "like a sovereign" with five or six male guests gathered around on cushiony divans, with liqueurs, cordials, and cognac on small tables, "enveloped in a cloud of fragrant tobacco smoke." It's not unreasonable to suspect, however, that in this case, the "smoking room" was *Vogue*'s euphemism for a private opium den.

If a man didn't have a smoking room to call his own, he would, of course, have been free to smoke in the privacy of his library. After the 1860s, when billiards became popular, smoking was also permitted in the Victorian billiard room. Another dark-paneled, masculine room, usually with a rather clubroom feeling, it was dominated by a green-topped billiard table and had cue sticks set in polished racks along the walls. Animal-skin rugs and mounted trophy heads of deer, moose, bear, or buffalo—not necessarily shot by the owner of the house—might have presided over the scene. Mark Twain's pale-crimson-walled billiard room offered the playful touch of billiard motifs, cue sticks and poles stenciled on the ceiling, while the coffered ceiling of the billiard room in the Flagler mansion in Florida was oak-grained and painted in gold,

green, and red.

Not surprisingly, the persistent exotic influences of the 1880s managed to creep into the Victorian billiard room as well, resulting in rooms with low Moorish divans covered with rich, dark-hued rugs and plentifully supplied with bright cushions, Oriental tapestries draping the doorways, or fireplaces faced in Mexican onyx. What was called "one of the handsomest rooms in New York" even boasted a ceiling of Moorish arches covered with glittery aluminum (the element was first isolated in the nineteenth century and rapidly found wide application), with the spaces between the arches painted pale blue and inset with silver stars. It was, perhaps, the range and excess of that particular billiard room that made it so noteworthy; its splendor was on an order that only the Victorians could have dreamed up, with lights set in Moorish-design antique silver, Moorish fretwork lining the walls, and thin medallions of onyx replacing glass window panes.

Another kind of decorative creativity was expressed in the trophy room, which was essential to gentlemen who wanted to display their prowess as huntsmen. In the 1890s, in fact, these rooms became something of a status symbol in the Victorian home. Modeled after the private hunt club, their decor usual-

Special Rooms
◆
201

ly consisted of oversized chairs and sofas upholstered in leather, rugged horn and antler furniture upholstered in skins, and engravings of wildlife, stuffed trophy heads, and stretched mounted pelts on the walls.

The Music Room

Music was one of the most absorbing pastimes in the nineteenth-century home, and no family with pretensions to culture and refinement could afford to be without a musical instrument, usually a piano or organ, in the parlor or sitting room, where it became a centerpiece for family and social entertainments—musicales, sing-alongs, and recitals. Music was also an important part of the courting ritual. To be able to sing and play was an admired skill in a woman of marriageable age—signs of her superior taste and refinement.

In middle-class homes, the very presence of a piano or organ in the back parlor was often enough to designate it "the music room." The Beckwith Imperial Grand, said to be the handsomest organ in the 1905 Sears Roebuck catalog, was such a parlor piece. It boasted bric-a-bracked shelves, pillars, and hand-carved ornamentation for a mere $51.95.

The great Victorian homes, however, had separate music rooms, which frequently were the settings for lavish formal entertainments. In general, this room was furnished much as the drawing room, with elaborately layered draperies and intricately patterned rugs, gleaming woodwork, gilded mirrors, and full portieres. A piano or harp (or both) would have replaced the fireplace or center table as focal point, and the room would also have been furnished with love seats and soft pillows, tea tables and occasional chairs.

Porcelains, inlaid screens, and the other usual accouterments of the drawing room filled out the corners of the typical Victorian music room. Frequently decoration had musical motifs. In general, however, less emphasis was placed on literacy of message in the music room than in the parlor. As social standing, cultural achievements, levels of taste and wealth would already have been established—anyone enjoying the pleasures of the music room would presumably have been first entertained in the parlor—the music room only had to reinforce those messages.

The Art Gallery

A new pursuit for the nouveau riche American Victorians was the serious collecting of art. As they progressed

Collecting of all kinds, whether porcelains for the parlor or paintings for the home art gallery, came into its own during the Victorian era. Here, the surprisingly vibrant shades of Victorian pottery—azure blues, turquoise, marigold—combine with nineteenth-century English tiles and the sunset hues of elegant Victorian art glass in this handsome collection.

as collectors and patrons, many began to set aside an entire room for the display of their acquisitions.

Sometimes music rooms and art galleries were combined, while elsewhere art galleries were integrated with the ballroom. Mrs. Astor's famous crimson and gold gallery, for example, also served as a ballroom for New York society's celebrated "Four Hundred" (which actually tallied only 311). Generally, these rooms ran true to form, illuminated by crystal chandeliers and lined with gilded settees and chairs. Tasteful variations were permitted, however. The art gallery of Chicago's Mrs. Potter Palmer, for instance, was furnished eclectically, according to the custom of the 1880s. In addition to its sumptuous collection of pictures and its full complement of side chairs and tables, it featured a splendid leopard-skin-draped sofa.

What was most distinctive about all these galleries, whether a grand ballroom setting, a corridor gallery, or simply a passageway through the halls, was the nineteenth-century tradition of picture hanging, based on the European "salon style." As might be expected of a society that shunned bare space, paintings, embraced in massively carved and thickly gilded frames, were stacked closely and irregularly one above the other, sometimes from the top of the dado to the tip of the ceiling

cornice, filling the space in between, often without an inch to spare.

Pictures generally were hung on wires, usually from a picture rail, a custom which has all but disappeared in our times, but which grew from the nineteenth century's development of plaster walls in homes as opposed to the eighteenth century's wood walls. Sometimes the picture rail was positioned at ceiling height, while at other times, it bordered the frieze. The latter arrangement was most favored, as it provided a suitable space for ornamentation between the rail and the ceiling. This custom of picture hanging prevailed not only in a gallery space but also in any area of the home, and it stemmed from a practical as well as a decorative basis: the picture rail permitted the Victorians an enviable degree of flexibility in arranging their wall art. Height, positioning, and spacing could be endlessly revised without making holes in the plaster walls.

Pictures hung low or at eye level were generally set flat against the wall, while those that were higher generally were tilted forward to enhance not only close examination of the brushwork but also full appreciation of perspective. The Victorians also tended to hang their paintings unusually high, making full use of the wall space afforded by their high-ceilinged rooms. Surprisingly, in view of their penchant for covering things, the metal wires were usually left bare, and in fact were appreciated for the interesting geometric patterns which they created on the already patterned walls.

Middle-class Victorians created small "art units" in their homes—usually in the corners of a room, in a hallway, or along a stairway wall—where they displayed inexpensive prints or engravings, family watercolors, and so on. The decorative custom of such a grouping (often a few pictures arranged over a table which displayed further objets d'art) grew out of the practical limitations of Victorian lighting. When pictures and objects were grouped in a picturesque arrangement, they could be easily illuminated by a single pool of light.

The Ballroom

The grandest of Victorian homes possessed a reception room of a different sort from that in which guests were greeted before entering the parlor. This reception room was the full-scale ballroom, the scene of costume balls, charity benefits, and other festivities that fashionable Victorian society delighted in.

In keeping with the extravagance of their purpose—and their great size—these rooms too were lavishly decorated. Ballrooms, which could have forty-five-foot-high ceilings, would have been decked out in carved and crested woodwork, their ceilings frescoed, their walls staggering under the weight of outsized mirrors, enormous paintings, and copious ornamentation.

The amazing number of flowers and amount of greenery set up for a festive party—in the ballroom and throughout the interior—was also a mark of Victorian decoration. Balustrades and galleries were decorated with evergreens and branches. Fireplaces, and even the hired musicians, were usually concealed behind elaborate flowering shrubbery. Sarah Hale, editor of *Godey's*, rapturously pronounced that when "tastefully done and with some artistic skill, almost a fairy-like scene is produced." James McCabe noted that no cost was spared in a ballroom's floral decoration. He found America's 1882 parlors covered with wreathes of smilax adorning the chandeliers, cornices, and mantels, and draping the artwork, while mantelpieces and shelves were buried in mosses and exotic ferns.

The Conservatory

The conservatory was a result of the Victorians' almost exaggerated obsession with flowers and nature's bounty. Their love of nature, however, wasn't merely a sentimental

The inviting terrace garden setting, with framed Victorian tiles and daisies flowering in Majolica jardinieres, is a modern image of the nineteenth-century conservatory, which supplied the lush greenery and tropical delights that crowded the Victorian home.

preoccupation; it had its own sound decorative basis. Growing plants and freshly cut flowers added a vital quality to the richly carpeted, copiously draped interiors, balanced the material splendor with nature's own splendid effects, and kept the rooms from being too enclosed, too sequestered. A doorway framed in stained glass, for example, providing a glimpse of a charming outside view, lent an appealing touch to an otherwise formal parlor, while fragrant orange trees and white jasmine, fuchsia, heliotrope, or potted plants, vines, and palms—all nineteenth-century favorites—contributed their color, fragrance, and beauty to the full bloom of the home. Greenery of different sorts even became symbolic of various styles in Victorian interior decoration. Tropical plants, such as orchids, palms, and other exotica, were associated with the exotic styles. Aspadistras were favored in darkened interiors because they could survive with very little light. The lily and the sunflower were the clichés of the aesthetically inclined, and poppies were appropriate to Arts & Crafts interiors.

The range of Victorian gardening efforts was vast. At holiday times the polished wood staircases leading up to the second floor were garlanded in greenery and red ribbons; at dances even the chandeliers swayed overhead with their burdens of fresh flowers. Victorians fortunate enough to live on country estates supplied their homes from their own greenhouses. City dwellers often had to be satisfied with what were called "fern rooms," created out of five-foot panes of glass set in wood or iron frames and mounted on casters for relocation from room to room.

The most common method of floral cultivation, however, was the Victorian conservatory, which was really a room in itself. Ideally the conservatory would have been set up on the first floor of the home, not too far from the drawing room so that visitors could catch a glimpse of the luxuriant plant growth through the half-closed parlor doors. Frequently a hallway or anteroom would have separated the conservatory from the parlor to prevent damage to the parlor brocades and upholstery from the warm moist air.

Typical Victorian conservatories had tiled floors and glass-paned walls, which were often enhanced with the stained glass that was so popular during the later nineteenth century. In addition to quaint plant stands of varying sizes and heights, the proper conservatory would have housed small-sized versions of the cast-iron fountains and urns found in Victorian gardens, along with wicker or bamboo chairs, wrought-iron garden sets, small rustic tables surrounded by rock gardens, rookeries, and trellises, and even a few caged songbirds. What was called a Wardian case would have occupied a center point in the conservatory. Basically enclosed terrariums, these were originally invented by Dr. Nathaniel Ward as a method for safely transporting plants to other countries. The condensation on the inside of the enclosure permitted plants, especially fragile ferns, to thrive. For women encumbered with the care of small children, a Wardian case was said to be a treasure, as it offered the refreshment of something beautiful and growing, while the glass protected the plants from small fingers. Wardian cases were also suggested as an "indescribable comfort" in an invalid's room, bringing a refreshing bit of the outdoors inside.

In keeping with the richness of home interiors, Victorian floral arrangements were generally massed and opulent rather than delicate. Frequently they featured bold juxtapositions of vibrant colors, such as vermilion, rose, sapphire blue, ochre and pale yellow, lavender, and claret red, edged with the greens of fern or ivy. White flowers, except for all-white flower constructions, were seldom used, and most arrangements tended to be wider than they were tall. Flowers were used in the parlors and sitting rooms, as dining room centerpieces were generally composed of fruits, cakes, and other sweets rather than flowers. By the closing years of the century, however, flowers had invaded the dining room as well—so much so that during the 1890s, one magazine commented that "dinner and lunch tables are so gorgeous and fragrant that the everyday meal would seem bare without some little bit of green growth or pleasant fragrance."

The American home of the late nineteenth century, with its tangled maze of rooms, from the sitting room and library to the gallery and conservatory, each with its clear-cut purpose and activity, satisfied the desire for specificity in the Victorian household. The grandest Victorian homes contained still further networks of rooms extending down sprawling hallways, branching off unexpected passageways or down long corridors. Behind each succeeding door, each passageway, was the promise of something new—another chamber, another room, to embrace, enjoy, and marvel at.

The unusual porcelain mounted on the wall and the tangle of vines would have appealed to the nineteenth-century's appreciation of the picturesque in nature.

Chapter 9

The Victorian Kitchen

If parents wish their daughters to grow up with good domestic habits, they should have, as one means of securing this result, a neat and cheerful kitchen. A kitchen . . . should have a large sink with a drain running underground, so that all the premises may be kept sweet and clean. If flowers and shrubs be cultivated around the doors and windows, and the yard near them be kept well-turfed, it will add very much to their agreeable appearance.

The American Woman's Home (1869)

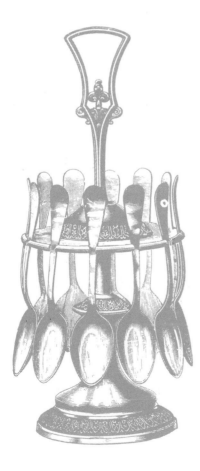

The dense arrangement of framed Victorian prints and the ornamental quality of colorful nineteenth-century and early-twentieth-century boxes and tins stacked on shelves easily convey Victorian character in a kitchen of today. A small butler's pantry, glimpsed through the open door, provides additional space for both food preparation and storage and features an old-fashioned oak icebox and a stained-glass window.

This sentiment of Catherine Beecher and Harriet Beecher Stowe's addresses a domestic situation which was quite new for that time—one that probably hadn't existed a mere generation earlier: a kitchen could be not only clean and marginally efficient, but also a "cheerful" and actually "agreeable" part of the American home. Several years later a popular women's magazine further legitimized this view: "The house is not furnished whose kitchen has not received the same attention as a kitchen, that its parlor receives as a parlor." Considering that kitchens of the previous Victorian decades had been viewed purely as rooms of function and little possible charm, such thoughts were almost revolutionary.

While family life in colonial days revolved around the warmth and aromas of the kitchen hearth, by the Victorian era the so-called heart of the home had unquestionably advanced to the parlor, its cozy center table being a cultural nexus for the joys and festivities of family life. The traditional kitchen, on the other hand, was a room hidden from public view, used almost exclusively by the servants who were then em-ployed by all but the very poorest families. A well-to-do, though by no means wealthy, family in the 1880s, for example, would have required at least one or two housemaids, a nanny for the children, and a cook and scullery maid in the kitchen, in order to maintain any semblance of respectability and style.

The Victorian lady of more substantial means spent very little actual working time in the kitchen herself, although it must be emphasized that she was far from idle. Hers was the supervisory position in the household, much in the manner of the chatelaine of an earlier time. Overseeing the staff, looking after the children's education, planning menus with the cook, supervising the purchasing, often even keeping the household books—all fell within her domain, as did dealing with such minutiae as instructing the new hired girl in exactly how the man of the house liked his soup served. But in most cases, through the 1860s, cooking and other domestic chores were done by servants.

In the years following the Civil War, with slavery abolished, with many servants deserting domestic service for what was felt to be the independence of factory jobs, and with the growth of a middle class (perhaps two or three servants graced middle-class homes, but not a whole staff), more women began

Rich mahogany-toned redwood cabinets and gleaming white surfaces create a nineteenth-century manor-house elegance in the kitchen of this Anaheim home, a look that is further enhanced by the nineteenth-century chandelier and the ornate wallpaper borders. The family extended the theme with a refrigerator encased in Honduran mahogany with the look of an old-time icebox.

to spend more time in the kitchen. Sometimes it was only to supervise and train their staff, which was beginning to be made up of newly arrived immigrants who were not used to the ways of the American Victorian home. Sometimes, however, this "new" lady of the house chose to work right alongside her diminishing staff. Many educated Victorian women had always preferred to take care of such exacting tasks as bread-making themselves. Whatever the reasons, more time spent in the kitchen served to point up its undeniably barren appearance, all the more apparent when contrasted with the plush comforts which filled the rest of the home. While women didn't yet expect luxury in their kitchen surroundings, *some* degree of cleanliness, comfort, and convenience came to be desired.

Further, some guidebooks timidly put forth the idea that even if a woman was seldom in the kitchen herself, there was all the more reason to make it comfortable for the sake of the servants. Perhaps, it was suggested, better meals might be forthcoming if the kitchen had a few framed prints on the walls, a homey chair to rest in, or bits of fabric lining the shelves for a touch of cheering color. As was pointed out in *The Household:*

Few servant girls will leave a mistress who makes their work pleasant and shows a proper consideration for their comfort. Then, with their work done, they can . . . for a time, forget they are working for others, but as if in a house of their own: this gives them a home-feeling and attaches them to the place.

Still another phenomenon prompted interest in kitchen decor: the birth, in the later decades of the nineteenth century, of a class of women unique to the American democracy—the respectable "lady" in charge of her own home without full-time servants to help her. It was this class that Harriet Beecher Stowe described in her little-known *House and Home Papers* (written under the pseudonym Clarence Crowfield, but copyrighted in her own name) as "ladies who did their own work," the very idea of which in Victorian times sounded like a contradiction in terms. The impact of that phrase almost misses its mark today until one comprehends the social climate at the time of its inception. This was an age in which well-bred young women would blush with shame to even be seen walking down the street carrying a parcel in their arms. But as "ladies" were beginning to toil in their own kitchens, efforts were made to improve the room's appearance.

From the few photographs of nineteenth-century kitchens that exist, and the even fewer actual examples that haven't been subject to modernization over the years, it's hard to believe that, even with the added attraction of a straight-backed chair or rocker, servants could ever become "attached" to the kitchen workplace. The Victorian kitchen, especially before the Civil War, was emphatically a working room, its ceiling low, its millwork simple, testifying to its status as the servant's domain. "Here the orders are issued for the day; from here the meals are produced for the family's table" was the no-nonsense maxim that applied.

The work of the kitchen, too, reads forth as a list of endless, strenuous tasks and tiring drudgery before commercial cleaning products, prepared foods, and other labor-saving devices revolutionized housekeeping. Servants made their own soaps, scoured and cleaned the pots and pans (a bit of an old clam shell was recommended for scraping), and put up the family jellies. They also cleaned the fireplace grates, washed and ironed the household linen, scrubbed the floors (for this, an old corset with the bones taken out served as an ideal cleaning rag), as well as ground the coffee, pounded the herbs, stirred the soups, and so on. The work day began long before 6:00 A.M., when pails of water were heated on the new cast-iron stoves and carried up to the family bedrooms for washing and bathing, and didn't end until the last dish was

cleaned and put away and all the family's personal needs had been fulfilled.

With all this going on, little about the kitchen was intended to be—or could be—purely decorative, although as the middle classes grew, small attempts were made. Plants, for instance, were suggested as one means of bringing the outdoors in. A pretty curtain, trimmed with scraps of an outgrown gown, could brighten a window outlook immeasurably.

The kitchen, however, remained firmly rooted as a workplace, not just by virtue of its functions, but by its location as well. Originally, Victorian kitchens were situated in the ground floor basements of the home to distance cooking odors and grease as far as possible from the upholstered parlor. In the 1860s, for example, a typical townhouse arrangement would have included in its basement the dining room, the pantry and china closets (known as the butler's pantry), all leading to the kitchen and laundry rooms which might look out onto a wide, open yard. Below that were the cavernous cellar storerooms, bins of food supplies, a "cold closet" for hanging meat and poultry, a locked butter box, and a hot air furnace. When the dining room was located upstairs, as it eventually came to be, the food was hoisted there by means of a dumbwaiter.

This tiny kitchen resembling a butler's pantry was created out of a stairwell space in a re-stored Boston home. The glass-front cabinets add an air of proper Victorian formality, as does the subdued lighting from the vintage globed brass fixture.

With the advent of plumbing and gas lines in the 1870s, the kitchen became a more sanitary place, often permitting it to be moved up to the main floor of the home, though usually it was still at the rear of the house, and the cellar storage was retained below. Now interest in the kitchen's appearance further increased. Despite the fact that the Centennial Exhibition of 1876 had promoted a patriotic interest in nostalgic kitchens with colonial themes (hanging pots and rustic-looking open hearths), that look didn't really catch on until well into the twentieth century. What did emerge, however, was the "typical" look of the late-Victorian kitchen—surprisingly sophisticated and with subtle "manor house" charm, its glass-front cabinet work and gleaming marble surfaces casting it in a much more urban vein.

Because of the ease with which they could be cleaned, painted surfaces predominated in this new Victorian kitchen. Walls were enameled in unobtrusive medium tones, such as beige, tan, gray, or cream, although sunny yellow and dark red are also mentioned as suitable in various sourcebooks. Wallpaper, in its few kitchen incarnations, was usually varnished so that it too could just be damp-wiped clean. Kitchen floors were made of hardwood, either oiled and then var-

nished, or painted, with a ceramic tile inset frequently set beneath the stove to guard against fire. All-tile floors or brick floors were other alternatives. They were either left bare to expedite cleaning or covered with a few rag rugs, carpet remnants, or decorated oilcloth.

Despite what comes across as an overwhelmingly utilitarian character, the Victorian kitchen was not always the cramped, ill-lit space it's usually depicted. Some undoubtedly were. But, though its ceilings were usually lower than those in the rest of the house, the room was actually quite sizable, especially in comparison with the space given over to city kitchens today. The room even had a simple, understated, functional beauty: not the appeal of precious materials, intricate craftsmanship, and ornament, but one of old-fashioned restraint, a near-formal quality of gracious austerity. The very setup, with its butler's pantry and service rooms intended for staff use, while usual then, conveys an orderly old-world dignity widely appreciated today.

Much of the appeal of the traditional Victorian kitchen is due not to its appearance as a whole, but to its individual architectural elements, which possess great charm in and of themselves. In addition to gleaming hardwood floors, foremost among these was the wainscoting which encircled the room, usually in thin vertical panels and, predictably, well advised for easy maintenance. Around the turn of the century, it frequently was replaced by an equally attractive tile dado. Kitchen wainscoting and the woodwork around the windows and doors added a sense of character to the otherwise featureless wallspace, and would have been either oiled and varnished or painted. A plate rail, attached about a foot below ceiling level, was another appealing period touch. Useful for the additional storage it provided, it also functioned, along with the wainscot, to divide the walls into areas suggesting the late-Victorian parlor configuration of dado, wallspace, and frieze.

Although there were fewer cupboards in Victorian kitchens than in those today (much of the china, silver, and tablesettings were on display in the dining room), one of the more elegant details of the late-Victorian kitchen was the use of glass-front cabinets. These promoted orderly household management, since everything inside them was necessarily visible to the eye. Not coincidental, then, is the fact that the packaging of the time was decorative—the boxes, tins, and canisters of the eighties, nineties, and new century were jewels of the fledgling advertising industry. Well

A Victorian country theme in an 1875 summer cottage is derived from such features as cabinets inset with nineteenth-century leaded-glass doors, a mix of several bright cotton chintzes on the walls and windows, and plenty of old-time accouterments, including the carved stove hood made from an old walnut bookcase, a working, coal-burning cast-iron stove, and an 1840s clock. The lower cabinets are simple, unfinished oak that the owners finished themselves, adding their own nineteenth-century ornamental trim and hardware. Floors and countertops are Italian ceramic tile.

The furnished-parlor look of this kitchen is achieved with the cozy armchair and rug, the elaborately framed paintings and fine porcelains, as well as the lace curtains and finished woodwork.

worth displaying and enjoying, they added a touch of color to the otherwise basically neutral room. If one wanted to conceal stored items, though, alternatives were available. In the July 1906 issue of *The Lady's World*, a reader wrote in to recommend a sliding curtain or window shade for glass-doored cupboards. "It's out of the way when not wanted, is easily dusted and altogether convenient," Miss C. H. enthused. Kitchen cabinets—and there were separate ones to house tinware, ironware, and earthenware—were usually painted in the same neutral or cream tones as the rest of the room, although Harriet Beecher Stowe strongly recommended woodgraining, a treatment she felt to be rich-looking yet still easy to care for. In her model kitchen plan, put into effect today at the Stowe historic home in Hartford, all the cabinetry, shelf surfaces, and woodwork are made of pine grained to resemble chestnut.

Stowe and other Victorian housewives also pondered the problem of kitchen shelving. One anonymous Victorian woman complained to her ladies' magazine that sometimes the shelves of an ordinary cupboard were so deep that "her baking powder hid behind the package of soda and the vanilla bottle couldn't be found at all." The nineteenth century's considered and quite sensible

solution was the introduction of very shallow, open shelving enabling all the items on hand to be seen at once, a practice adopted by many housewives. As the concern for cleanliness and hygiene grew, open shelves fell into disfavor, however, and doors were attached to these shelves in the first step toward the now-standard built-in cabinet.

Victorian kitchens had other types of storage, too. Before the whitewashed glass-door cabinets of the late-Victorian kitchen, standing cupboards, especially corner cupboards, were used. These were popular in the early-Victorian years (through the 1840s), but remained in use in rural areas of the country through the turn of the century. Kitchen dressers—what we'd call a server today—were also used, contributing to the more roomlike look of the space and indicative of the direction of Victorian taste. The memoirs of Mabel Osgood Wright, for example, recall days in the 1860s spent in her family's "big, sunny [New York] kitchen to which the willow-ware and pewter plates on the dresser gave the brightness of a living room," presumably a very desirable effect. Willow-ware refers to the Blue Willow pattern, the popular Victorian china with drooping trees, bridges, pagodas, and other scenic designs. Originally imported as part of the China trade, it was

The Victorian Revival breakfast corner in this kitchen, with its golden oak table and chairs and old-fashioned hanging fixture, easily conveys warmth and charm. The blue-and-white china set out on antique lace, the lace panel in the window, and the rich textures of the hand-painted walls and woodwork, grained to resemble old oak, are all in the Victorian tradition.

first manufactured in England in 1780. By the 1840s willow-ware had become so plentiful and readily available that it was a familiar sight in most middle-class American homes. In this case, for example, it had been relegated downstairs by the acquisition of a new, more fashionable gilt-bordered set. The dresser mentioned was probably a Welsh dresser—a long, shallow, handsome storage piece suitable for storing and displaying daily tableware, such as bowls, pitchers, pie plates, pudding dishes, custard cups, and other odds and ends of china and earthenware.

The old-time kitchen pump and bucket were replaced by a sink made of granite, cast iron, soapstone, or coated porcelain, complete with faucets. Next to the sink stood a long wood table to hold newly washed dishes. Elsewhere in the room stood another sturdy worktable, its top scrubbed, its legs polished and varnished. This table, used for chopping, cutting, and preparing food, would often hold a drawer in which utensils and measuring cups were stored. Still another table, of the marble-topped variety (or some sort of alternative marble-topped counter), was used for pastry rolling. Because these were frequently broken, few examples survive today. Large households also had what was known as a linen press—a tall cupboard that held table linens. Still

other furnishings included a carved oak clock, wallpockets and hanging shelves, and a rocking chair, usually placed near the warmth of the heated stove.

Before the introduction of the stove in the early part of the nineteenth century, cooking was done over an open-hearth fire. By the middle of the century, however, these old-time hearths were being bricked up and replaced with portable, iron cookstoves: big, black cast-iron affairs, resplendent with gleaming nickel-plate ornamentation. Although their arrival caused much excitement, they were initially bewildering to their new owners. When a cookstove was installed in the basement kitchen of the White House in the 1850s, during President Fillmore's administration, the cook reportedly couldn't get the hang of its use, and Fillmore himself had to take time away from more pressing duties of state to trot down to the local patent office and find out how to operate the new stove's knobs and pulleys.

An icebox, and later an early version of the refrigerator, was also part of the Victorian kitchen. Iceboxes of the 1840s were fairly simple: wooden boxes with the food inside simply placed on a block of ice. By the 1850s, it was known that the more effective way of food preservation was to keep the ice on top, with the

air permitted to circulate around it. An actual refrigerator of sorts had evolved by the 1860s and remained in use with few variations until nearly 1914. This was a deep, insulated wood cabinet filled with pieces of crushed ice, with a provision for drainage installed. The most attractive versions, not surprisingly, were crafted like furniture, such as an elaborate wood-paneled icebox with porcelain and metal fittings.

Other items in the Victorian kitchen addressed specific household problems, most notably keeping food and other items free from mice or vermin. Candles, for instance, were stored in tubular punched-tin or black cast-iron holders to keep them from being eaten by mice. Pie safes—standing cupboards with perforated tin or wire "windows"—kept baked goods free from flies. Still another item no city kitchen reportedly would be without was the kitchen hedgehog which slept curled up by day, but by night was turned loose to scurry around the darkened room, eating any cockroaches that crossed its prickly path.

From the 1860s on, the Victorian kitchen was also the recipient of masses of patented appliances: cast-iron apple corers, raisin stoners, spice graters, bean slicers, and fruit choppers to name but a few. While ground coffee could be purchased

Above and opposite: *The owners of this apartment ingeniously used their vast collection of Victorian tiles to carry a nineteenth-century theme into their kitchen. A reproduction Victorian wallpaper has been inset into the cabinet panels, and pieces from the owners' collection of richly colored Victorian majolica—first made in 1851 and now undergoing a collecting revival—are displayed.*

*The canned goods, stored in an adjacent pan-
try closet, and the china and silver in the nineteenth-century English sideboard, instead of in
wall-hung kitchen cabinets, preserve this
kitchen's gracious qualities. The walls are covered with a washable "ostrich-skin" wallpaper
and hung with a collection of Victorian animal
prints, while porcelains, restored wood floors,
and Victorian woodwork complete the theme.*

from one's local grocer, during the
1870s a small home coffee grinder
became one of the most fashionable
conveniences to own.

Perhaps the feature that most distinguishes the proper Victorian kitchen
from those of the preceding and
succeeding centuries was that it was
in actuality a network of rooms surrounding a main kitchen area. In
townhouses or city homes, for instance, there was the butler's pantry, a way station of sorts, located
between the kitchen and the dining
room. In the butler's pantry, one
found ceiling-high glass-doored
cabinets (sometimes actually made
of mahogany in the homes of the
wealthy), in which the daily tableware, serving dishes, and glassware
were stored. These items might instead be kept in small, closetlike
rooms—the china closet, silver
room, glass closet, etc.—off the
main butler's pantry. In that case,
the main butler's pantry became a
supplementary serving area or a
place for assembling the finishing
touches of the food preparation. In
this way, the butler's pantry also
added a touch of high Victorian
drama to a formal dinner. It was felt
that by fully containing any hint of
the sights and smells behind closed
doors, each successive course would
gain in impressiveness and impact
upon its appearance at table. The

butler's pantry would also have been a likely place for the call box, the Victorian system for summoning servants. When a bell was pulled or a pulley was pushed in any of the house's rooms, a number would pop up in the pantry call box telling the staff members just which room needed their service. This system was also popular in many Victorian hotels and other large establishments.

Some Victorian kitchens had two types of pantries: one for the dishes, silver, and cutlery as described above, and a food pantry used to house supplies of staples. This little room, often little more than a walk-in closet, would be lined ceiling to floor with neatly labeled jars of pickled or preserved fruits and vegetables, glazed stoneware crocks, tins and canisters of coffee, tea, sugar, bottles of cider vinegar, and the like. On the floor were boxes and barrels of other provisions, and in many cases this pantry also contained the icebox. Pantries, of course, were not confined to city homes. One version, built in 1885 for an eighteen-year-old bride in a Dakota settlement town, was especially well equipped, with wrap-around shelving as "well-made and fitted as boughten furniture," and deep built-in bins for flour and corn meal.

Still another service room off the main kitchen was the scullery, which either combined with the laundry or adjoined it. This was an important adjunct, as cleaning the home took up a substantial part of the nineteenth-century servant's day. This was where the dirty work of the household was done, from laboriously polishing the silver (before the days of silver creams) and shining the brass andirons and fenders, to peeling the vegetables and boiling the laundry (the only way to get the garments anywhere near clean). Here the heavy-duty pots were stored, as well as brooms, brushes, and ostrich-feather dusters. Ostrich-feather dusters were used for light dusting, while flat brushes were for bannisters and wide ones for blacking the stove. Churns, washtubs, washboards, clothes racks, mangles, and other cleaning supplies were housed here, too. Finally, the scullery might also contain a big stone or granite sink with a draining board, a cold-water pump, and sometimes a second stove, which came in handy for heating water and during the months when jelly-making and preserving went on. The old-fashioned irons would also be heated on top of this stove, which made ironing especially difficult, as one couldn't regulate the amount of heat.

Even before World War I brought an end to the Victorian way of life, the reduction of kitchen staff

The deck off the kitchen of this San Francisco home, ca. 1882, overlooks a stylized nineteenth-century garden of boxwood and English ivy. More English ivy completely covers the latticework fence, while home-grown geraniums in clay pots are arranged on the deck. Clay camels and porcelain hens and chickens, part of the owners collections, are displayed on the old-fashioned iron garden furniture.

This turn-of-the-century chestnut storage cupboard, with etched-glass panes, is as much at home in a living room as in a kitchen.

and the multitude of miraculous new home inventions that were changing the tempo of domestic life were, in turn, changing the nature, layout, and appearance of the kitchen. The heightened sanitary awareness late in the era had the greatest influence, turning the direction of kitchen decor, like bathroom design, toward the cold and clinical. By the turn of the century, chilly white tiles had begun to replace the traditional wainscoting, accompanied by plain white painted walls, bare white enamel cabinets, exposed institutional plumbing and piping (exposed pipes were easier to keep clean), all surrounding a furiously scrubbed central worktable. The typical kitchen of the early twentieth century was becoming characterized by its almost laboratorylike atmosphere, as barren as the rest of the Victorian house had been full.

The Victorian Revival Kitchen

Although many people would question the sense of reproducing an authentic period-perfect kitchen in a private home today, most homeowners interested in the Victorian Revival do want their kitchens to reflect the flavor of the era in which they were built in some way, without sacrificing modern convenience.

What exactly a Victorian Revival kitchen looks like, however, is open to educated interpretation. What is most clear is what it's not. Few would dispute the fact that a Victorian kitchen is far from a colonial one, with its open hearth and hanging utensils, but the two actually do have elements that overlap: natural materials would certainly predominate (instead of today's synthetics), and the presence of a pie safe or corner cupboard would be equally at home in both. Few would argue either that, in truth, the type of kitchen most in tune with the *philosophical spirit* of the highly progressive nineteenth century would be spaceage sleek in design, up-to-the-minute in everything that modern technology could supply. Yet, neither of these decorative routes fully satisfies the nostalgic direction of the Victorian Revival or its craving for luxury and ornamentation in all areas of the home.

The Victorian Revival kitchen reflects most of all the urban nature of Victorian America, translating its love of luxury and opulent materials into the practicality and functionalism of the room. What works most often is anything that suggests by association a more "finished" effect—parlor materials, for example, such as marble or marbleized surfaces, richly decorated tilework instead of butcher-block woods, lace or brocaded curtain fabrics instead of gingham or calico, mahogany finishes instead of simple pine. Highly polished wood floors topped with Oriental-style rugs also strongly and accurately evoke nineteenth-century feeling, as they, too, suggest parlor formality. While linoleum is indeed a nineteenth-century product, its common use within popular memory recalls the twentieth century more than the nineteenth. The same goes for braided rag rugs: also a fully authentic Victorian accent, these are betrayed by their almost irrevocable popular association, for despite their legitimacy in the Victorian setting, they have too often taken on a "country" connotation, rather than a Victorian one.

Certain furnishings can also impart a nineteenth-century feeling, especially when "real" furniture, as opposed to anything "kitcheny," is used. Golden oak pedestal tables and pressed-back oak chairs, common to turn-of-the-century tastes, can be at once practical, authentic, and handsome. The same goes for an oak, walnut, or mahogany server, an elegant formal armoire or wardrobe used as a storage space for silver and crystal, a marble-topped commode, a Welsh cupboard, or a traditional pie safe. The use of fine art, especially in heavy, "dressy" gilt frames, or in the form of dignified porcelains put on display—the treatment of the room as a bona fide living space rather than just a functional ad-

junct—helps it blend with the rest of the Victorian Revival home and avoid standing out as an obviously modern addition.

Lighting also plays an important part in the Victorian Revival kitchen. Most contemporary kitchens are vastly overlit. Without sacrificing efficiency, a lower level of lighting in the Revival kitchen helps create a more gracious atmosphere. The simple hanging light fixtures the Victorians used over the kitchen's central worktable (often similar in style to a two-armed brass billiard lamp with plain glass shades) impart a glow to the painted walls and woodgrained effects the Victorians favored. When these techniques are employed today, lighting should be adjusted in kind. If supplementary light was needed, simple wall lamps would have supplied it, a treatment as valid today as it was a hundred years ago.

Another accent suggestive of, and appropriate to, a Victorian Revival kitchen is the display of old-fashioned nineteenth-century kitchen appliances, in moderation, for the visual appeal of their basic form, shape, and workmanship. This is not an authentic nineteenth-century practice, but in fact parodies a rather bizarre late-nineteenth-century precedent in reverse: the fad in the 1880s for decorating common kitchen tools and hanging them up as ornaments in *other* areas of the

A Victorian spice box serves the same purpose today as it did a hundred years ago.

This stove from the early 1920s—porcelain-coated steel and cast iron, with nickel trim—is still fully functional.

house, such as the parlor or bedroom. One woman describes in letters to her cousin this amazing new variety of decoration, relating that "one friend of Martha's has in her room . . . a potato masher gilded and covered with plush, on which she hangs her jewelry at night. . . . Above her chiffonier hangs a wooden butter paddle . . . the inside of this is painted, as is a miniature chopping bowl. The scene in the bowl is Niagara Falls." Devices like a gilded rolling pin were said to refer to the fact that a family no longer had to make its own bread, but had the means to purchase it.

Other ways of extending Victorian urban comfort into the kitchen center on the nineteenth century's traditional use of architectural effects—details once taken for granted, but appreciated today as evidence of long-gone nineteenth-century craftsmanship. Such detailing includes glass-doored cabinetry, charming tin ceilings, plate rails, and the wainscoting and polished wood-

work that help create the old-world formality of Victorian life in the kitchen. Also included in this concept is the use of tilework backsplashes, woodgraining effects, and brass accents. As for kitchen windows, they can be covered with simple curtains made of muslin or, for a touch of color, red window shades, both authentic and appropriate today. *The American Woman's Home*, well known for its dislike of heavy curtains in all areas of the home and for its interest in, and approval of, plants and greenery, suggested bare windows bordered with vines. Greenhousing, too, wouldn't be out of place.

While today few homes retain the original configuration of rooms that gave such character to the nineteenth-century kitchen, and few have their sizable space, many retain or can easily fabricate these elements in conjunction with modern appliances, to integrate the charm of the century past with present-day convenience.

Chapter 10

The Victorian Bathroom

A bathroom worthy of Venus herself opens from this ideal sleeping apartment. Walls, floor and ceiling are of pink Carrara marble with a frieze of carved cupids gamboling among garlands of superbly executed flowers and fruit. The "tub" is reached by going down three marble steps, and is surrounded by groups of blossoming pink camellias and yellow mimosas, and a silver fountain in the shape of a dolphin replaces the ordinary douching apparatus. This room is lighted from the ceiling through a pink silk vellum, and at night tiny electric lights fashioned like rosebuds turn the whole place into a bower of light.

Vogue (Society Supplement) (1893)

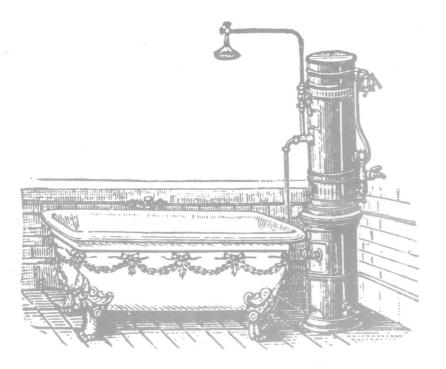

An uninhibited use of rich, floral fabric transforms a spare bedroom into a spacious master bath in a turn-of-the-century country retreat. The old-fashioned footed tub, swagged with a canopy, is the central focus of this shamelessly romanticized Victorian room, flaunting its highly furnished "parlor" look. Even the draped corner table contributes with a Victorianesque tabletop vignette.

The ornate bathroom described on the preceding page, which certainly rivals our most lavish contemporary examples, was installed nearly one hundred years ago, when bathroom ornamentation was at its height of sumptuousness. Bathrooms, first pioneered in affluent American homes in the 1840s and 1850s, had become standard in better middle-class homes by the 1860s. It took another twenty years, however, before they received such lavish attention. While a bathroom this extraordinary was hardly the rule, many prosperous Victorians of the 1880s and 1890s were beginning to express the decorative spirit of the age by devoting considerable energy to the embellishment of their bathrooms. Such mundane fixtures as plumbing pipes were cast with leafy vines and floral designs, and porcelain toilet bowls were painted with scenic landscapes and even Aesthetic motifs. The bathroom fast became a source of status—a luxury to be shown off proudly to visitors. Often, when a new and proper "water closet" was installed in a family's home, guests were invited upstairs for a demonstration of how this miracle of modern invention worked.

The bathroom was wholly an invention of the Victorian era, before which such rooms were virtually nonexistent in this country. Thomas Jefferson devised something of an "inside toilet" at Monticello in the early 1800s: an elaborate system of ropes and pulleys that wheeled his chamber pot along a tunnel to an outside dumping ground. And, in 1851, President Fillmore installed the first bathroom in the White House (regarded by the wary public of the time as an alarmingly monarchical luxury), but these were outstanding exceptions. For most Americans of the time, outhouses and chamber pots were the rule. Daily washing was conducted at one's bedchamber washstand, and, when more extensive bathing was needed, portable hip baths and tin tubs—sold in the 1880s through the Sears Roebuck catalog for about $5.50—were warmed in front of the bedroom fire or on the kitchen stove. Servants toted hot water for washing or shaving upstairs, and also emptied the chamber pots. Also called slop bowls, chamber pots were regularly scalded with boiling water, then thoroughly dried in order to ensure cleanliness. They were then discreetly hidden beneath the bed or tucked away in a cabinet commode. Such sanitary measures remained in use in many rural areas into the early years of the twentieth

Above and opposite: *The delicate Art Nouveau chandelier, upholstered chair, and fringed lampshades further assist in lending this bath its furnished look. The john is discreetly tucked away, Victorian-style, in one of the closets; the floor is hand painted in a faux-marble finish.*

century. In cities, poorer folk had the option of using the public baths, where five cents bought the "luxury" of hot and cold water, a cake of soap, and a towel of dubious cleanliness.

By the second third of the nineteenth century, however, the proper Victorian bathroom had begun to evolve. Although some forward-looking house planners set aside space in the home for a regular bathroom, most early "bathing rooms" in older homes were created from already existing space, most often an unused bedroom. The rooms that emerged had much more to admire than just the expansive size they inherited from their parent bedchamber. Many retained the wood-burning fireplaces, glossy, paneled wainscoting, stained-glass windows, and high ceilings of their former existence. These preexisting features dictated to a great extent the nature of what became proper bathroom decor.

Because this was an entirely new kind of room, no precedent existed for the Victorians. Given a room which looked, in its bare-bones state, much like any other room in the Victorian home, they proceeded to furnish the new bathrooms in much the same manner as the other rooms, all the while keeping an eye toward the concealment of its less-than-delicate purpose. The bath-

room's wood floors were covered with elegant Oriental rugs. Walls were painted in any of the fashionable colors, such as Pompeiian red, then hung with gilt-framed paintings. Most significant, however, were the massive furniturelike encasements which were created by craftsmen to camouflage the toilet, tub, and sink and to make the room resemble other, more familiar, areas of the home as much as possible. Because the appearance of bathroom enclosures was familiar to most people, fears the Victorians harbored about the hygiene of bringing the outhouse indoors were allayed, as was the uncertainty about the healthful merits of regular bathing.

The Victorian taste for magnificence gave preferential treatment to the elaborate Renaissance Revival style, which entailed the widespread use of marble for furniture tops as well as on the walls and floors of the new room. A mirror-backed, marble-topped dresser made in 1880 was nearly identical to one created for a bedroom, but with the notable addition of a sunken single or double bowl and brass or nickle-plated faucets mounted on its top. A smaller washstand sink might also have boasted a marble splash-back, while its lower cabinet concealed unsightly plumbing from public view. Still another variation was the built-in, rather than freestanding, enclosure.

The Victorian practice of encasement naturally applied to the humble toilet. Concealing it with a wooden enclosure built to resemble a chair satisfied the nineteenth-century reticence about such matters, while it fooled no one. Lillie Langtry, for example, was typically, if grandly, Victorian about it when she specified that the top of the custom-built armchair made to fit over the john in her West Hampstead home be upholstered in nothing less than *royal* blue velvet, as if anticipating her visitors. Odd as it may seem, even as late as the 1890s some Victorian homes retained the custom of a built-over chair. In 1895 at Biltmore, the Vanderbilt estate in North Carolina, a slender, cane-seated chair was placed over the porcelain tank-topped toilet bowl, creating a fashionable disguise.

The first Victorian bathrooms were exactly what the name implies—rooms for bathing and nothing more. The toilet was set off either in a tiny separate room or in a closet that adjoined the main space (the custom of segregating the toilet persists in Europe). This practice again reflected the lingering Victorian uncertainty about the wisdom and hygiene of bringing the john indoors. By the 1870s, however, that revolutionary concept had come to be more fully accepted, and all the bathroom fixtures came to be housed in the same room, although the toilet might still be set off from the other fixtures in its own enclosed alcove (hung with portieres or enclosed behind a door with inset panels of etched glass) or concealed behind a wall partition or screen.

The earth closet—as opposed to the water closet—was another Victorian invention, one enthusiastically advocated during the 1860s in Beecher and Stowe's *American Woman's Home*. It basically looked like a wooden potty chair that used a mixture of dry earth, charcoal, and stove ashes instead of flushing water. Earth closets were said to offer an advantage to those who couldn't afford the expense of indoor plumbing, which was continually breaking down, while allowing for the accumulation of what was called "valuable matter."

Victorian bathtubs were also originally enclosed in furniturelike surrounds, varnished to a high gleam to prevent warping. It was this look, more than any other, that contributed to the opulent appearance of even the smallest Victorian bathroom. In 1886, even the Sears Roebuck catalog offered an inexpensive wood-boxed tub to those with a craving for luxury and willing to discard their portable, tin-lined hip baths. Some Victorian tub units even began to feature the novelty of a shower attachment, usually a large

Above and opposite: *At first glance, this luxurious bedroom-to-bath conversion may seem contemporary, but it fits squarely within the nineteenth-century spirit of clean, tiled surfaces that began to prevail in the late 1890s. Victorian touches in this shower room include the traditional black-and-white tile work and the brass and porcelain shower head flanked by nineteenth-century-style ship's light fixtures. Even the cube of old-fashioned Castile soap is at home in this setting.*

boxed hood that attached to the wood-framed tubs and partially concealed a kerosene or gasoline heater. We know that during the 1870s, Judge David Davis, of Bloomington, Illinois, installed one of these early shower units, as well as a separate foot bath, in his twenty-room mansion. Water was supplied by a tank in the attic, which was filled in turn by a manually operated basement pump, all so the judge might have his bath. Other Victorians had tubs attached to unusually ornate water heaters, embossed with nickel plating and fanciful designs, much like old-time kitchen stoves. Some people regarded these heaters as dangerously combustible, however, and clung to the old practice of having water heated on the kitchen stove and carried upstairs.

As more frequent bathing became fashionable—bodily cleanliness was a message carried to the American public with fervor by the periodicals of the 1870s through the 1890s—still other variations on the bathtub appeared. The zinc-lined Mosely folding bathtub of 1893, for example, unfolded, Murphy-bed style, out from a dresser, and came with a heater and a full-length beveled-glass mirror. The Sears Roebuck folding tub, ca. 1900, also came with its own impressive-looking heating unit. And there were the rocking

tub and the cradle tub, both of which supposedly made bathtime more soothing and palatable for infant and adult alike.

Since Victorian bathrooms were spacious, furniture was often added, further increasing its roomlike appearance. Armoires, bureaus, and dressers, used to hold towels and toiletries, were not uncommon, and the use of other-than-bathroom furniture became one of the keynotes of bathroom style. Spool-turned or brass towel racks, small cabinetlike commodes, chairs, washstands, and men's shaving stands also moved from the bedchamber and dressing room when the Victorian family installed its first bathroom. The bathroom was also as susceptible as any other room to the decorating fads and fancies of the era. "Art" wallpaper, ornamental friezes and ceiling borders, and bonsai plants (reflecting the Japanese craze) were just some of the typical affectations; and since a room without art—even the bathroom—was a room with something missing, a few framed prints or even paintings were usually added to give the strange new room a more familiar feeling.

As the Victorians continued to search for ways to improve their homes, the bathroom interior began to change. The look that emerged in the 1890s was in keeping with the overall lighter look that was begin-

ning to be advocated for the rest of the interior. Much of this updating of the bathroom stemmed from the same hygienic considerations that were changing kitchen decor around this time as well. In the bath, the change sometimes combined effectively with the grand old-style enclosures; sometimes it replaced them completely. Generally, however, bathroom design was moving toward a more open, sanitary, twentieth-century style.

The hardwood floors and wainscots were replaced by gleaming tile floors and dados. Hospital-like cleanliness was of paramount importance. Plumbing, instead of being concealed, was now exposed, bright and shiny as new coin, in an effort to prevent germs from congregating in enclosed places. Historians even report that some bathrooms were built with round, rather than square, corners to prevent the accumulation of dirt in those hard-to-clean spaces. The enclosures themselves began to disappear slowly. Elegant enclosed sinks were replaced by models with sculpted pedestals or simply by marble slabs supported by spindly silver-colored legs. Toilets emerged from underneath their housings of built-over chairs, while the newest type of bathtub, the claw-footed, porcelain-coated variety, replaced the boxed-in look.

Despite these changes, the later Victorian bathroom retained its highly ornamental spirit, particularly in its use of brass hardware. The faucets, plumbing, doorknobs, and hinges all reflected Victorian pride in attention to the smallest details, like the buttons on a dress. Bathroom windows even received special treatment—shuttered, covered with Venetian blinds, or draped with a simple curtain. In city townhouses or rowhouses, a pane of richly colored stained glass was a popular window treatment—a colorful, ornamental touch that ensured both light and privacy.

Ornamental Victorian tilework continued in its established role as a focal point of the bathroom. During the 1870s and 1880s, bathroom tilework was used to create elaborate, picturesque friezes encircling the upper portion of the bathroom walls and surrounding sinks and tubs. The rich colors and designs of these tiles were often picked up in the painted porcelain washbasin or even in the decorative painting on the toilet bowl. Later, tilework became simpler, but was still a focal point. One frequent application was a simple glazed gray or white tile dado, topped by a decorative tile border. Today, many examples remain of floors tiled in small, crisp black and white hexagons, rectangles, or squares, a covering that was durable, attractive, and waterproof.

When the Victorian toilet was removed from its built-over armchair, it too became subject to creative decoration. Some were sculpted, while others were painted, with designs glazed into the pottery itself. Fancifully shaped toilets were often given fanciful names as well, like The Sultan, ca. 1896, with its delicate floral leaves and classic Greek geometrics, or the Pedestal Lion Closet, also from the 1890s, which featured the bowl resting atop a sphinxlike sculpted lion. An earlier model created during the 1880s was the Dolphin, whose scalloped bowl rested in a gaping dolphin's mouth. The toilet seats of the gentry were made of polished walnut and mahogany, while the servants' johns were made of untreated white pine.

While all this embellishment was going on, it has to be remembered that even by the 1890s, the bathroom was still a relatively modern convenience. While many houses of the 1890s had indoor plumbing, there still were far fewer bathrooms per home than houses of similar size and stature would have but a few years later. An upper-middle-class establishment with a large family and staff of servants, for example, would generally be served by no more than a bath and a half. The Biltmore estate in North Carolina was an extraordinary exception, with a bath for each of its thirty-one bedrooms. That each bath was relatively simple in terms of decor, for the times, makes the number no less astounding.

Even with the new, more simplified approach to bathroom decoration, the room was now "simple" only by nineteenth-century tastes. Photos of "simplified" Victorian bathrooms in the new mode still convey great charm, even luxury, with their white, marble-slabbed sinks, ceiling moldings, and elegant brass fixtures. A New York City bathroom of 1902, which belonged to an art dealer, conveyed that feeling. Though spare and in the newer style, its wainscoted walls and decorative tile border and its clean, tiled floors and simple fringed window shade made it seem furnished, comfortable, and even elegantly luxurious by contemporary standards. Enclosed cabinets and mirrors framing the marble-topped sink area added a note of Gilded Age luxury from the previous decade, while the tub was one of the new, claw-footed variety. Another interesting furnishing was a carved wood shaving stand, with adjustable mirror, which stood in the corner.

As the century progressed, bathrooms became more commonplace, and interest in the functional took precedence over the ornamental, causing the typical Victorian bathroom to become smaller, plainer,

and less elaborately decorated. When money was no object, however, the Victorian imagination continued to run free. One fanciful millionaire installed a bathroom during the closing years of the nineteenth century that featured an embroidered linen canopy suggestive of a Napoleonic campaign tent over the tub, as well as gold-plated faucets which offered one the choice of either fresh or sea water. Henry Morrison Flagler's bath at Whitehall (1902) was a vast, seventeen-by-eleven-foot space floored and faced in marble, with upper walls and windows covered with the same gold moiré silk damask used in the adjoining bedroom. The toilet stand was green onyx and the seat was polished maple—apt testimony to the striking Victorian sense of ornament, opulence, and comfort, all carried to the fullest, even in this most functional of spaces.

The Victorian Revival Bathroom

In the course of this century, the bathroom, like the kitchen, has undergone extensive structural changes, making it more functional, but also diminishing its original, Victorian charm. As a result, up until a few years ago, even if the rest of the house was restored to full nineteenth-century splendor, the bathroom often remained separate and

Above: *A nineteenth-century painted wash set and chamber pots are used today as pitchers and planters.*

Opposite: *The original marble sink and tilework join the freestanding oak-trimmed tub and old-fashioned heater (ca. 1880–1890) to create this elegant bath. The faux-bamboo table holding the pitcher and washstand is actually walnut, as is the late-Victorian mirror, rescued from an old dresser and adorned with brass hooks from a hall tree. Other reminiscences of the Gilded Age: a whatnot shelf on ropes filled with family pictures, a brandy bottle revived to hold bath salts, and the old-time sitz bath.*

A traditional Victorian wooden tub enclosure like this still imparts the elegance of an earlier time to a bath, especially when the room is dressed up with polished-brass fixtures and with porcelains and framed artwork hanging on its walls. The mirror above the tub originally graced a Victorian sideboard.

apart from the rest of the rooms—cold and impersonal, furnished with bland, modern accessories. Even if one wanted to retain the bath's original fixtures—the claw-footed tub, the pedestal sink, the marble-topped vanities, the rich network of decorative tilework on the walls or floors—these nostalgic features were often long gone or beyond repair.

Today, however, the bathroom is as open to Victorian Revival interpretation as is any other room in the house. Like the kitchen, its treatment is a subject more for creative interpretation than for documentary restoration, as it has to combine both romantic Victorian touches with the comforts and conveniences of today. At the same time, the range of new ways to evoke the aura of the nineteenth century has increased. Options in terms of Victorian-style reproduction bathroom accessories alone—the old-fashioned tank toilets, the freestanding porcelain tubs, the hardware, the lighting—are more available than ever.

As in the Victorian Revival kitchen, architectural details set the scene for the bathroom; anything that suggests the ornamentation, richness of detail, or fondness for luxurious materials that characterized the interiors of the nineteenth century has a part in the Revival bath. These include embossed-tin ceilings, ornamental moldings and cornices, and plaster ceiling medallions. Nineteenth-century woodwork around the windows, doorframes, and walls—stained in darkened rich shades (and set off with cream-white tiles)—also conveys a Victorian feeling. Other attractive—and authentic—details to consider include ornamental tilework and a decorative tile frieze, and floors in marble, tile, or wood (or wood painted to resemble marble). The less formal feeling of a country Victorian bathroom can be achieved with a whitewashed wood floor with a colorful stenciled border or allover floral pattern and a painted wall and stenciled border above the wainscot.

Proper lighting is also important when converting a plain or stripped-down modern space into a bathroom possessing nineteenth-century charm. A Victorian-style chandelier, too small or unimpressive for the parlor or dining room, for instance, can often add just the right touch of opulence to a Victorian Revival bath. Fringed silk lampshades on light fixtures and period-style wall sconces on either side of the sink are also in keeping with the feeling. Accents that pick up and reflect the light—such as antique mirrors in ornate Victorian frames (or a modern mirror in an old-fashioned

frame) and etched-glass, stained-glass, or beveled-glass panels in windows or doors—all help create the glow of the last century. The warmth of brass hardware—faucets, spigots, door pulls—also enhances a Victorian setting in a more sophisticated vein, while a simple, four-spoked faucet handle in pure, white porcelain suggests the more casual side of the century.

Further warmth and richness can be created by floor coverings. Instead of fuzzy contemporary bathmats, an Oriental-style rug or runner lends a look of parlor pattern to the room. A country Victorian braided rug, a rag rug, or even grass-rafia matting are other possibilities.

Wall treatments extending to include the ceilings, even in a small-sized bath, are another way to achieve the furnished, "filled" feeling of Victorian style. Covering the walls and ceilings with wallpaper, in fact, is one of the best ways to evoke the sumptuousness of the Belle Epoque era, especially in bathrooms in older homes where the walls are often cracked or damaged. In general, richer, darkened shades—emerald greens, berry tones, deep golds, and chocolate browns—in strong, medium to large patterns provide the color and boldness of nineteenth-century style. Fabric is another alternative, especially dressier fabrics like damasks, brocades, moirés, or taffetas (or wallpapers that simulate those looks), while lighter, small-patterned papers or fabrics have their place in the country Victorian bath. In these rooms, scrubbed pine, wicker, painted walls, and a wallpaper border are all appropriate treatments. Matching fabric, of course, or lace panels can be swagged and draped for curtains, shower curtains, or even a shirred vanity skirt (to disguise unsightly plumbing). Panels of lace or fabric, backed by a liner, can also lend a romantic touch while camouflaging modern shower doors.

The use of furniture in the bathroom is probably the quickest way, however, to create a nostalgic atmosphere in the bath. Generally, the more opulent Victorian Revival bathrooms rely on their luxurious "parlor" moods, with mahogany or walnut furnishings, richly patterned rugs, swagged or draped curtains, deep-colored wallpaper, and accents of marble, brass, and mirror. The elegant, old-fashioned look of the Victorian furniture enclosure for the bath can be obtained by setting a porcelain sink in a marble-topped oak or mahogany dresser, an old Victorian bureau, a cupboard, or even a nineteenth-century sideboard; by adding a varnished wood surround to the tub; and by storing towels or bath linen in a vintage cupboard or armoire. An old-fash-

An exquisite jewel-box richness is the hallmark of this tiny but opulently furnished bath. Its built-in cabinetry has been handgrained to resemble tortoise shell and is complemented by creamy marble surfaces and old-fashioned brass faucets. The mirror reflects beautiful Chinese wallpaper and a hanging shelf, which hails from the Aesthetic era, used to hold fragrances, grooming aids, and other sundries.

ioned chair, a bench, or even a small settee adds to the highly furnished look. In less formal Victorian bathrooms, furnishings of scrubbed pine or wicker work equally well: a wicker cabinet or shelf unit for towels or bath accessories, or a bamboo table to hold soaps, ivory-handled brushes, and combs. And, of course, there is the whole range of pedestal sinks, freestanding porcelain tubs, and marble vanities.

In a small-sized bathroom where furniture isn't practical, a slender pedestal sink and a mounted wall cabinet are a solution that suggests the period, along with an elegant light fixture and an overall wallpaper, to achieve a "furnished" look. These smaller rooms also benefit from attention to the small details which have even greater decorative impact in scaled-down spaces: tassels or fringe added to door and cabinet pulls or window shades, wallpaper edged with braid or borders, doorknobs made of embossed brass, crystal or painted porcelain, a decorative light switch, old-fashioned brass or porcelain soap dishes, even towels trimmed with touches of crocheted lace or ribbon instead of those that are plain. If the bath is small but has a high ceiling, a plate rail running around the upper reaches of the room, displaying blue and white Victorian porcelain or other nineteenth-century collectables, can add a charming touch.

Simple botanical prints, framed Victorian postcards, nineteenth-century greeting cards, or inexpensive chromos can also be hung in the bathroom in the way one would throughout the Victorian-inspired home. Along with open bowls of old-fashioned fragrances—orange or apple peel, lilac, lavender, rosebud, or lemon vebena, kept fragrant in the moist atmosphere of the bath—a room lushly evocative of the Victorian era should be complete.

Victorian smoking room and trophy room motifs create a unique look in this highly original Victorian Revival bath. The fur throw draped over the towel rack and the specimens of nineteenth-century taxidermy mounted in glass cases on the walls complete the theme.

Bibliography
♦
248

Bibliography

In addition to the list of books that follows, back issues of *The Old House Journal*, *Nineteenth Century Magazine*, the magazine *Antiques*, and *Victorian Homes* have been helpful to me in researching this book. I have also relied extensively on popular magazines from the Victorian era itself including issues of *Godey's Lady's Book* (1850s and 1860s), *Harper's Bazar* (1864–1900), *Vogue* (1893–1915), as well as individual issues of *Good Housekeeping*, *The Decorator & Furnisher*, *The Ladies' Home Journal*, *Frank Leslie's Illustrated Newspaper*, *Woman's Home Companion*, *The Ladies' World*, *The Delineator*, *The Modern Priscilla*, and others.

In addition, many novels by nineteenth-century authors have either influenced my opinions or corroborated my conclusions. These include: the novels of Edith Wharton such as *The Custom of the Country*, *The Age of Innocence*, and *The House of Mirth*; Henry James's *The Bostonians*, *The Portrait of a Lady*, and *The Ambassadors*; the many novels of William Dean Howells, including *Their Wedding Journey*; the works of Mark Twain, particularly, *Life on the Mississippi*, *A Connecticut Yankee in King Arthur's Court*, and *The Innocents Abroad*; Oscar Wilde's only adult novel, *The Picture of Dorian Gray*; all of the popular books of Louisa May Alcott: *Little Women*, *Little Men*, *Jo's Boys*, *Eight Cousins*, and *Rose in Bloom*, as well as her lesser-known works; and Laura Ingalls Wilder's autobiographical *Little House* children's books, which depict everyday American life during the 1870s and 1880s. Another part of my picture of nineteenth-century manners and morals was acquired from the "sentimental" novels which were part of the popular fiction of the day. These include: *The Fashionable Adventures of Joshua Craig*, by David Graham Phillips (1909); *Not Like Other Girls* and *Nellie's Memories*, by Rosa Nouchette Carey (ca. 1890s); *Marcia Schuyler*, by Grace Livingston Hill Lutz (1908); *Dorothy Dale: A Girl of Today*, by Margaret Penrose (1908); *Molly Brown's Freshman Days*, by Nell Speed (1912); *Countess Kate*, "by the author of *The Heir of Redclyffe*" (1866); *Dick's Sweetheart*, by "The Duchess" (ca. 1890s); *A Gingham Rose*, by Alice Wood Ullman

(1904); the *Betty Wales, Freshman* series, by Margaret Warde (1904); *The Making of a Marchioness*, by Frances Hodgson Burnett (1901). And finally, one novel by a contemporary author: Jack Finney's classic *Time and Again*.

Adams, Carol. *Ordinary Lives, 100 Years Ago.* London: Virago Press, 1982.

Advice to a Young Gentleman on Entering Society. Philadelphia: Lea and Blanchard, 1839.

The American Heritage History of Antiques, from the Civil War to World War I. New York: American Heritage, 1969.

The American Heritage History of the Confident Years. New York: American Heritage, 1969.

Arrowsmith, James. *The Paper-hanger's Companion: A Treatise on Paper-hanging.* Philadelphia: Henry Carey Baird, 1856.

Avery, Gillian. *Victorian People in Life and Literature.* New York: Holt, Rinehart & Winston, 1970.

The Bazar Book of Decorum. New York: Harper, 1970.

Beecher, Catherine E., and Harriet Beecher Stowe. *The American Woman's Home.* 1869. Watkins Glen, N.Y.: American Life Foundation, 1979.

Birmingham, Stephen. *The Grande Dames.* New York: Simon and Schuster, 1982.

Birmingham, Stephen. *Life at the Dakota.* New York: Random House, 1979.

Bishop, Robert, and Patricia Coblentz. *American Decorative Arts: 360 Years of Creative Design.* New York: Abrams, 1982.

Bishop, Robert, and Patricia Coblentz. *The World of Antiques, Art and Architecture in Victorian America.* New York: Dutton, 1979.

Blum, Stella, ed. *Victorian Fashions and Costumes from "Harper's Bazar," 1867–1898.* New York: Dover, 1974.

Boger, Louise Ade. *The Complete Guide to Furniture Styles.* New York: Scribner's, 1969.

Bridgeman, Harriet, and Elizabeth Drury. *The Encyclopedia of Victoriana.* New York: Macmillan, 1975.

Brown, Henry Collins. *Brownstone Fronts and Saratoga Trunks.* New York: Dutton, 1935.

Brown, Henry Collins, ed. *New York in the Elegant Eighties (Valentine's Manual of Old New York).* Hastings-on-Hudson, N.Y.: Valentine's Manual, Inc., 1927.

Browne, Junius Henri. *The Great Metropolis: A Mirror of New York.* Hartford, Conn.: American Publishing Co., 1869.

Busbey, Katherine. *Home Life in America.* New York: Macmillan, 1910.

Byron, Joseph. *Photographs of New York Interiors at the Turn of the Century, from the Byron Collection of the Museum of the City of New York.* Text by Clay Lancaster. New York: Dover, 1977.

Cable, Mary. *Top Drawer: American High Society from the Gilded Age to the Roaring Twenties.* New York: Atheneum, 1984.

Carson, Gerald. *The Polite Americans: A Wide-angle View of Our More or Less Good Manners over 300 Years.* New York: Morrow, 1966.

Cathers, David M. *Furniture of the American Arts and Crafts Movement.* New York: New American Library, 1981.

Cook, Clarence. *The House Beautiful.* 1878. North River Press, 1980; distributed by Caroline House Publishers.

Cooper, Nicholas. *The Opulent Eye: Late Victorian and Edwardian Taste in Interior Design.* London: Architectural Press, 1976.

Cornforth, John. *English Interiors, 1790–1848: The Quest for Comfort.* London: Barrie & Jenkins, 1978.

Corson, Richard. *Fashions in Makeup, from Ancient to Modern Times.* London: Peter Owen, 1972.

Cromie, Alice. *Restored America: A Tour Guide. The Preserved Towns, Villages and Historic City Districts of the United States and Canada.* New York: American Legacy Press, 1979.

Crow, Duncan. *The Victorian Woman.* New York: Stein and Day, 1972.

Cruse, Amy. *The Victorians and Their Reading.* Boston: Houghton, Mifflin, 1935.

De Wolfe, Elsie. *The House in Good Taste.* New York: Century Co., 1913.

Downing, A[ndrew] J[ackson]. *The Architecture of Country Houses.* 1850. New York: Dover, 1969.

Downing, Andrew Jackson. *Victorian Cottage Residences.* (pub. in 1842 as *Cottage*

Residences). New York: Dover, 1981.

Drepperd, Carl W. *Victorian: The Cinderella of Antiques*. Garden City, N.Y.: Doubleday, 1950.

Dresser, Christopher. *The Art of Decorative Design*. 1862. Watkins Glen, N.Y.: The American Life Foundation, 1977.

Dubrow, Eileen, and Richard Dubrow. *American Furniture of the 19th Century: 1840–1880*. Exton, Pa.: Schiffer Publishing, 1983.

Dudden, Faye E. *Serving Women: Household Service in Nineteenth Century America*. Middletown, Conn.: Wesleyan University Press, 1983.

Eastlake, Charles Locke. *Hints on Household Taste in Furniture, Upholstery and Other Details*. 5th ed. London: Longmans, Green, 1878.

Elex, Geoffrey. *The Ruined Maid: Modes and Manners of Victorian Women*. Herfordshire, Eng.: The Priory Press, 1970.

Etiquette for Americans, by A Woman of Fashion. Chicago: Herbert Stone and Co., 1898.

Ewing, Elizabeth. *Dress and Undress: A History of Women's Underwear*. 2d ed. New York: Drama Book Specialists, 1981.

This Fabulous Century. Vol. 1: 1900–1910. New York: Time–Life Books, 1974.

Forge, Suzanne. *Victorian Splendour: Australian Interior Decoration, 1837–1901*. Melbourne, Australia: Oxford University Press, 1981.

Freeman, Larry. *New Light on Old Lamps*. Watkins Glen, N.Y.: American Life Foundation, 1984.

Freeman, Larry. *Victorian Silver*. Watkins Glen, N.Y.: Century House, 1967.

Freeman, Sarah. *Isabella & Sam: The Story of Mrs. Beeton*. New York: Coward, McCann & Geoghegan, 1978.

Garrett, Elisabeth Donaghy, comp. *The "Antiques" Book of Victorian Interiors*. New York: Crown, 1981.

Gernsheim, Alison. *Victorian and Edwardian Fashion: A Photographic Survey*. 2d ed. New York: Dover, 1981.

Gloag, John. *Victorian Comfort: A Social History of Design, from 1830–1900*. London: Adam and Charles Black, 1961.

Goff, May Perrin, ed. *The Household: A Cyclo-pedia of Practical Hints for Modern Homes*. Detroit: Detroit Free Press, 1981.

Gowans, Alan. *Images of American Living: Four Centuries of Architecture and Furniture as Cultural Expression*. Philadelphia: Lippincott, 1964.

Green, Harvey. *The Light of the Home: An Intimate View of the Lives of Women in Victorian America*. New York: Pantheon Books, 1983.

Grow, Lawrence. *The Old House Book of Kitchens and Dining Rooms*. New York: Warner Books, 1981.

Hale, Sarah Josepha. *Manners; or Happy Homes and Good Society All the Year Round*. 1868. New York: Arno Press, 1972.

Haller, John S., Jr., and Robin M. Haller. *The Physician and Sexuality in Victorian America*. New York: Norton, 1974.

Halttunen, Karen. *Confidence Men and Painted Women: A Study of Middle-Class Culture in America, 1830–1870*. New Haven: Yale University Press, 1982.

Handlin, David P. *The American Home: Architecture and Society, 1815–1915*. Boston: Little, Brown, 1979.

Harland, Marion. *Eve's Daughters; or Common Sense for Maid, Wife and Mother*. New York: Anderson & Allen, 1882.

Harrison, Fraser. *The Dark Angel: Aspects of Victorian Sexuality*. London: Sheldon Press, 1977.

Hill's Manual of Social and Business Forms. Chicago: Hill's Standard Book Co., 1884.

Houghton, Walter. *The Victorian Frame of Mind, 1830–1870*. New Haven: Yale University Press, 1957.

Jeffrey, Julie Roy. *Frontier Women: The Trans-Mississippi West, 1840–1880*. New York: Hill and Wang, 1979.

Jensen, Amy La Follette. *The White House and Its Thirty-Three Families*. New York: McGraw–Hill, 1962.

Jones, Mrs. C. S., and Henry T. Williams. *Household Elegancies*. 1875. Reprint. Watkins Glen, N.Y.: Century House, 1967.

Kouwenhoven, John A. *Adventures of America, 1857–1900. A Pictorial Record from "Harper's Weekly."* New York: Harpers, 1938.

Labine, Clem, and Carolyn Flaherty, eds. *The Old-House Journal Compendium*. Woodstock, N.Y.: Overlook Press, 1980.

Late Victorian Interiors & Interior Details. (Facsimile of Wm. B. Tuthill's *Interiors and Interior Details*). 1882. Watkins Glen, N.Y.: American Life Books, 1984.

Late Victorian Needlework for Victorian Houses. (Facsimile of *The Lady's Handbook of Fancy Needlework*). Watkins Glen, N.Y.: American Life Foundation, 1979.

Lewis, Ethel. *The White House: An Informal History of Its Architecture, Interiors and Gardens*. New York: Dodd, Mead, 1937.

Lichten, Frances. *Decorative Art of Victoria's Era*. New York: Scribner's, 1950.

Lockwood, Charles. *Bricks and Brownstones: The New York Rowhouse, 1783–1929. A Guide to Architecture Styles and Interior Decoration for Period Restoration*. New York: Abbeville Press, 1972.

Loftie, M. J., Lucy Orrinsmith, and Lady Barker. *The Dining Room, the Drawing Room, the Bedroom and Boudoir*. London: Macmillan, 1878.

Lucie-Smith, Edward. *Furniture: A Concise History*. New York: Oxford University Press, 1979.

Lynes, Russell. *The Tastemakers: The Shaping of American Popular Taste*. New York: Dover, 1949.

Maas, John. *The Gingerbread Age*. New York: Bramhall House, 1957.

Maas, John. *The Victorian Home in America*. New York: Hawthorn Books, 1972.

Marcus, Steven. *The Other Victorians: A Study of Sexuality and Pornography in Mid-Nineteenth Century England*. New York: Basic Books, 1964.

Mayhew, Edgar de N., and Minor Myers, Jr. *A Documentary History of American Interiors from the Colonial Era to 1915*. New York: Scribner's, 1980.

McCabe, James D., Jr. *Lights and Shadows of New York Life, or the Sights and Sensations of the Great City*. 1872. New York: Farrar, Straus & Giroux, 1970.

McCallister, Ward. *Society As I Have Found It*. New York: Cassell, 1890.

McClinton, Katharine Morrison. *Collecting American Victorian Antiques*. DesMoines, Iowa: Wallace-Homestead, 1978.

McCorquodale, Charles. *History of the Interior*. New York: Vendome Press, 1983.

Merriman, Effie W. *Modern Entertainments*. New York: F. M. Lupton, 1898.

Minnegerode, Meade. *The Fabulous Forties, 1840–1850: A Presentation of Private Life*. New York: Putnam's, 1924.

Moore, Katharine. *Victorian Wives*. London: Allison and Busby, 1974.

Moreland, Frank A. *The Curtain-Maker's Handbook*. Reprint of *Practical Decorative Upholstery*, 1890. New York: Dutton, 1979.

Mumford, Lewis. *The Brown Decades*. 1931. Reprint. New York: Dover, 1975.

19th Century America: Furniture and Other Decorative Arts. (Exhibition Catalog.) New York: Metropolitan Museum of Art, 1970.

Norwalk, Mary. *Kitchen Antiques*. New York: Praeger, 1975.

Oakley, Ann. *Woman's Work: The Housewife, Past and Present*. New York: Vintage Books, 1976.

Pearl, Cyril. *The Girl with the Swansdown Seat: An Informal Report on Some Aspects of Mid-Victorian Morality*. London: Robin Clark, 1980.

Peterson, Harold L. *Americans at Home, from the Colonists to the Late Victorians. A Pictorial Source Book of American Domestic Interiors*. New York: Scribner's, 1971.

Richards, Caroline Cowles. *Village Life in America, 1852–1872. Including the Period of the American Civil War as Told in the Diary of a Schoolgirl*. New York: Holt, 1913.

Roe, Frederic Gordon. *Victorian Corners: The Taste and Style of an Era*. New York: Praeger, 1969.

Ross, Ishbel. *Crusades and Crinolines: The Life and Times of Ellen Curtis Demorest and William Jennings Demorest*. New York: Harper & Row, 1963.

Rusk, Katherine Knight. *Renovating the Victorian House*. San Francisco: 101 Productions, 1982.

Ruskay, Sophie. *Horsecars and Cobblestones*. New York: Beechhurst Press, 1948.

Saint-Laurent, Cecil. *A History of Ladies Underwear*. London: Michael Joseph, 1960.

Savage, George. *Dictionary of 19th Century Antiques and Later Objets d'Art*. New York: Putnam's, 1978.

Schwartz, Marvin D., Edward J. Stanek, and Douglas K. True. *The Furniture of John Henry Belter and the Rococo Revival*. New York: Dutton, 1981.

Seale, William. *Recreating the Historic House Interior*. Nashville: American Association for State and Local History, 1979.

Seale, William. *The Tasteful Interlude: American Interiors through the Camera's Eye, 1860–1917*. Nashville: American Association for State and Local History, 1981.

Service, Alastair. *Edwardian Interiors: Inside the Homes of the Poor, the Average and the Wealthy*. London: Barrie & Jenkins, 1983.

Sherwood, Mary Elizabeth. *Manners and Social Usages*. 1884. New York: Arno Press, 1975.

Sigourney, Mrs. L. H. *Letters to Young Ladies*. New York: Harper, 1839.

Simon, Kate. *Fifth Avenue: A Very Social History*. New York: Harcourt Brace Jovanovich, 1978.

Sironen, Marta K. *A History of American Furniture*. East Stroudsburg, Pa. and New York: Towse, 1936.

Skinner, Cornelia Otis. *Madame Sarah*. Boston: Houghton Mifflin, 1967.

Sklar, Kathryn Kish. *Catharine Beecher: A Study in American Domesticity*. New York: Norton, 1973.

Smith, Jane S. *Elsie de Wolfe: A Life in the High Style. The Elegant Life and Remarkable Career of Elsie de Wolfe, Lady Mendl*. New York: Atheneum, 1982.

Spofford, Harriet Elizabeth Prescot. *Art Decoration Applied to Furniture*. New York: Harper and Brothers, 1878.

Squire, Geoffrey. *Dress and Society, 1560–1970*. New York: Viking, 1974.

Steegman, John. *Victorian Taste: A Study of the Arts and Architecture from 1830 to 1870*. Cambridge: MIT Press, 1971.

Stowe, Harriet Beecher [Christopher Crowfield, pseud.] *House and Home Papers*. Boston: James R. Osgood and Co., 1872.

Swedberg, Robert, and Harriett Swedberg. *Victorian Furniture: Styles and Prices*. Book I and Book II. Revised eds. Des Moines, Iowa: Wallace-Homestead, 1976 and 1983.

Thornton, Peter. *Authentic Decor: The Domestic Interior, 1620–1920*. New York: Viking, 1984.

Treasures of Use and Beauty. [By a core of Special Authors.] Detroit: F. B. Dickerson Publishers, 1883.

Vicinus, Martha, ed. *Suffer and Be Still: Women in the Victorian Age*. Bloomington: Indiana University Press, 1973.

Ward, Mrs. H. O. [Clara Sophia (Jessup) Bloomfield–Moore]. *Sensible Etiquette of the Best Society*. Philadelphia: Porter & Coates, 1878.

Wellman, Rita. *Victoria Royal: The Flowering of a Style*. New York: Scribner's, 1939.

Wharton, Edith, and Ogden Codman, Jr. *The Decoration of Houses*. 1897. New York: Arno Press, 1975.

Wildeblood, Joan. *The Polite World: A Guide to English Manners and Deportment from the 13th to the 19th Century*. New York: Oxford University Press, 1965.

Wright, Lawrence. *Clean and Decent*. New York: Viking, 1960.

Wright, Mabel Osgood. *My New York*. New York: Macmillan, 1926.

Young, John H. *Our Deportment, or the Manners, Conduct, and Dress of the Most Refined Society*. Detroit: F. B. Dickerson Publishers, 1882.

A variety of sources and directions are available to those who wish to further explore the social and cultural backgrounds of the Victorian Revival in order to better understand nineteenth-century life and style. The following five-part directory of those people and places that responded to my queries represents a starting point. These appendices consist of several selective listings:

A. Museums in the United States that house notable collections of nineteenth-century furniture and furnishings. Many display their collections in painstakingly restored period rooms, thereby enabling one to see the pieces in the context of authentic Victorian environments.

B. A state-by-state listing of **historic Victorian homes,** from prairie cottages to High Victorian extravaganzas, whose interiors reflect the rich variety of styles that flourished throughout the nineteenth century. While each represents a different approach to—and state of—restoration, each also offers insight into the domestic styles of the past in its particular region.

For those inspired to re-create aspects of Victorian splendor in their homes, listing **C,** a guide to some leading **antique dealers** who specialize in Victorian antiques and furnishings of high quality, should be helpful. Listing **D** refers to some top **specialists in the Victorian home arts**—restoration experts and consultants on Victorian design, as well as artists who work in the mediums that made the nineteenth-century home unique, including stained glass, stenciling, decorative-painting techniques, and so on. (Those looking for manufacturers' reproductions of nineteenth-century architectural elements and interior furnishings and accessories should consult restoration catalogs which provide the most comprehensive, up-to-date listings and therefore are not included here.)

Finally, for readers who have become encouraged to delve further into the life and times of Victorian America, listing **E,** a roster of **organizations and publications** dealing with various aspects of Victorian life, has also been included.

APPENDIX A.
MUSEUMS

Baltimore Museum of Art
Art Museum Drive
Baltimore, Maryland 21218
The museum's Victorian gallery showcases furniture by Belter, Roux, and other leading cabinetmakers. Also featured are a Gothic Revival period room and decorative items, including silver and Tiffany glass.

Boston Museum of Fine Arts
465 Huntington Avenue
Boston, Massachusetts 02115
The American Decorative Arts wing includes nineteenth-century furnishings and decorative arts.

Brooklyn Museum
188 Eastern Parkway
Brooklyn, New York 11238
The museum houses four Victorian period rooms: the Milligan parlor and library, a Civil War dressing room, and the noted Rockefeller Room. American Victorian furnishings are best represented by Rococo Revival and Gothic Revival styles.

Chicago Art Institute
Michigan Avenue and Adams Street
Chicago, Illinois 60603
The museum is strong in the Herter Brothers' furnishings and all the Victorian revival styles.

Cincinnati Art Museum
Eden Park
Cincinnati, Ohio 45202
A period room of the 1870s is found here, and Rookwood and German ceramics, Bo-

hemian glass, silver, Arts & Crafts items, and many Rococo Revival furniture pieces are sprinkled throughout the museum.

Cleveland Museum of Art
11150 East Boulevard
Cleveland, Ohio 44106
Galleries here are set up in chronological order, housing paintings, furnishings, and decorative items. Although primarily of French origin, American furnishings are represented as well.

Cooper-Hewitt Museum,
The Smithsonian Institution's National
Museum of Design
2 East 91st Street
New York, New York 10128
Although this extensive collection of nineteenth-century items is not on exhibition, it can be viewed by appointment.

Denver Art Museum
100 West 14th Avenue Parkway
Denver, Colorado 80204
The collection concentrates mostly on American furniture, 1850 through 1900, featuring many Aesthetic and Reform pieces, with other styles also represented.

Detroit Institute of Arts
5200 Woodward Avenue
Detroit, Michigan 48202
The museum's small collection concentrates on Gothic Revival style and those up to the 1870s.

Essex Institute
132 Essex Street
Salem, Massachusetts 01970
Although a parlor set is the main exhibition piece of Essex's Victorian collection, the museum also has in storage five to six pieces of almost every major Victorian style, with an emphasis on Renaissance Revival. The museum also runs the Ropes Mansion in Sa-

lem, decorated in those styles favored in 1894 and 1927.

Grand Rapids Public Museum
54 Jefferson Avenue, SE
Grand Rapids, Michigan 49503

This collection houses six Victorian period rooms as well as decorative arts from the nineteenth century. Besides the extensive collection on exhibition, the museum has many more pieces in storage that are available for viewing by scholars and researchers by appointment.

Henry Ford Museum
Greenfield Village
20900 290 Oakwood Boulevard
Dearborn, Michigan 48121

This museum covers fourteen acres and houses an extensive collection of everything from steam engines and furniture to glass and ceramics. Greenfield Village in itself a living museum with many historic houses.

High Museum of Art
1280 Peachtree Street, NE
Atlanta, Georgia 30343

The museum houses the Virginia Carroll Crawford Collection of decorative arts, 1825 to 1917, an outstanding collection of ceramics, textiles, and glassware, as well as furniture by Belter, Roux, Pabst, the Herter Brothers, among others.

Houston Museum of Fine Arts
1001 Bissonnet
Houston, Texas 77005

The museum's Bayou Bend collection features period-room displays of American decorative arts and furnishings from colonial times to the Victorian era.

Hudson River Museum
Trevor Park-on-Hudson
511 Warburton Avenue
Yonkers, New York 10701

The museum, which houses four Victorian period rooms, is part of an Eastlake mansion with an extensive collection of Eastlake furniture. Other Victorian styles are also represented, as well as a treasure trove of nineteenth-century decorative objects, including textiles, glass, and silver.

Louisiana State Museum
751 Chartres Street
New Orleans, Louisiana 70116

The museum galleries contain extensive collections of nineteenth-century glass, ceramics, and metalwork. Furniture is housed in the 1850 House on Jackson Square.

Lyman Allyn Museum
625 William Street
New London, Connecticut 06320

A good selection of items in this collection is on permanent display, including glass, Parian wear, and Belter pieces.

Margaret Woodbury Strong Museum
1 Manchester Street
1 Manhattan Square
Rochester, New York 14607

This unusual museum is devoted entirely to documenting life in Victorian America. It houses an extensive collection of nineteenth-century decorative arts, including textiles, ceramics, draperies, and hardware, as well as furniture.

Metropolitan Museum of Art
Fifth Avenue at 82nd Street
New York, New York 10028

The American Wing galleries include nineteenth-century glass, silver, and furniture, some displayed in elaborate period rooms representing the Empire, Rococo, and Renaissance Revival styles.

Minneapolis Institute of Arts
2400 Third Avenue, S
Minneapolis, Minnesota 55404

Nineteenth-century period rooms are on view, as well as the third-floor galleries that exhibit decorative arts of the period.

Museum of the City of New York
Fifth Avenue at 103rd Street
New York, New York 10029

The collection includes nineteenth-century period rooms and galleries with furniture and decorative arts, including paintings, silver, and porcelains, and an impressive collection of Victorian toys and dollhouses.

New York State Museum
State Education Department
Cultural Education Center
Albany, New York 12230

The collection includes several galleries of nineteenth-century furniture.

Newark Museum
49 Washington Street
Newark, New Jersey 07101

This extensive collection of fine nineteenth-century furnishings and decorative arts adjoins the Ballantine House, where one can see the furniture in elaborate restored period rooms, ca. 1880s.

Philadelphia Museum of Art
26th Street and Benjamin Franklin Parkway
Philadelphia, Pennsylvania 19101

The American wing houses a number of collections of nineteenth-century furnishings in a variety of styles, including pieces by the Herter Brothers, Pabst, and Tiffany.

Renwick Gallery
Smithsonian Institution
17th Street and Pennsylvania Avenue, NW
Washington, D.C. 20560

The Smithsonian's decorative-arts museum includes a floor of nineteenth-century furniture and frequent special exhibitions.

Rhode Island School of Design
Museum of Art

224 Benefit Street
Providence, Rhode Island 02903
Pendleton House, the American wing, has period rooms with nineteenth-century furnishings and decorative arts.

St. Louis Art Museum
Forest Park
St. Louis, Missouri 63110
The museum's extensive collection of nineteenth-century furnishings can be viewed by appointment only.

San Antonio Museum of Art
200 West Jones Street
San Antonio, Texas 78299-2601
The galleries house nineteenth-century furnishings from the region, including horn furniture.

Virginia Museum of Fine Arts
Boulevard and Grove Avenues
Richmond, Virginia 23221
This collection features Art Nouveau rooms as well as nineteenth-century furniture, which is scattered throughout the galleries.

Wadsworth Atheneum
600 Main Street
Hartford, Connecticut 06103
The third-floor galleries exhibit nineteenth-century furniture and decorative arts.

Winterthur
Main Street
Odessa, Delaware 19730
This vast collection of colonial American furnishings recently has been expanded to include some American Empire holdings.

APPENDIX B.
HISTORIC HOUSES
(in alphabetical order by state)

ALABAMA

Bellingrath Gardens and Home
Route 1, Box 60
Theodore, Alabama 36582
Magnificently furnished fifteen-room post-Victorian mansion, built by Coca-Cola bottler Walter Bellingrath in 1935 and 1936, featuring an impressive collection of Rococo Revival furniture as well as china, flatware, and objets d'art.

ARIZONA

Century House
240 Madison Avenue
Yuma, Arizona 85364
Home of E. F. Fanguinetti and his family from 1890 to the 1960s. Due to continued family occupation, many original furnishings are intact. The house has reconstructed redwood floors; decor is divided between two periods: some rooms (for example, parlor) are in 1870s style, while others date from the 1910s.

Customs House
1st Avenue and Riverfront
Yuma, Arizona 85364
Built in 1859, it was abandoned in 1885 and occupied by the United States Department of the Interior from 1895 to 1955. Now fully restored in 1875 Renaissance Revival style, the rooms are decorated in a military style with a magnificent bed used by an officer of the time. All floors are originally from the 1870s.

Pioneer Arizona Living Museum
Black Canno Stage, Box 1677
Phoenix, Arizona 85029
Historic village with twenty-six buildings of interest, including an 1890s home built by

cattleman John Marion Sears, moved to this site for preservation; a miner's cabin (reconstruction of an 1880 home); a ranch, ca. 1870. All completely furnished.

ARKANSAS

Clayton House
514 North 6th Street
Fort Smith, Arkansas 72901
Built in 1852, this house was later bought by Clayton, who added to the home in 1882 to make room for his six daughters. Some of the more interesting features are the black walnut floating staircase, the reconstructed fresco, the original rug in the ladies' parlor, and the children's room complete with toys.

CALIFORNIA

The General Phineas Banning
Residence Museum
401 East M Street, P.O. Box 397
Wilmington, California 90748
An 1864 Greek Revival home beautifully restored and furnished with a fine, eclectic collection of American pieces, 1830 to 1900, reflecting several generations of occupancy and the changing taste of the Victorian decades. Of special note are the teen-age boy's and the young girl's bedrooms and the personal quality of decor throughout.

Camron-Stanford House
1418 Lakeside Drive
Oakland, California 94612
Built in 1876, this two-story Italianate house represents the lives of five nineteenth-century families, including that of the David Hughes family (Hughes gave the golden nuggets to create the golden spike that joined the transcontinental railroad). Four period rooms are extensively furnished to reflect the period 1875 to 1885, with Turkish furniture, draped paisley

shawls, tea tables, a Renaissance Revival parlor cabinet, a horn chair, and a Damascus table. The art gallery is of special note, as is the outstanding collection of nineteenth-century lighting fixtures.

Queen Anne Cottage
Los Angeles State and County Arboretum
301 North Baldwin Avenue
Arcadia, California 91006

Now lovingly refurbished with period pieces, this cottage was built in 1885 as the guest house of the Rancho Santa Anita (now a 127-acre arboretum). Features original stained-glass windows, marble mantels and hearth tiles, and encaustic-tile mosaic floors, as well as a music room with a piano, a melodeon, and a harp.

Villa Montezuma Museum/
Jesse Sheperd House
1925 K Street
San Diego, California 92012

Built in 1887 by author and musician Jesse Sheperd, this extravagant Queen Anne-style house has been restored to reflect the style and taste of the 1880s. Unusual features include stained-glass windows and a tiled-floor conservatory housing exotic plants.

The Wahaley House
2482 San Diego Avenue
San Diego, California 92110

Constructed in 1857, the house still maintains nearly half the original furnishings, including a Battenburg lace bedspread over 150 years old, as well as many pieces bought from Andrew Jackson by the Wahaley family.

Whittier Mansion
California Historical Society
2090 Jackson Street
San Francisco, California 94109

A thirty-room home completed in 1896, its Classical Revival style is not typical of San Francisco Victorian homes. Of special note is the original woodwork in the dining room, the golden oak in the reception area, and the Honduran mahogany in the living room. The rooms are not presented as period rooms, although some nineteenth-century furniture is on view, including an 1860s folding chair, and a settee and chair from the 1870s.

COLORADO

The Molly Brown House Museum
1340 Pennsylvania Street
Denver, Colorado 80203

Built in 1889 and purchased by the Browns in 1894 (for $30,000), this house has been restored to its original late-nineteenth-century look, based on photographs from 1910. All furnishings and accessories are from the period. Special features include golden oak wainscoting and staircase, gilded radiators and a gilded Anaglypta-covered foyer, original stained-glass windows, and many excellently furnished rooms.

The Grant/Humphreys Mansion
770 Pennsylvania Street
Denver, Colorado 80203

Built in 1902, this forty-two-room mansion was remodeled extensively in the 1920s, eliminating much of its turn-of-the-century charm. The drawing room, however, features original silk damask wallcoverings and a chandelier, and the original mahogany fireplace remains in the library.

CONNECTICUT

Alsop House
Davison Art Center
317 High Street
Middletown, Connecticut 06457

This Greek Revival house, built in 1838, has an overall feeling of pre-Victorian restraint, but several rooms have been refurnished with nineteenth-century pieces, the bulk of which are American Empire, including a Duncan Phyfe sofa and dining table.

Gillette Castle State Park
East Haddam, Connecticut 06423

Built in 1914 by actor William Gillette, whose portrayal of Sherlock Holmes brought him fame. The home is a medieval-style castle, of the type admired by the Victorians, decorated in a Victorian fashion for the Christmas season.

The Lockwood-Mathews Mansion
205 West Avenue
Norwalk, Connecticut 06850

Although not fully furnished, original wallpaper, stencil work, parquet floors, marble fireplaces, extraordinary frescoed walls, etched glass, and woodwork are just some of the features of this sixty-room mansion, built in the late 1860s as a country estate. Of special note are the richly inlaid sliding doors enclosing the music room; the floors in the library; and the eight-piece Herter drawing room set, original to the house but reacquired in 1985.

The Harriet Beecher Stowe House
77 Forest Street
Hartford, Connecticut 06105

Built in 1871, in Cottage style, the Stowe house is of particular interest due to Mrs. Stowe's co-authorship with her sister Catherine of the influential book *The American Woman's Home*. Furnished with care, the house contains many original features, including a tufted sofa, a dining room set, and a violet-patterned china tea set designed by Mrs. Stowe. The kitchen has been restored with wood graining, narrow shelving, and so on, according to instructions in *The American Woman's Home*.

The Mark Twain House
351 Farmington Avenue
Hartford, Connecticut 06105

Built in 1874 in a small literary community

known as Nook Farm, this impressive nineteen-room home retains the spirit and sensibility of an elegant, slightly eccentric, family retreat. Although the furnishings alone make the trip worthwhile, the real treat here is the restored decorative stenciling and wallpapers that were part of the decor masterminded by Louis C. Tiffany in the 1880s. Of special note are hallway stenciling resembling mother-of-pearl inlay; embossed wallpaper in the dining room; the elegant parlor, billiard room, impressive library, and even children's rooms. The conservatory resembles neighbor Mrs. Stowe's ideal.

FLORIDA

The Henry Morrison Flagler Museum
Whitehall Way, P.O. Box 969
Palm Beach, Florida 33480

Henry Morrison Flagler was a co-founder with John D. Rockefeller of Standard Oil, and, befittingly, his home, completed in 1901, was one of the great American palaces. The ground floor rooms, particularly the opulent banquet room and library, tend to reflect Victorian tradition more than do the second floor bedrooms. In addition to period rooms, special collections of porcelains, paintings, silver, glass, dolls, lace, and costumes are exhibited.

GEORGIA

Bulloch Hall
180 Bulloch Avenue
Roswell, Georgia 30075

Bulloch Hall, a Greek Revival house built in 1840, was the family home of Theodore Roosevelt's mother (she was married here, Christmas 1853). Today it has ten rooms on view, in the process of being furnished to reflect the period 1840 to 1860, when the Bulloch family lived here. Special features include the basement kitchen (where cooking was done in a Dutch oven and open fire)

and the extensive landscaped gardens, antebellum style, as well as an arbor, a shrub garden, and an herb and vegetable patch.

The Green-Meldrim House
St. John's Parish
Madison Square
Savannah, Georgia 31401

A fine example of Gothic Revival architecture, this house was built in the 1850s by Charles Green, a wealthy cotton merchant, and today is the parish house of the St. John's Episcopal Church. During its day, it was considered the most elaborate house in Savannah, and today still features beautifully carved black walnut woodwork on the main floor, as well as silver-plated doorknobs, hinges, and escutcheon plates and marble mantels in every room. Other details include the ornate chandeliers, gold-leaf-framed mirrors, and skylight above the staircase. During the Civil War, the house was the headquarters of General Sherman.

Hay House
934 Georgia Avenue
Macon, Georgia 31201

Built from 1855 to 1861, this twenty-four-room mansion was one of the most opulent in antebellum Georgia and is still furnished much as it was in the 1860s. Of special note are exquisite plasterwork throughout the home; nineteen carved marble mantels; high, dark ceiling and Renaissance Revival cabinetry in the dining room; as well as stained glass characteristic of the 1880s and 1890s, rather than of the 1850s.

The Rankin House
1440 Second Avenue
Columbus, Georgia 31906

The lower floor of this 1860 house has been restored in the style prevalent during the 1850s to 1870s, although it is not excessively Victorian. Period gaslight chandeliers and fine reproduction carpeting are of interest here, as are the rosewood piano in the mu-

sic room and the center hall's unusual solid walnut double staircase.

Wren's Nest
1050 Gordon Street, SW
Atlanta, Georgia 30310

Wren's Nest, a four-room home built in 1870 and expanded with an additional three rooms and a wraparound porch in 1884, was the home of Joel Chandler Harris, famous for writing the Uncle Remus tales. It holds an abundance of original Harris family furnishings, books, roll-top desk, photographs, and memorabilia. For the person looking for original wallpaper, these parlors are a good place to start.

ILLINOIS

Glessner House
Chicago Architecture Foundation
1800 South Prairie Avenue
Chicago, Illinois 60616

A unique townhouse built around an inner courtyard, Glessner House was designed by Boston architect H. H. Richardson in 1886. The house features many beautifully restored rooms, including a master bedroom and bath suite on the ground floor, decorated in an English Arts & Crafts motif, as well as a stipple-painted library and a kitchen with a Garland stove, encaustic-tile floor, and glazed-tile walls.

Ulysses S. Grant Home
State Historic Site
509 Bouthillier Street
Galena, Illinois 61036

Built in 1859 and acquired by the Grants in 1865, this five-bedroom house exhibits the library, parlor, dining room, and kitchen with 90 percent of the furnishings originally belonging to the Grant family. Of special note are the white, gold, and pink Haviland china made for the president's daughter's White House wedding in 1874 and the restored parlor. Also on view throughout the home are family portraits. Note: Nearby, the Belvedere House, a restored and furnished 1857 mansion, is also open to the public.

Lincoln Home
National Historic Site
426 South 7th Street
Springfield, Illinois 62703

The Lincoln home, built in 1839 and enlarged by Lincoln in 1856, was occupied by the Lincoln family from 1844 to 1861. Sixty-five pieces of furniture bought by the Lincolns can still be found in this restoration, as can other furniture from the period and two sections of original wallpaper.

INDIANA

President Benjamin Harrison Memorial
Home
1230 North Delaware
Indianapolis, Indiana 46202

Completed in 1875, this sixteen-room brick mansion stands on a double lot conveniently close to Harrison's law office. Although the home is only sparsely decorated with paintings and bibelots, it has been restored with many of the family's original furnishings and mementos. Of special interest is a handsomely furnished guest bedroom.

James Whitcomb Riley House
528 Lockerbie Street
Indianapolis, Indiana 46202

Built in 1872, and one of only two preservations in the country ("preservation" meaning that the house has not been restored but remains as it was when the family lived here), this house is decorated in a way representative of the 1870s. Many rooms can be seen in their original state, including the library, drawing room, and dining room.

IOWA

General Dodge House

605 Third Street
Council Bluffs, Iowa 51505

The General Dodge House, the home of the wealthy railroad man, is considered by many authorities to be one of the ten finest Victorian restorations today. The fourteen-room, three-story mansion, completed in 1870 (at a then-lavish cost of $35,000), features almost all the Victorian styles: Eastlake, Renaissance Revival, Rococo, Cottage, Empire, and Centennial. Special features include the beautifully restored double parlors, in the style of the 1870s; the elegant dining room with crystal, china, and silver; and the library, considered one of the most authentically restored rooms in the home.

Martin Flynn Mansion
Walnut Hill
Living History Farms
2600 NW 111th Street
Des Moines, Iowa 50322

Built in 1870 in the Italianate style, this mansion has been restored as part of a recreated town of the 1870s, which is part of a museum of Iowa farm history. The mansion kitchens are soon to be restored and used by authentically clad "cooks," while "maids" bustle about as "Mrs. Flynn" receives visitors who have come to call.

Terrace Hill
(Iowa governor's residence)
2300 Grand Avenue
Des Moines, Iowa 50312

Completed in 1869, this home was in private hands until 1970, when it was given to the state of Iowa to be converted into a permanent residence for the state's governor. The main floor rooms, particularly the drawing room, which showcases a handsome Belter parlor suite and a huge silver and crystal chandelier, have been refurbished to reflect elements of nineteenth-century splendor.

KENTUCKY

The Brennan House
631 South Fifth Street
Louisville, Kentucky 40202

A lovely Italianate townhouse built in the 1860s and occupied by the same family for ninety years. Furnishings and decor remain mostly as they were during the Brennans' time, including family portraits, musical instruments, Tiffany lamps, pier mirrors, and objets d'art. Sound-and-light displays bring back the sensual feeling of the era.

LOUISIANA

Beauregard-Keyes House
1113 Chartres Street
New Orleans, Louisiana 70116

Built in 1826 and restored in 1860, this house, owned by novelist Francis Parkinson Keyes, is filled with furnishings, porcelain, dolls, and fans from the years of the Keyeses' occupancy. Later bought by Pierre Beauregard, the house also contains a generous sampling of this Southern general's furnishings and memorabilia.

Gallier House
1118-32 Royal Street
New Orleans, Louisiana 70116

Begun in 1857 and completed three years later, this house has an abundance of original fixtures reflecting the life of the Victorian South in a grand style. Wood floors, wallpaper fragments, unusual ceiling medallions, and cornices are just some of the highlights. Furnishings include Belter and Belter-style furniture, but all the pieces fall into the mid-Victorian era. The house is known for its continuing the practice of disrobing: every June, the rich damask draperies are replaced with airy lace curtains, and the furniture is dressed with cool muslin slipcovers.

Rosedown Plantation and Gardens
Highway 10 and U.S. 61, P.O. Box 1816
St. Francisville, Louisiana 70775

An opulent sixteen-room plantation house on a vast estate, built by Daniel Trumbull, a wealthy cotton planter, and his wife. Today it is restored to its original condition with crystal chandeliers, silver, marble statuary, and the like. Of note are Gothic Revival furniture in the bedroom (originally built for Henry Clay); twenty-eight acres of formal gardens, including flowers and an herb garden. Nearby, several smaller homes of the period are also open to the public, including Laurel Hill from the early 1800s and enlarged in 1873; Hazelwood, ca. 1832, a smaller plantation house; The Old Taylor House, ca. 1876; the Wakefield Plantation, ca. 1834; and Evergreenzine, ca. 1885.

San Francisco Plantation Foundation
P.O. Box AX
Reserve, Louisiana 70084

This 1850s home is also known as the Marmillion Plantation and has been lavishly restored to reflect stylish Southern living of the 1850s and 1860s. Of special interest are the elegant rosewood furniture, fanciful frescoed ceilings, grained and marbleized woodwork, an 1852 sewing machine, and a cast-iron swivel-spring rocking chair once exhibited at the Crystal Palace.

The Shadows-on-the-Teche
117 East Main Street
New Iberia, Louisiana 70560

A Classic Revival house completed in 1834 and originally owned by sugar planter David Weeks. The house remained in the Weeks family until 1958 and consequently has retained much of its original charm and furnishings. Restored to antebellum splendor by the last owner, the house now features outstanding Victorian window treatments and interior decoration, as well as an assortment of nineteenth-century furnishings.

MAINE
The Victoria Mansion

109 Danforth Street
Portland, Maine 04101

Also known as the Morse-Libby House, this magnificent villa was completed in 1863 as a summer home and is one of the most outstanding examples of High Victorian style and richness that can be seen today. The opulent furnishings are from the period, many having been made especially for this house, including an enormous étagère in the sitting room that covers nearly an entire wall. Special features include a Turkish room, the brightly painted and molded music room ceiling and walls, and a marble-topped double sink in a bedroom.

White Columns
Maine Street
Kennebunkport, Maine 09046

An 1853 Greek Revival house notable because it was owned by one family until deeded to the Kennebunkport Historical Society in 1981. Original furnishings are a blending of Victorian pieces with those of an earlier era which had belonged to the owner's parents. The parlor still has its handmade French wallpaper, specially woven carpet, and ottomans worked in needlepoint by the original owner. Also of interest is the massive black walnut bedroom suite, made to order for the master bedroom.

MARYLAND
The Peale Museum
(Baltimore's Historic Museum)
225 Holliday Street
Baltimore, Maryland 21202

The fourth-floor gallery of this museum contains rowhouse period interiors, ca. 1840 to 1933, including a kitchen, 1875; an opulent Victorian parlor, 1870s; a parlor, 1840s; a bedroom, 1890; and a bathroom, 1911. The museum is part of the Baltimore City Life Museums, which also oversees the 1840 house, a living history site depicting the reconstructed nineteenth-century row-

house of wheelright John Hutchinson; the Carrol Mansion, opulently furnished to reflect the 1820s and 1830s; the nineteenth-century H. L. Mencken house; and others.

MASSACHUSETTS
Wistariahurst
238 Cabot Street
Holyoke, Massachusetts 01040

A rambling structure, ca. 1848, moved piece by piece and floated down the Connecticut River from Williamsburg to its present site. Interior treasures include a massive round dining table with griffin-clawed feet and hand-carved dining chairs, a leather room with walls that are indeed covered with hand-painted and embossed leather, and—a seeming incongruity—a room of Shaker furniture.

MICHIGAN
The Grosvenor House
211 Maumee Street
Jonesville, Michigan 49250

A ten-room house built between 1872 and 1874 with original Renaissance Revival furnishings, including a bed with a jewel box concealed in the footboard. Also of note are the turn-of-the-century bathroom and telephone and the large closets, unusual in the 1870s. Extensive servants' quarters include service rooms, dressing rooms, and so on.

Honolulu House
107 North Kalamazoo Street
Marshall, Michigan 49068

Built just before the Civil War, the Honolulu House has retained almost all its original plasterwork, which includes exceptional wall paintings and decorative ceilings. While some of the pieces present were made locally, the dining room set was made originally in 1876 for the display at the American Centennial exhibition.

MISSISSIPPI

Waverly Plantation
West Point, Mississippi 39773

An eclectic mix of Greek and Gothic Revival features, with a spectacular octagonal entryway, this plantation house was built in 1882 and has been restored and furnished with period pieces. Featured are such details as a parlor designed with a wedding alcove, handgrained floors, porcelain keyhole covers, and marbleized baseboards.

MISSOURI

Campbell House
1508 Locust Street
St. Louis, Missouri 63103

Built in 1851 and purchased by fur trader Robert Campbell, this house is still complete with the family's fine furniture and memorabilia. Much of the parlor furniture is Rococo Revival, with hand-carved scrolls, fruits, and flowers. The massive dining room sideboard features the traditional Victorian fish and fowl motifs.

Samuel Cupples House
3673 West Pine Boulevard
St. Louis, Missouri 63103

A forty-two-room mansion built in 1890, remarkable for its exterior stone carving and wood carving inside. Although the present furnishings don't reflect the layered abundance of the 1890s, the fireboxes and trim on the twenty-two fireplaces exhibit some of the best work of the famed St. Louis ironwork. All ten stained-glass windows are by Tiffany. The house also had indoor plumbing.

The Glenn House
325 South Spanish Street
Cape Girardeau, Missouri 63701

Built in 1883 as a Victorian Eastlake structure, its curved veranda, turret, and stained-glass windows and main entrance were added around 1900. The house has been beautifully restored with appropriate period furniture and much attention to details such as stenciling, wallpaper borders, and woodgraining. Of note are the stunning entryway, dining room, conservatory, and upstairs bedrooms.

Martin Franklin Hanley House
10 North Bemiston Avenue
Clayton, Missouri 63105

An eight-room Greek Revival farmhouse built in 1855 and occupied by the same family until 1968. Most of the massive, beautiful furnishings belonged to the family, and detailed records and photographs have aided in restoring the house to reflect aspects of the decades from the 1850s through the 1890s. The house has not been aggrandized but has kept its middle-class farmhouse flavor with pine plank floors and separate outdoor kitchen and outhouse.

Oliver House
224 West Adams Street
Jackson, Missouri 63755

Converted from a one-and-a-half-story saltbox, built between 1833 and 1848, into its present Federal style with Greek Revival façade around 1855, this simple little house is being restored to reflect Victorian home life from the 1850s to the early 1900s. Furnishings reflecting its gradual "Victorianization" include such details as a late-Victorian mantel added to the parlor.

The John Wornall House
146 West 61st Street Terrace
Kansas City, Missouri 64113

An imposing 1858 Greek Revival farmhouse which, though it now stands in the city, offers insights into the lives of prosperous Victorian farm families. Furnished simply, it includes such architectural features as a stone fireplace painted to look like brick and a dining room pass-through into the kitchen.

MONTANA

The Conrad Mansion
P.O. Box 1195
Kalispell, Montana 59901

A Normal Revival structure built in 1895, this house remains very much as it was at the turn of the century, with original parlor furniture, marble lavatories, sleigh beds, and canopied fourposter in the bedroom.

NEBRASKA

General Crook House
Fort Omaha
Omaha, Nebraska 68111

Built in 1879 for the commanding officer of the Department of the Platte, a last outpost on the Western plains, this was not a family house but was designed for entertaining. Furnishings are of the period with documented reproductions of carpets, drapery, and upholstery. Of note are steerhorn furniture in the general's study, an Eastlake-style parlor set, and the Rogers group in the parlor.

Fairview
Sumner at 50th Street
Lincoln, Nebraska 68508

Home of the "Great Commonor," William Jennings Bryan, this house was completed in 1903 and features ornate carved furniture, cushions piled on overstuffed chairs, and bearskin rugs, all aptly reflecting the time. Although the house is only partially restored, much of the vast collection of Bryan's curios from his travels is still on display, including a decorated ostrich egg which was suspended from the chandelier in the front parlor.

NEW HAMPSHIRE

Strawberry Bank
P.O. Box 300
Portsmouth, New Hampshire 02801

(Located on Marcy Street near Portsmouth's waterfront)
Strawberry Bank, a historic waterfront neighborhood, is made up of a number of small restorations that were originally on, or moved to, this site. Among these, the Victorian Governor Goodwin Mansion, moved here from a mile away, displays many original pieces collected by Goodwin between 1830 and 1896. Although eclectic, the collection is rich and varied.

NEW JERSEY

Acorn Hall
68 Morris Avenue
Morristown, New Jersey 07960

Dr. John Schermerhorn built this Italianate mansion in 1853, and then sold it three years later after his wife died in childbirth. Descendents of the new owners lived in the house until 1971, when it was donated to the historical society. Beautifully restored, many of the elegant furnishings date from the first owners, including the printed velvet parlor carpet. Of note are a well-appointed parlor typical of the 1850s, a music room, and Gothic Revival bookcases in the library. Upstairs, a crib and other nursery furniture which belonged to the second owner's children, including a charming bedroom set of painted cottage furniture, can be seen. Also of interest are the gardens and grounds, created in a Victorian style.

The Ballantine House
49 Washington Street
Newark, New Jersey 07101

Completed in 1885, this house's exteriors and interiors are an eclectic blend of all the revival styles, but perhaps most typical of the elegance and grandeur of 1880s Victorian taste. One of the best and most complete of the late-nineteenth-century restorations, it retains much of the personal quality of the original home. Painstaking cleaning of carved woodwork, repainting and gluing of canvas and plaster ceilings, and rebuilding of ornamental plaster were undertaken. Furnishing follows many photographs of the original rooms, which include a furnished reception room, library, drawing room, and dining room.

Bridgeton, New Jersey

This town is the largest National Historic Distric in America, boasting over six thousand Victorian homes. Most are private, but many can be seen by appointment. Among the public Victorian sights are a brick walk, a zoo, an amphitheater, a bandstand, and a restored train station which serves as an information center. Along the streets, shops have been restored as well. Special events such as fairs, Christmas walking tours, and the like are frequently scheduled.

Cape May, New Jersey

Historic Cape May is a restored nineteenth-century resort that is one of the few cities designated a National Historic Landmark in the United States. The town is well known for its hundreds of Victorian homes, many of which are being carefully restored as charming bed-and-breakfasts, inns, and guest houses. In addition to the Emlen Physick Estate (see below), the town is host to an extensive variety of Victorian activities: special tours such as Mansions by Gaslight, Cottages by Twilight, and a Christmas Candlelight Tour, as well as Victorian craft and antique fairs, Victorian dinners, concerts, and so on. Every October, a ten-day Victorian Week is held, featuring restoration and decorative-arts seminars and workshops, and other special events. (For more information, contact The Mid-Atlantic Center for the Arts, Cape May, N.J., P.O. Box 164, Cape May, N.J. 08204.)

Emlen Physick Estate
1048 Washington Street
Cape May, New Jersey 08204

Built in 1881, this sixteen-room Stick-style home was designed by the well-known Victorian architect Frank Furness. Although the house is presently in the process of acquiring a full complement of furnishings appropriate to the period, impressive features include the rich woodwork and paneling in the entry, Lincrusta wallcoverings, and an original Furness bedroom suite. Also note the collection of toys, costumes, books, and other Victorian memorabilia.

Ringwood Manor
Ringwood, New Jersey 07456

Completed in its present form in 1878, this fifty-one-room summer house was the home of famous ironmaster families for over two centuries. Befitting a generational house, interiors have been furnished in a variety of styles, including the many different revival periods of the nineteenth century. Of special note is an impressive paneled nineteenth-century dining room

NEW YORK

Cottage Lawn
435 Main Street, P.O. Box 415
Oneida, New York 13421

A charming Gothic Revival cottage, designed in 1849 by Alexander Jackson Davis, with furnishings that reflect the years 1865 to 1890. Unique features include a gymnasium (added in 1854) and a banking room attached to the house.

The 1890 House
37 Tompkins Street
Cortland, New York 13045

A magnificent château-style mansion with towers, turrets, and gables, plus interiors by Tiffany to delight the eye. Features spectacular stained glass throughout, even in the children's rooms, as well as decorative stenciling and oak and cherry woodwork. Furnishings are in opulent 1890s styles. Of note are the fernery and sun parlor added in the 1920s, as well as a formal gold parlor and music room, an informal sitting room, an inglenook beneath the stairs, and a medieval dining hall.

The Millard Fillmore House
East Aurora, New York 14502

Our thirteenth president built this simple, Federal-style cottage in 1825 with his own hands, and the house still contains his original window panes and sturdy plank floors. Some rooms have been arranged to approximate the 1826 to 1830 period; others are furnished with the Empire and later Victorian furniture belonging to the Fillmores after his tenure as president.

Fountain Elms
310 Genesee Street
Utica, New York 13502

An 1850 Italianate house with four period rooms superbly restored to reflect that period's best in woodwork and wallpapers, furniture, curtains, lighting, and upholstery. Includes a drawing room set by Belter, and other furniture by Phyfe and Quervelle, all signed, labeled, or otherwise documented. The parlor features Victorian silver, porcelains, and sculptures by Hiram Powers. Beautifully decorated for Christmas, when even the dollhouse boasts a tiny tree.

Granger Homestead
295 North Main Street
Canandaigua, New York 14424

Built in 1816 by Gideon Granger, Postmaster General for Presidents Jefferson and Madison, four generations of the Granger family lived in this house. Although its eight rooms contain some Federal and Sheraton furnishings, it also reflects its period of Victorian occupancy in such details as early-Empire furniture, a Victorian bed and parlor set, and a piano from 1841.

Lyndhurst
635 South Broadway
Tarrytown, New York 10591

This 1838 mansion, surrounded by extensive landscaping, greenhouses, and gardens, represents the zenith of Gothic Revival architecture in this country. It began as a "pointed style" building under its first owners and grew under the hand of Victorian architect A. J. Davis into the mansion it is today. Third owner, railroad magnate Jay Gould, made only minor changes to the mansion, and the furnishings today represent the different families and tastes of the era. Of special note is the Davis-designed Gothic Revival furniture in the dining room.

Olana
R.D. 2
Hudson, New York 12534

The country estate of Hudson River School painter Frederic Edwin Church was built between 1870 and 1874 and commands a spectacular view of the Hudson River and the Catskill Mountains. The thirty-seven-room house, which includes a handsome east parlor, a library, an art studio, and a gallery, was designed almost entirely by Church himself and took many years to decorate. The design was influenced strongly by his trips to the Near East: the Islamic arches and the Persian decoration throughout reflect nineteenth-century eclecticism and extravagance at its utmost.

Old Merchant's House
29 East 4th Street
New York, New York 10003

Built in 1832 in New York's first exclusively residential neighborhood, the eight-room Old Merchant's House was inhabited continuously from 1835 to 1933 by members of the Tredwell family. Interiors, furnishings, and family possessions are intact, showing the gradual "Victorianization" of the home and making it an excellent documentation of the social history of the times. Of note are the Victorian draperies and gilded cornices, the carpeting in the Greek Revival-

style parlors, and the downstairs kitchen. The house has been open to the public since 1936.

Richardson-Bates House
135 East Third Street
Oswego, New York 13126

A Victorian Italianate house built in the 1860s through the 1880s for Maxwell Richardson, mayor of Oswego. The exterior was originally painted pink with green trim and features Florentine balconies and stained-glass windows, all guarded by pairs of sphinxes. Inside, 90 percent of the furnishings are original to the house, including embossed wallpaper from Paris, hand-carved cherrywood paneling in the library, golden oak in the dining room, and fine Renaissance Revival furniture in the drawing room.

Theodore Roosevelt Home
28 East 20th Street
New York, New York 10003

This brownstone is an exact reproduction of Theodore Roosevelt's boyhood home, completely reconstructed on its original site and restored to reflect the period of 1865 to 1872. Featured are a Rococo Revival formal parlor, a dining room with horsehair-upholstered seating, and a bedroom suite in elegant satinwood created by Leon Marcotte. About 40 percent of the furnishings are original, half of those belonging to Roosevelt relations. The rest of the pieces, however, accurately reflect the period. Completed in 1923, this reconstruction was supervised by one of Roosevelt's sisters, and therefore is tempered to a degree by the prejudices of that decade.

Rosehill
534 South Main Street
Geneva, New York 14456

An elegant twenty-room Greek Revival mansion built in 1839 on the shores of Lake Seneca, its predominantly Empire furnishings, wall-to-wall carpeting, and appropriate wallpapers and textiles make it an excellent example of early-Victorian style. Many of the furnishings are original to the house, including an eight-piece parlor set by Alexander Roux which had belonged to the owners in the 1850s and was recently discovered and returned.

Sagamore Hill
Box 304
Oyster Bay, New York 11771

Built in 1885 by Theodore Roosevelt (who moved in two years later), this home has been refurnished to depict the 1910 time period. Ninety percent of the furnishings in this twenty-five-room house are original, including linens and rugs. Of special note are the monumental Gothic bench, a carved bed by Daniel Pabst of Philadelphia, a Herter chest in the parlor, and chairs made of moose antlers, as well as the many family portraits.

The Seward House
33 South Street
Auburn, New York 13201

Built in 1816 by Judge Elijah Miller, Seward's father-in-law, the house is filled with mementos of Seward's illustrious career, from the staircase given to him by California's forty-niners to his certificate of appointment as Secretary of State signed by Lincoln, and a samovar presented by the Russian minister with whom Seward negotiated the purchase of Alaska ("Seward's Icebox"). Extensive furnishings—Federal to late Victorian—reflect the five generations of the Seward family who occupied the house from 1816 to 1951. Of note are the drawing room, library, dining room, upstairs Victorian bedroom, ca. 1860s style. The house retains the original basement kitchen.

Sonnenberg Gardens and Mansion
151 Charlotte Street, Box 496

Canandaigua, New York 14424

A forty-room mansion built in 1887 as a summer home, the house is now a wondrous profusion of affluent High Victorian taste—furniture, bric-a-brac, curios, plants, and so on—with period rooms ranging from the Renaissance to the nineteenth century. The extensive gardens are considered to be among the finest examples of Victorian landscape architecture.

Sunnyside
Sleepy Hollow Restorations
150 White Plains Road
Tarrytown, New York 10581

Sunnyside was a tenant farmer's house when Washington Irving bought it in 1835 and modified it into the charming cottage it is today, complete with a bathroom and bathtub with running water (unusual in those days). The house is handsomely furnished with Federal, Empire, and Victorian revival pieces and remains much as Irving left it—even the books in his study remain as he arranged them. Other details are the curtained book alcove in the library, a Rococo Revival sleigh bed, the charming kitchen.

The Vanderbilt Mansion/
The Franklin D. Roosevelt Historic Site
Route 9
Hyde Park, New York 12538

The Vanderbilt mansion, which shares a site with the Roosevelt home, was designed by McKim, Mead and White and is a fine example of Beaux Arts architecture. Upon being purchased by Frederick Vanderbilt in 1895, the home became a showplace; today it retains much of its original furnishings. Highlights include an Italianate main hall and north foyer, a French Empire mantel in the Mauve Room, original plaster ceilings, wallcoverings, and rugs. The neighboring family estate of Franklin Delano Roosevelt is an enlarged two-story frame house, purchased by FDR's father in 1867, and over-

looking the Hudson River. Inside, the house is overflowing with original furnishings in elaborate settings, and collections of art objects, curios, and the like.

NORTH CAROLINA

Biltmore House
Asheville, North Carolina 28803

A 250-room French Renaissance château built by George Vanderbilt, grandson of Cornelius. Completed in 1895, the mansion is the centerpiece of a vast working estate totaling over 7,500 acres, its gardens designed by Frederick Law Olmstead. The house itself was designed by Richard Morris Hunt, and 1000 workers toiled for five years to execute his design. Interiors have remained much as they were during Vanderbilt's lifetime: art treasures grace every room; in the library, one can see the massive carved fireplace and Pelligrini's 450-square-foot ceiling painting; in the morning room are the ivory chessmen Napoleon used while a prisoner on St. Helena. Of special interest is the "downstairs"—the kitchens, laundry, and pantries, as well as the wine cellars, servants' rooms, swimming pool, bowling alley, and gymnasium. Also of interest are the trophy, billiard, and smoking rooms.

OHIO

Rutherford B. Hayes Presidential Center
Speigel Grove
Fremont, Ohio 43420

Built in the 1850s, this house was given to the nineteenth president by his uncle in 1873 and is furnished in an elegant, restrained manner with Victorian antiques belonging to the Hayes family. This is also the first presidential library in the United States, with over 60,000 volumes, 50,000 photographs, over 1 million manuscripts, and a large collection of the president's correspondence, scrapbooks, and diaries. The museum site also includes the neighboring Dillon House, built in 1873 (now a guest house for the center), which has been carefully restored to reflect the character of late-nineteenth-century style.

Lawnfield
8095 Mentor Avenue
Mentor, Ohio 44060

Lawnfield, the home of the twentieth president, James A. Garfield, underwent extensive remodeling in 1876 and again in 1880. In the twenty rooms on view, one can see Garfield's 120-compartment Wooten desk and, in his study, a customized leather chair (one arm of the chair was lower than the other so one could sit with a leg slung over comfortably), as well as family portraits in the parlor, lacquered furniture, a fainting couch, and so on. All furnishings are original to the house. Of special note are two children's bedrooms.

John Wright Mansion
Historic Lyme Village
State Route 113 East
Bellevue, Ohio 44811

Completed in 1882, this Second Empire-style farmhouse was built by the owner himself of bricks fired in his kilns and timber felled in his forests. When completed, the fifteen-room mansion rose three stories, with a graceful stairway, walk-in closets (rare in those days, when each room was taxable), and two bathrooms with running water. There were also steam radiators, heated by a furnace that burned huge logs, and gas lamps lit by acetylene produced right on the grounds. The top floor housed an immense ballroom with a stage at one end. It is now part of a preserved nineteenth-century village.

OREGON

Beekman House
206 North Fifth Street

Jacksonville, Oregon 97530

In Country Gothic style, this house, built in 1875 for Wells Fargo agent C. C. Beekman, contains belongings that intimately reflect the way life was at the time. Visitors to the house chat with costumed interpreters playing the parts of members of the family: old Mrs. Beekman, a maid cooking on the wood stove, or one of the music pupils who took lessons from Beekman's daughter. Period furnishings reflect the history of the home from the 1870s through the early part of the twentieth century.

Bush House
600 Mission Street, SE
Salem, Oregon 97302

Completed in 1878, this home was built in a simplified Italianate style and had many of the nineteenth century's most forward-looking modern conveniences, including central heating and sinks with hot and cold running water in every bedroom. The wallpapers that were imported from France and shipped around Cape Horn are among the many original furnishings on view. Of note are ten one-of-a-kind marble fireplaces and beautifully restored parlor and drawing room.

PENNSYLVANIA

The Ebenezer Maxwell Mansion
200 Tulpehocken Street
Philadelphia, Pennsylvania 19144

Built in 1859, this mansion incorporated the latest innovations of the day—pipes to carry water into the house, central hot-air heating, gaslights, and such. The new owners redecorated in the 1870s, painting and stenciling all the ceilings and walls of the main rooms with motifs reminiscent of Egyptian, Japanese, and Classical designs. The first floor has been beautifully restored and furnished to reflect the style of the original owners from 1858 to 1867. The second floor shows redecoration touches

from the 1870s, allowing visitors to see the changes over twenty years from wallpaper to paint, and Rococo Revival to Renaissance Revival. The gardens have also been restored to reflect the mid- to late nineteenth century.

The Harry Packer Mansion
Packer Hill
Jim Thorpe, Pennsylvania 18229

Built in 1874, this fifteen-room house has been fully restored and has many wonderful items of interest: the library with mahogany woodwork, original English ceramic sink bowls, a walnut mantel in the reception room, and beautiful parquet floors throughout the house. Many furnishings are original, dating from 1874 or to the redecorating done in the 1880s. For those looking for specific styles, this house has Rococo, Eastlake, and Renaissance Revival rooms on show.

RHODE ISLAND

Beechwood
580 Bellevue Avenue
Newport, Rhode Island 02840

Built in 1852, the original structure burned, and the house was rebuilt in 1875. Designed by A. J. Downing and remodeled by Richard Morris Hunt in 1890, this Astor house has a large private ballroom decorated with over 800 mirrors and windows to resemble the Hall of Mirrors at Versailles. The music room, in ebony and gold, is in contrast to the white and gold of the ballroom, with its original carpets and repainted Wedgewood panels. Frescoed walls can be found throughout the house. An added feature is the living play performed in every room. Professional actors live, act, and react in the house to provide the viewer with a feeling of what it was like to visit this house during the nineteenth century.

Château-Sur-Mer

Bellevue Avenue
Newport, Rhode Island 02840

One of the finest Victorian mansions that can be seen today, this palatial residence was originally built in 1852 and enlarged and redecorated in 1872. The result was a château that nearly tripled its original size and that is touched with a fascination for the Eastlake philosophy. The house is a treasure trove of Victorian luxury, with objects collected by the family throughout the years. Of special interest are the extraordinary woodwork and the famous "Butternut" bedroom with a seventeen-piece suite designed by Leon Marcotte.

Kingscote
Bellevue Avenue
Newport, Rhode Island 02840

A romantic Gothic Revival "cottage" in the grand Newport style, the interiors of this 1839 home offer wonderful examples of the Gothic Revival style, from the wooden Tudor arches and columns to the elaborated mantelpiece in the southeast bedroom. A perfect environment for its mid- and late-Victorian furnishings, with such details as a McKim, Mead and White dining room added in 1881, as well as stained-glass windows, new mantelpieces, and Morris wallpapers of this same period.

SOUTH CAROLINA

Calhoun Mansion
16 Meeting Street
Charleston, South Carolina 29401

An elaborate Italianate twenty-five-room Renaissance Revival mansion built in 1876 at a cost of $200,000, this house features unusual woodwork and inlay throughout, a tiled entryway, ornate plaster and wood moldings (even in the closets), and elaborate chandeliers. Other details include a forty-five-foot-high covered ballroom skylight, an Eastlake-style staircase, and a fifty-foot central hallway.

Edmonston-Alston House
21 East Battery
Charleston, South Carolina 29401

Built in 1828 and redesigned in a Greek Revival mode in 1838, this house museum overlooking Charleston harbor is furnished with a mix of family furniture and decorative arts that reflects both the late eighteenth century and the early Victorian Empire style of the 1830s. Rooms on view include a double parlor on the second floor, a library, a dining room, and a morning room.

SOUTH DAKOTA

Beckwith House
Museum of Pioneer Life
Mitchell, South Dakota 57301

This house, built in 1886, exhibits a variety of Victorian design elements with many of its original furnishings intact. It features well-restored rooms and many beautiful examples of Eastlake-style furniture, as well as Victorian wallpapers, window treatments, rugs, and so on.

Cramer-Kenyon Heritage House
509 Pine Street
Yankton, South Dakota 57078

Built in the late 1880s, this house remains virtually unchanged since the day it was redecorated in 1890. Its high cove ceilings, sliding parlor doors, elaborate woodwork, and wallpaper are said to be among the state's finest examples of nineteenth-century style.

Mellette House
421 Fifth Avenue Northwest
Watertown, South Dakota 57201

This 1883 Italianate mansion was restored as a museum in 1943 by the first governor of South Dakota, and is now in almost original condition. Among the furnishings are Empire and Renaissance Revival furniture as well as pictures, family heirlooms,

and other memorabilia.

The Pettigrew Home and Museum
131 North Duluth Avenue
Sioux Falls, South Dakota 57102

The front and back parlors of this Queen Anne-style home are being restored to their original grandeur of 1890 and the early 1900s, highlighted by a beautiful 1874 Steinway grand piano. (Restoration began July 1, 1985.)

TENNESSEE

The Fontaine House
680 Adams
Memphis, Tennessee 38105

Built in 1870, this three-story Second Empire home houses seventeen rooms of Victorian furnishings, including pieces by Huntzinger and Belter. Of special note are the restored Victorian wallpapers throughout the home, as are the collections of clothing, accessories, and so on.

The Hermitage
4580 Rachels Lane
Hermitage, Tennessee 37076

This was the plantation home of Andrew Jackson, built in 1819 and occupied by him until his death in 1845. Of special interest are the graceful spiral staircase, unusual scenic wallpaper from Paris (ca. 1837), and horsehair-covered Empire sofas, all in the hall, as are other wallpapers and draperies throughout the house which date from the 1830s and the porcelain, crystal, mirrors, kitchen utensils, and bedroom furniture (ca. 1845) from the Jackson occupancy. All furnishings are original.

The Magevney House
198 Adams Avenue
Memphis, Tennessee 38103

This white-clapboard frame cottage, built in 1837, is typical of the pre-Civil War, middle-class homes of this area. Inside, one finds rooms furnished 1850s style. Many of the original furnishings, pine floors and woodwork, rag rugs, and mahogany bureau are on view. Brick slave quarters as well as the detached kitchen are also preserved.

The Mallory-Neely House
652 Adams Avenue
Memphis, Tennessee 38105

Built in the 1850s, the Mallory-Neely House underwent many expansions during the nineteenth century. Original carpets, wallcoverings, and ornate plaster ceilings are still there to see and admire, as are many original furnishings, including exquisite examples of nineteenth-century furniture. Among the furnished rooms are eleven bedrooms bedecked with rosewood and chintz, gold and white parlors, a pink flowered and ribboned reception room, a dining room decorated with hand-tooled-leather walls, and a music room. A "must see" for anyone in the area.

Oaklands Historic House Museum
900 North Maney Avenue
Murfreesboro, Tennessee 37130

Oaklands, an antebellum mansion and one-time plantation, originally was a four-room house built in the early 1800s and expanded with a series of additions, the last in 1862. The present twelve-room home features furnishings and decoration that predate 1865, the year chosen for its restoration. Sheraton, Empire, Victorian, and primitive styles are all present, with many pieces that belonged to the original owners, the Maney family.

James Knox Polk Home
301 West 7th Street
Columbia, Tennessee 38401

This beautiful home of the eleventh president and first lady was built in 1816 and lived in by the Polks during the 1820s. The interior architecture, mantels, and paint colors have been restored to reflect that early period, while the furnishings, selected by Mrs. Polk, reflect a mix of those years with the White House years, 1845 to 1849. Of note are the patterned crimson carpeting in parlor and dining room, crimson draperies, elegant rosewood parlor furniture, pier mirrors, French clocks, and chandeliers. All furnishings belonged to the Polk family.

TEXAS

Sam Houston Park
1100 Bagby Street
Houston, Texas 77002

In this park, seven Victorian structures can be seen along with a copy of the turn-of-the-century bandstand that once stood on this spot. These buildings show the visitor examples from a wide variety of Victorian styles and periods. From public to private buildings, all have been restored to their original Victorian beauty.

Old City Park
1717 Gano Street
Dallas, Texas 75215

On the Old City Park walking tour, visitors can visit twenty-seven Victorian buildings with interiors that range from the 1850s to the turn of the century, from upper middle class to log cabin. This is a wonderful opportunity for those looking to compare and contrast the variety of nineteenth-century styles. Victorian gardens, fountain, and bandstand are also found in the park.

Thistle Hill
1509 Pennsylvania Avenue
Fort Worth, Texas 76104

Thistle Hill, a landmark Texas mansion and "cattle baron's legacy," was built in 1903 as a wedding gift from cattleman W. T. Waggoner to his daughter. The house features stained-glass windows and an impressive entry stairway, and plans are under way to restore it to its 1912 appearance.

VERMONT

The Park-McCullough House
North Bennington, Vermont 05257

A thirty-five-room Empire mansion, built in 1865, that features a magnificent central hall with a sweeping double staircase, oak and chestnut paneling, Italian marble fireplaces, bronze chandeliers, and a stained-glass skylight. Much of the original furniture is on display, including some clothing and a number of family portraits. Formal Victorian gardens are also of interest.

VIRGINIA

Centre Hill Mansion
1 Centre Hill Court
Petersburg, Virginia 23803

First built in 1823 in the Federal style, this house was extensively renovated in the Greek Revival style in 1840, and redone once again in a Georgian Revival style between 1900 and 1936. The interiors of the twenty-five rooms all retain elements of each owner's taste, including double parlors with Greek Revival plaster ornamentation, a rosewood piano (ca. 1886), and furniture in the various other nineteenth-century styles.

Stonewall Jackson House
8 East Washington Street
Lexington, Virginia 24450

Jackson and his wife purchased this Federal townhouse in 1858 and made it their home until 1861, when he marched off to the Civil War. It has been restored with carefully documented furnishings which either are original or match the house's inventory. Included are rag rugs and parlor rugs, transparent window shades, and marble-topped tables belonging to the family.

Maymont House
1700 Hampton Street

Richmond, Virginia 23220

Twelve of the thirty-three opulent rooms in this 1893 mansion are on view, all with original furnishings belonging to the owners, Major and Mrs. James H. Dooley. Of special note are the outstanding frescoed ceilings, stenciling, woodwork, and stained glass. The Swan Room sports a swan-shaped bed and a one-of-a-kind Tiffany & Co. dressing table and chair. Outside, one finds Italian and Japanese gardens and arboretum.

Wickham-Valentine House
1015 East Clay Street
Richmond, Virginia 23219

Built in 1812 and 1813, this ten-room home features nineteenth-century furnishings throughout—many from the period 1850 to 1870—belonging to the home's various owners. Of special interest is the drawing room with Rococo Revival furniture, richly carved Italian marble mantel, and carved window cornices.

WASHINGTON, D.C.

Decatur House
748 Jackson Place, NW
Washington, D.C. 20006

The second floor of this 1818 home represents the taste of the Edward Beale family (1872–1956), featuring a double parlor with painted ceiling and a north drawing room, its floor inlaid in twenty-six woods with the seal of California, and its two Philadelphia Centennial gasoliers, Belter chairs, and paintings.

Frederick Douglass Home
1411 W Street, SE
Washington, D.C. 20020

The fourteen furnished rooms in this 1855 house reflect its occupancy by Frederick Douglass (1817–1895), the escaped slave who became an honored statesman. The house includes Douglass's 2,000-volume li-

brary, a restored kitchen, pantry, and parlor, all with furnishings that reflect the period from 1870 to 1900.

WISCONSIN

Galloway House
336 Old Pioneer Road
Fond du Lac, Wisconsin 54935

A thirty-room Victorian museum, originally built in 1847 and extensively remodeled between 1860 and 1880, this elaborate home is a classic Midwestern version of a Victorian Italianate villa. Details include the open walnut stairway; a parlor with original hand-stenciled ceiling, carpet, and light fixtures; a grand piano; and other original furnishings. This house contains one of the first bathrooms installed in the state.

Pabst Mansion
2000 West Wisconsin Avenue
Milwaukee, Wisconsin 53233

A grand Flemish Renaissance mansion belonging to the famous Pabst Brewery family, this home featured thirty-seven rooms, with fourteen fireplaces and thirteen baths—highly unusual for 1893, when it was completed. The interiors are lavish, with wood carvings, ornamental plasterwork and ironwork, and the dining room's Lincrusta-Walton wallcoverings. Furniture in the dining room, as well as the parlor and music room, is original to the house; the rest of the furniture was donated to the mansion and reflects the period from 1890 to 1904, the year Pabst died.

APPENDIX C.
ANTIQUE DEALERS

Circa 1890
265 East 78th Street
New York, New York 10021
(212) 734-7388

Specialty: Wicker furniture

David Hanks and Associates
156 Fifth Avenue
Suite 625
New York, New York 10010
(212) 255-3218

Specialty: Victorian furniture; nineteenth-century silver
Note: This company also does art consultation.

Didier Aaron, Inc.
32 East 67th Street
New York, New York 10021
(212) 988-5248

Specialty: Eighteenth- and nineteenth-century European and American furniture; Old Masters

Elizabeth and Richard King, Inc.
Antique American Wicker Furniture
Tracy Road
Northeast Harbor, Maine 04662
(207) 276-5288

Specialty: Late-nineteenth- and early-twentieth-century wicker

Florian Papp
962 Madison Avenue
New York, New York 10021
(212) 288-6770

Specialty: Late-eighteenth- to early-nineteenth-century English furniture; High Victorian

Gene Tyson
19 East 69th Street
New York, New York 10021

(212) 744-5785
Specialty: Oriental and European furniture; nineteenth-century English; Regency

Hays House of Wicker
8565 Melrose Avenue
Los Angeles, California 90069
(213) 652-1999
Specialty: Nineteenth century; reproduction American wicker

James II Galleries, Ltd.
15 East 57th Street
New York, New York 10022
(212) 355-7040
Specialty: Victorian accessories, such as jewelry, dinner sets, canes, screens, wine coolers

Joan Bogart Gallery
Gallery Address:
617 Seaman Avenue
Baldwin, New York 11510
Mailing Address:
Box 265
Rockville Centre, New York 11571
(516) 764-0529
Specialty: American High Victorian furniture; majolica; Parian; lamps; cast-iron garden furniture; chandeliers; Victorian wicker

Jordan Volpe
457 West Broadway
New York, New York 10012
(212) 505-5240
Specialty: American Arts & Crafts furniture; American pottery; Tiffany; studio fixtures

Kent Shire Gallery
37 East 12th Street
New York, New York 10003
(212) 673-6644
Specialty: Nineteenth-century English furniture and accessories

M. H. Stockroom
654 Madison Avenue

New York, New York 10021
(212) 752-6696
Specialty: English Regency; Victorian objects, prints, and small furniture

Margot Johnson Antiques
American Standard Building
40 West 40th Street
New York, New York 10018
(212) 703-5472
Specialty: All fine late-nineteenth-century furniture

Mimi Findlay Antiques
1556 Third Avenue
New York, New York 10128
(212) 534-6705
Specialty: Nineteenth-century furniture and interiors

Pugley & Sons
4900 California
San Francisco, California 94118
(415) 752-3668
Specialty: American decorative arts; Victorian furniture; American Arts & Crafts furniture
Note: This company also does museum-quality restoration of American nineteenth-century furniture.

R. Brooke
139½ East 80th Street
New York, New York 10021
(212) 535-0707
Specialty: English Victorian furniture and accessories

Richard and Eileen Dubrow Antiques
Box 128
Bayside, New York 11361
(718) 767-9578
Specialty: Fine Victorian furniture, especially Belter pieces; Wooten desks

Richard McGeehan
Box 181

Bedford Hills, New York 10507
(914) 241-3815
Mailing Address:
P.O. Box 1000
Old Chelsea Station
New York, New York 10113
(718) 875-1441
Specialty: American nineteenth-century furniture, silver, and decorations

A Summer Place
29 Whitfield Street
Guilford, Connecticut 06437
(203) 453-5153
Specialty: Nineteenth-century wicker furniture

Walters Wicker Wonderland
991 Second Avenue
New York, New York 10022
(212) 758-0472
Specialty: Victorian wicker and rattan

The Wicker Lady
1197 Walnut Street
Newton, Massachusetts 02161
(617) 964-7490
Specialty: Nineteenth-century wicker furniture

APPENDIX D.
RESTORATION SPECIALISTS, DESIGN CONSULTANTS, ARTISTS, AND CRAFTSPEOPLE

Artistic License
1489 McCallister Street
San Francisco, California 94115
(415) 922-5219
This is a guild of skilled artisans trained in Victorian architectural and decorative-arts restoration. Members who specialize in different areas can be contacted through the guild. Specialties of the various artists and artisans, just a few of whom are listed here, include Victorian stained glass, woodwork, ornamental plaster, lighting, stencil, wall-

paper, restoration carpentry, and ornamental painting.

Bradbury & Bradbury*
Box 155
Benicia, California 94510
(707) 746-1900
Specialty: A complete line of exceptional nineteenth-century reproduction wallpapers, with accompanying art borders, dado papers, and friezes, as well as a wallpaper-design service

Conti Construction
4250 North 6th Street
Kalamazoo, Michigan 49009
(616) 375-6399
Specialty: Architectural and interior restoration

Gary Kleppel
368 Congress Street
Boston, Massachusetts 02210
(617) 426-8887
Specialty: Decorative finishes, murals, and furniture painting

Gentle Arts
936 Arabella Street, P.O. Box 15832
New Orleans, Louisiana 70115
(505) 895-7003
Specialty: Cleaning and restoring textiles and costumes, especially lace

Helene Von Rosensteil
382 11th Street
Brooklyn, New York 11215
(718) 788-7909
Specialty: Expert textile and costume cleaning, restoring, and mounting

Henry A. Dornsife & Sons, Interior Designers
974 Hollywood Circle
Williamsport, Pennsylvania 17701
(717) 322-1550
Specialty: Under the auspices of Samuel J.

Dornsife, the eminent Victorian-design historian, this firm specializes in the preservation, restoration, decoration, lighting, and landscaping of public and private nineteenth-century buildings.

J.R. Burrows & Company
The Victorian Revival Showroom on Copley Square
25 Huntington Avenue
Room 527
Boston, Massachusetts 02116
(617) 262-6171
Victorian Revival design consultants, this company also has a showroom featuring American and English Victorian Revival wallpapers, reproduction carpets, tiles, and other home furnishings.

J. & R. Lamb Studios
P.O. Box 291
Philmont, New York 12565
(518) 672-7267
Specialty: Stained-glass restoration and reproduction

Jill Pilaroscia*
855 Alvarado Street
San Francisco, California 94114
(415) 285-4544
Specialty: Designer; interior and exterior color specialist

John David Modell*
284 Page Street
San Francisco, California 94102
(415) 621-5295
Specialty: Nineteenth-century architectural restoration

Ken Phillips
6501 Hamilton Avenue
Pittsburgh, Pennsylvania 15206
(412) 361-8888
Specialty: Stained glass

Larry Boyce & Associates*

P.O. Box 421507
San Francisco, California 94142
(415) 923-1366
Specialty: Unusual ornamental painting and stenciling, especially ceiling treatments

Louise Freedman
368 Congress Street
Boston, Massachusetts 02210
(617) 426-8887
Specialty: Design and plaster restoration

Old World Restoration
The Columbia-Stanley Building
347 Stanley Avenue
Cincinnati, Ohio 45226
(513) 321-1911
Specialty: Fine-art restoration and conservation (oil painting, gold-leaf frames, china, porcelain, marble)

The Rambusch Company
40 West 13th Street
New York, New York 10011
(212) 675-0400
Specialty: High-quality decorative painting, stained-glass design, and the like

Restoration Stenciling
1416 East Second Street
Port Angeles, Washington 98362
(206) 457-6676
Specialty: Stenciling, graining, marbleing, and gilding

Victorian Interior Restoration
1713 East Carson Street
Pittsburgh, Pennsylvania 15203
(412) 381-1870
Victorian-design consultants and craftsmen specializing in interior restoration of residential and small commercial spaces. Services include complete nineteenth-century

*Member of Artistic License in San Francisco. See entry for more information.

design planning, restoration surveys, construction, and so on. The firm's retail outlet stocks historic wallcoverings, chandeliers, hardware, and carpeting. This company is active on the east coast and throughout the Midwest.

APPENDIX E.
ORGANIZATIONS AND
PUBLICATIONS

The American Life Foundation
Box 349
Watkins Glen, New York 14891

A nonprofit foundation involved in the study of American life, republishing nineteenth-century books on life and style in Victorian America.

The Antique Trader
P.O. Box 1050
Dubuque, Iowa 52001
(319) 588-2073

A weekly newspaper of advertisements and auction news covering antiques and collectors' items, many of which are nineteenth century, such as Victorian furniture, art glass, silver, and china.

Antiquity Reprints
P.O. Box 370
Rockville Centre, New York 11571
(516) 766-5585

Seller of reprints of Victorian architectural plan, or "pattern," books. Publishes an annual catalog and a syndicated newspaper column entitled "Homestead Hints."

The Atheneum
219 South Sixth Street
East Washington Square
Philadelphia, Pennsylvania 19106
(215) 925-2688

A research center housing nineteenth-century popular literature, drawings, manuscripts, correspondence, photographs, periodicals, trade catalogs, domestic man-

uals, pattern books, travel accounts of overland journeys, and the like. Also presents lectures, chamber-music concerts, and exhibitions, and publishes several books each year.

Living History Magazine
P.O. Box 2309´
Reston, Virginia 22090

This magazine is mainly targeted at living history reenacters and interpreters; also includes book reviews and an events calendar.

The National Trust for Historic
Preservation
1785 Massachusetts Avenue, NW
Washington, D.C. 20036
(202) 673-4000

This organization holds conferences and seminars, and publishes *Historic Preservation* magazine and a newspaper, *Preservation News.*

The Northeast Victorian Studies
Association
c/o Professor Hartley Spatt
Humanities Department
SUNY Maritime
Bronx, New York 10465
or
Professor Earl Stevens
English Department
Rhode Island College
Providence, Rhode Island 02903

A newsletter, *Victorian Studies*, and conferences are sponsored by this association.

The Old House Journal
69A Seventh Avenue
Brooklyn, New York 11217
(718) 636-4514

Articles dealing mostly with restoring, maintaining, and nineteenth-century items; publishes an annual comprehensive catalog and buyer's guide.

Tracy Halcomb / Shades of the Past

P.O. Box 502
Corte Madera, California 94925
(415) 459-6999

Specializes in hand-made traditional and Victorian-inspired lampshades crafted from new and antique silks, embroideries, and so on.

Victorian Accents
661 West Seventh Street
Plainfield, New Jersey 07060
(201) 757-8507

An excellent mail-order source for books on nineteenth- and early-twentieth-century architecture, interiors, gardening, and so on.

Victorian Homes
550 Seventh Avenue
Brooklyn, New York 11215
(718) 499-5789

Called "the magazine for romantic living," the only magazine devoted exclusively to today's Victorian-home owner. Covers decorating how-tos, crafts, fashion, food, travel ideas, and so on. Also features articles on antiques and historic houses.

The Victorian Society in America
East Washington Square
Philadelphia, Pennsylvania 19106
(215) 627-4252

Sponsors conferences and tours, publishes a newsletter, *The Victorian*, and conducts a summer school in both America and England.

Index